MUSCLE CAR LEGENDS

Paul Zazarine, Tom Corcoran, and Anthony Young

Lowe & B. Hould
Publishers

This edition published in 2002 by Lowe & B. Hould Publishers, an imprint of Borders, Inc., 515 East Liberty, Ann Arbor, MI 48104. Lowe & B. Hould Publishers is a trademark of Borders Properties, Inc.

First published by MBI Publishing Company, Galtier Plaza, Suite 200, 380 Jackson Street, St. Paul, MN 55101-3885 USA

Library of Congress Cataloging-in-Publication Data Available

ISBN 0-681-89057-6

On the front cover: This 1970 Hemi 'Cuda looks right at home at the beach. *Mike Mueller*

On the frontispiece: The trademark GTO exhaust splitters, an extra-cost option in 1964. *Paul Zazarine*

On the title page: A 1967 Pontiac GTO convertible. *Mike Mueller*

On the back cover: Under the hood of this 1970 Hemi 'Cuda resides the unique Chrysler engine that gives this car its muscle. *Mike Mueller*

On pages 8–9: Rear view of the 1967 GTO. *Mike Mueller*

On page 131: Competition Shelby Mustang 5R105, owned by Jim Bridges. *Tom Corcoran*

On pages 132–133: A 1968 Shelby Mustang GT-350. *Tom Corcoran*

On page 255: Dodge named its fresh air induction system after its famous factory drag-racing team, the Ramchargers. This set-up, shown on the 1970 Coronet R/T, fed the 426 Hemi below. Note the 426 with the Hemi on the air-cleaner cover. *David Gooley*

On pages 256–257: Assembly layout drawing for one of the first-generation Hemis, the DeSoto FireDome V-8. *Chrysler*

Printed in Singapore

Contents

Shelby Mustang

Hemi

GTO 1964–1967

The package for 1964: license plate tag bracket from Royal Pontiac and a bolt-on set of Hurst wheels.

Acknowledgments

During the course of writing this book on 1964–1967 GTOs, I was assisted by a number of friends whose help was instrumental in completing this project. Without sounding like an overdone Academy Award speech, I'd like to thank Donald Farr at Dobbs Publications for use of the *Musclecar Review* archives, Ed Lechtzin and Reg Harris at Pontiac Motor Division, Michael Dregni at Motorbooks and Greg Pernula for helping me find the ending. My love and thanks go especially to my wife, Nancy, who endures the long hours I spend in my office, pecking away at the word processor and emerging only briefly for food or sleep.

My thanks also to all the folks in the GTO hobby who allowed me to photograph their cars for this book, especially Bob Bassett, Jr., Richard Gill, John Truesdell, Eric White, Chuck Roberts, the late Bill Sherman, Milt Schornack, Dr. Stephen Bailey, Steve Brown, Bob Milloy and Ed Rowe.

Back in 1981, I spent over four hours interviewing Jim Wangers. The transcript runs 178 pages in length, and Jim covered just about every topic regarding Pontiac's performance history. You'll find excerpts from that interview interspersed throughout the book. But what intrigued me the most while rereading the interview in 1990 was Jim's concerns and opinions about the state of Pontiac's health back in the early 1980s. Pontiac had suffered through most of the 1970s with a lousy product mix and a tremendous lack of image, and by the early 1980s, the division was in damage control. All through the interview, Jim kept pounding away at what was wrong with Pontiac and what they needed to do to survive. "If they are not successful in reimaging that entire division around the new Trans Am," he told me, "I predict Pontiac is terminal." Jim then laid out the strategy he felt was needed to resurrect Pontiac and rebuild it into the performance division of General Motors.

During the interview ten years ago, as I listened to him talk about Pontiac's problems, I thought this was mostly a case of sour grapes. Jim wasn't in the loop at Pontiac anymore and, I assumed, he was frustrated because he could no longer bang on somebody's desk and get results like he had almost twenty years before.

Boy, was I wrong.

In 1983, Pontiac radically reimaged the division, and built a new reputation on performance with the Trans Am and sophistication with the STE. All of the things Jim had said Pontiac needed to do to survive had come to pass. There had been no sour grapes, and the frustration I had heard in his voice was there because he couldn't save the car company that he loved so much and had worked so hard for. It was only then that I realized Jim Wangers truly was an automotive marketing genius. Although he was part of a team at Pontiac that created some great cars, the GTO was Wangers' greatest achievement. Without his genius, his nurturing and his total devotion, the GTO would not have realized its destiny as America's premier musclecar.

This book is dedicated to him.

The Rise of Pontiac Performance

Long before Detroit had ever thought of a car like the Pontiac GTO, the movement toward high-performance automobiles was already under way. In the years preceding World War II, the birthplace of speed was in southern California. Young men whose names have become pillars of today's performance aftermarket industry—such as Edelbrock and Iskendarian—were modifying flat-head Fords and building "rods" that exceeded the performance of even the most expensive production automobiles.

After the war, as Detroit produced cars to quench the thirst of a war-weary public, the word performance began creeping into the car maker's advertisements. The introduction of the high-compression Oldsmobile and Cadillac V-8 engines were the first shots fired in the horsepower wars that would escalate for more than two decades. In the early 1950s, Chrysler countered with the Hemi engine. Although displacing less than 350 ci at the time, the new Hemi was a boon to hot rodders and drag racers, who soon learned how to coax more power from it. Back in Detroit, product planners looked to the high-performance engines as a selling tool to attract buyers of large, luxurious models. The lower-priced models like Chevrolet, Plymouth and Pontiac had no V-8s. These cars were offered only with straight-sixes or straight-eight engines. They were sensible cars, and Detroit's perception was that sensible buyers wanted reliability and economy, not performance.

All of that changed in the fall of 1954 with the introduction of the 1955 models. The 1955 model year stands as a

milestone for several reasons. A considerable number of car lines were restyled in 1955, marking more contemporary styling that appealed to the huge numbers of World War II veterans who were now in their mid- to late-thirties and growing more affluent. They could afford new cars, and they flooded dealer showrooms in droves. The industry set new sales records in 1955 thanks in part to the exciting new styling that appeared on Ford, GM and Chrysler products.

There was another, more significant revolution going on in 1955—the emergence of performance in the low-priced field. For the first time, Chevrolet and Pontiac offered V-8 engines. The small-block Chevrolet engine went on to become the cornerstone of street performance, and those southern California hot rodders who had built their passion for speed into profitable aftermarket parts businesses recognized the small-block Chevy as a gold mine of opportunity. Within a few years, a plethora of parts was offered to modify the Chevy Mouse Motor. New performance components are still being introduced today, nearly four decades after the 1955 model year.

While Pontiac's new V-8 didn't draw attention like Chevrolet's, it was a significant break from the past for a company that possessed a staid image of reliable

Call it the Wide Track Tiger, call it the Goat, call it The Great One—the GTO gave a new name to Pontiac as a performance automobile maker. It also revived Pontiac at a time when the future looked dim. By 1967, when this car was built, the GTO was at the top.

It's The Talk of the Test Drivers!

THE FABULOUS '56 PONTIAC WITH A BIG AND VITAL GENERAL MOTORS "AUTOMOTIVE FIRST"!

Believe us—it isn't easy to impress a test driver!

But they're cheering Pontiac in a big way.

What's set them buzzing is that big and vital General Motors "First" combining:

Pontiac's new big-bore Strato-Streak V-8 with the terrific thrust of 227 horsepower.

General Motors' new Strato-Flight Hydra-Matic* that gentles this mighty "go" to smoothness beyond belief.

You don't need a test track to prove that here is the lift of a lifetime.

Traffic tells you. Here's "stop-and-go" response as fast as thought itself. *A hill helps.* High or low, it's left behind without a sign of effort. *And passing definitely pins it down.* Gun it and in-

stant, flashing power sweeps you swiftly by the loitering car ahead. No drag, no lag—just safe and certain "go"!

There's plenty more to charm you. The safety of big new brakes, a steady ride, advanced controls. Glamorous new beauty.

But, above all, it's that fabulous new "go" that gets you!

Drive a Pontiac today for a glorious double thrill. There'll be pride in your heart, a torrent at your toe-tip. What more could anyone want?

*An extra cost option.

'56 PONTIAC

PONTIAC MOTOR DIVISION OF GENERAL MOTORS CORPORATION

The new overhead Pontiac V–8 was introduced in 1955, replacing the straight-six and straight-eight engines that had powered Pontiacs since 1926. Introduced at 287 ci, it was enlarged to 316 ci in 1956, 347 ci in 1957, 370 ci in 1958 and 389 ci in 1959. It forever changed Pontiac's image and its fortunes.

The "torrent in your toe-tip" advertising embellishment may have been hyperbole in 1956, but it did signal the emergence of high performance at Pontiac, not only in the product itself, but in the advertising image presented to the public. The top of the line was the NASCAR engine, introduced in January 1956 with dual four-barrel carburetors and rated at a sizzling 285 hp.

yet boring transportation. In fact, sales had been so soft for so long that General Motors management had at one time considered slowly killing off the product by merging Pontiac with Oldsmobile, allowing the dealer body to either switch to Olds franchises when possible or simply closing them down.

Instead, a commitment was made to resuscitate Pontiac, and a changing of the guard was made in 1956. Semon "Bunkie" Knudsen, whose father had been with Pontiac two decades before, was moved into the office of general manager on July 1, 1956, and told to turn things around or possibly go down as the

last general manager the Pontiac Division would ever have. Knudsen went right to work. His first step was to evaluate Pontiac's product line-up and the perceived image of those products by the buying public. To increase sales and improve market penetration, Knudsen knew he had to turn his back on thirty years of image and build a new look. Younger customers were the target, and if Knudsen could win these buyers, the future belonged to Pontiac.

Within the first ninety days of his reign, Knudsen had stripped the chrome "suspenders" from the hood of the 1957 models, which were about to go into production. These chrome stripes were

By 1962, Pontiac ruled the high-back tracks of NASCAR, with drivers like Fireball Roberts and Joe Weatherly piloting the Smokey Yunick-prepared 421 ci Super Duty Catalinas. Pontiac General Manager Bunky Knud-sen was a firm believer that "racing on Sunday and selling on Monday" was one of the keys to Pontiac's success in rising to the number-three sales slot behind Chevrolet and Ford.

legendary Tri-Power carburetion setup of three two-barrel carburetors. It also pumped up the horsepower and displacement of its engines and cleaned house at Daytona's 1957 Speed Week and NASCAR events. Knudsen personally directed the stock-car and drag-racing programs at Pontiac, searching out the best builders and tuners. Pontiac's blitzkrieg paid off, dominating stock-car racing and gathering the attention of the automotive press, which reported to enthusiasts that "Grandma's car" was now the hottest ticket going.

The successes enjoyed by Pontiac on the racetrack were paying dividends in the showroom as well. The introduction of the Wide Track Pontiacs in 1959 set the cars apart from the rest of the industry. These Hot Chiefs with their new engines were developing a reputation for performance that rubbed off on even the most mundane members of the Pontiac product line-up. By 1959, Pontiac had moved into the number-four spot behind Chevrolet, Ford and Plymouth, up from sixth place just four years before.

Knudsen had also influenced the styling of Pontiac. The first models under his direction debuted in 1959, and by 1963, Pontiac styling had broken new ground by using clean lines, an absence of excessive chrome trim and flaring the rear quarter panels. These styling cues would be picked up by every other manufacturer during the 1960s.

For his efforts, Knudsen was rewarded the top post at Chevrolet in 1961, and Estes moved into the general manager's chair. DeLorean was appointed chief engineer. The agenda for Pontiac set by Knudsen was accelerated by his successors. By 1962, Pontiac and its new line-up of Super Duty engines were literally ruling the racetracks and drag strips of America. Out of the ivy-covered walls of the Pontiac Engineering building emerged radical camshafts, aluminum exhaust headers, special lightweight aluminum body components, and lightened frames and wheels. Many of these parts were also offered for street applications, and the major performance magazines were now featuring articles and covers on the hot Pontiacs.

By this time, Wangers, DeLorean, Estes and others within Pontiac were riding the crest of a successful wave that had carried the division to the number-three

a throwback to the Silver Streaks that his father had been involved with at Pontiac in the early 1930s. Removing the chrome was more than a styling ploy; it broke the bond with tradition and paved the way for new interpretations of what Pontiac signified as a car maker.

Knudsen also hired a group of young engineers to fulfill his vision for a new Pontiac. He had determined that for Pontiac to succeed, it had to cash in on the success the industry had enjoyed in 1955. The excitement of performance, of youthful styling that was a departure from the heavy, bulbous lines of the past, couldn't be understood by men who clung to high collars and French-tip shoes. In September 1956, Knudsen hired Elliot "Pete" Estes as chief engineer. Estes had been involved in the design of the high-compression Olds V–8 and favored high performance. Knudsen also brought aboard a bright young engineer from Packard, John Z.

DeLorean, to become director of Advanced Engineering.

Soon the word was out that things were happening at Pontiac, and that attracted more young engineers, product planners and designers. It also attracted a young man named Jim Wangers who had some unique ideas about how to image and sell cars. Wangers had been at Campbell-Ewald, Chevrolet's advertising agency, and was instrumental in the campaign to change Chevy's image in 1955 by emphasizing performance. After a short stint at Chrysler, Wangers was recruited by McManus, John and Adams, Pontiac's advertising agency.

Within eighteen months of Knudsen's arrival, a barrage of high-performance packages and programs began to hit the automotive world. Thanks to Estes, who brought the concept of multiple carburetion with him from Oldsmobile, Pontiac introduced in 1957 the now-

A harbinger of things to come was the 1963 Tempest, dressed out for road-racing or drag-strip action. Equipped with the Super Duty 421 ci engine but still using the stock rear transaxle and "rope" driveshaft, these Super Tempests paved the way for what would eventually become the GTO.

sales position. Wangers was finely attuned to the street scene, and he reported to DeLorean what the emerging generation of gearheads was doing and how he thought Pontiac could be a part of it. Wangers met George Hurst and introduced him to the engineers at Pontiac. Soon Pontiac became the first car maker to use Hurst's new floorshifter. Virtually everyone on the street was converting to Hursts, and Pontiac's adaptation of the stout stick was an indication of just how much in touch Pontiac—and Wangers—was with the high-performance scene.

Pontiac was on an incredible roll, with huge successes on the tracks, a *Motor Trend* Car of the Year Award under its belt and a hot performance image that staked its booming showroom sales to continued dominance on the tracks. They were the envy of the industry, and just when it appeared nothing could go wrong, Pontiac was dealt a blow that threatened to crumble the dynasty Knudsen and his successors had so carefully built.

1964 GTO

The Instant Performance Automobile

Pontiac had hitched its image to performance, and while they still built four-cylinder Tempests and nine-passenger Safari station wagons, the aura of Super Duties and Tri-Power Bonnevilles rubbed off on even the most mundane cars in the product line-up. The success of these pavement-melting Pontiacs was directly related to the division's domination on the tracks. In NASCAR, Fireball Roberts and Joe Weatherly had piloted Pontiacs to the winner's circle before tens of thousands of rabid car enthusiasts. On the NHRA drag strips, Jim Wangers' victory in Stock Eliminator at the 1960 NHRA Nationals drew considerable attention from the automotive press. The emerging popularity of Super Stock racing showcased the power of the 389 ci, followed by the 421 ci Super Duty Pontiac engines and drivers like Arnie Beswick, Arlen Vanke and Hayden Profitt.

The racing and performance image carefully cultivated by Pontiac was suddenly threatened by the January 24,

The GTO hardtop featured clean and functional styling that looked great from any angle.

1963, GM corporate edict that specified Pontiac and sister division Chevrolet absolve themselves from all racing activities. Any backdoor support of other racing teams carrying the division banner was also to be terminated. With one stroke of the corporate pen, the careful work of five years had just been torpedoed by GM management.

History records success as the convergence of luck and timing, and both of these factors played a part in the birth of the GTO. Ever since the Tempest had arrived in 1961 with its four-cylinder engine derived by splitting the Pontiac V–8 in half, "rope" driveshaft and rear transaxle, the idea of dropping a 389 into the engine bay had been discussed. A handful of 421 powered Tempests had been built in 1963 for drag racing in the Factory Experimental class; however, these cars still utilized the rear transaxle, and were never considered for production. The year before, Pontiac Engineering had even gone as far as submitting an application to the FIA (the international racing federation) for a 389 ci powered Tempest to go road racing.

General Motors planned to abandon the radical drivetrain layout for the Tempest in the 1964, reverting back to a

For the man who wouldn't mind riding a tiger if someone'd only put wheels on it—Pontiac GTO

This piece of machinery is something our Engineering Department slipped a motherly big Pontiac 389-incher into and named the GTO.

It comes in hardtop, sports coupe and convertible form, based on the Le Mans—only sleekened down some and fitted with a special set of red-circle high-performance tires.

The looks you can see for yourself. The big deal is under the hood: 325 bhp at 4800 rpm and 428 lb-ft of torque at 3200 rpm. That's just the standard 4BBL engine. There's also a version with 348 bhp* at 4900 rpm and 428 lb-ft of torque at 3600 rpm.

*optional at extra cost.

This one does deep-breathing exercises through a 3-2BBL setup. Both make bad-tempered noises through dual pipes. As illustrated above, pairs of exhaust splitters on each flank, just behind the rear wheels, are available dealer installed*.

A 3-speed transmission is standard, stirred by a Hurst shifter on the floor. Extra-cost variations include an automatic with shift on the column . . . an all-synchro 4-speed on the floor . . . or a choice of any one of them sprouting out of a console.

Give yourself a blast of tonic. Sample one of these here big pussycats. PONTIAC MOTOR DIVISON • GENERAL MOTORS CORPORATION

standard drivetrain, powered by a base six-cylinder with the 326 ci engine as an option. Since the 326 and 389 engines shared the same exterior dimensions and used the same motor mounts, Pontiac Engineering began experimenting with a 389 powered 1963 Tempest, simply as an engineering experiment. The work of Pontiac engineers Bill Collins and John DeLorean couldn't have come at a better time. While their project was simply an experiment, they had unknowingly laid the groundwork for a Super Tempest. DeLorean already had a name for it—GTO.

It was Wangers' vision that solidified the creation of the GTO, based on the engineering experiments. Wangers recognized Pontiac would have to transfer its performance image from the racetrack and put it on the street, thanks to GM's ban on racing. He also saw the budding "youth market" that he believed would snap up a low-priced car that was the antithesis of what its parents drove. Make it affordable, give it flash, give it image and give it the powertrain to blow away virtually any car on the street. As he had in the past, Wangers passed his idea on to DeLorean of dropping the big Pontiac 389 engine into the new Tempest and turning it loose on the streets. It was the recipe for success, and DeLorean recognized it instantly. The engineering experiment was on its way to becoming a production reality.

While the concept of slipping a big engine under a small hood sounds simple enough, no car maker had ever seriously attempted to bring the combination to production. The Pontiac team had one other obstacle—a GM edict that restricted engine displacement and horsepower output in mid-sized cars. That wasn't all. Any new models had to have the approval of the corporation, and a car that didn't meet corporate guidelines didn't stand a chance of getting the GM nod. DeLorean and Wangers realized *options* were not subject to approval. They also knew it was easier to ask forgiveness than permission, so a concentrated team effort was made to

A device for shrinking time and distance
Pontiac GTO

The 1964 GTO brochure was straightforward about what the GTO was all about. "To be perfectly honest," Pontiac warned, "the GTO is not everyone's cup of tea. Designed as a piece of performance machinery, its purpose in life is to permit you to make the most of your driving skill. Its suspension is firm, tuned more to the open road than to wafting gently over bumpy streets. Its dual exhausts won't win any prizes for whispering. And, unless you order it with our lazy 3.08 low-ratio rear axle, its gas economy won't be anything to write home about. If all this dismays you, then you're almost certainly a candidate for one of our 27 other Pontiac Pontiacs and Pontiac Tempests. But if you're tuned in to our particular wave length, if you start vibrating when you're at the controls of a sudden automobile, if you've driven enough different kinds of performance to know what it's all about, then you've got GTO written right across your forehead."

Pontiac had led the way with clean styling and sparse use of chrome beginning with the

1963 Grand Prix. The 1964 GTO continued that tradition.

Unlike most other high-performance cars of the time, the GTO's office was luxurious, with door-to-door carpeting, plush seats and aluminum-turned applique on the instrument panel.

Previous page
One of three body styles was the sport coupe. The bright trim around the windows and wheel openings on this Singapore Gold 1964 was standard as part of the LeMans package, from which the GTO option was ordered.

Next page
The standard GTO engine displaced 389 ci and utilized a single Carter AFB four-barrel carburetor. It was rated at 325 hp.

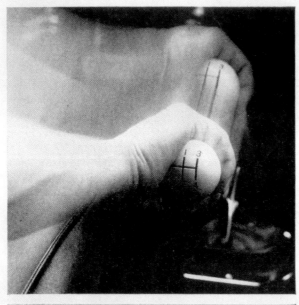

GTO is for kicking up the kind of storm that others just talk up.

Standard Equipment: engine: 389-cu. in. Pontiac with 1-4BBL; bhp—325 @ 4800; torque—428 lb-ft @ 3200 rpm/dual-exhaust system/3-speed stick with Hurst shifter/heavy-duty clutch/heavy-duty springs, shocks, stabilizer bar/special 7.50 x 14 red-line high-speed nylon cord tires (rayon cord whitewalls optional at no extra cost)/14 x 6JK wide-rim wheels/high-capacity radiator / declutching fan / high-capacity battery (66 plate, 61 amp. hr.)/chromed air cleaner, rocker covers, oil filler cap/bucket seats/standard axle ratio 3.23:1 (3.08, 3.36*, 3.55* to 1 available on special order at no extra cost). **And some of our extra-cost Performance Options:** engine: 389-cu. in. Pontiac with 3-2BBL (Code #809); bhp—348 @ 4900;

Available only with heavy-duty options at slight additional charge.

torque—428 lb-ft @ 3600; 3.55:1 axle ratio standard with this engine option/4-speed with Hurst shifter (gear ratios 2.56:1, 1.91:1, 1.48:1, 1.00:1, and 2.64:1 reverse)/2-speed automatic with 2.20:1 torque converter/Safe-T-Track limited-slip differential (Code #701)/3.90:1 axle ratio available on special order with metallic brake linings, heavy-duty radiator and Safe-T-Track/handling kit—20:1 quick steering and extra-firm-control heavy-duty shocks (Code #612)/high-performance full transistor (breakerless) ignition (Code #671)/tachometer (Code #452)/custom sports steering wheel (Code #524)/exhaust splitters (Dealer installed)/wire wheel discs (Dealer installed)/custom wheel discs, with spinner and brake cooling holes (Code #521)/console (Code #601).

the GTO makers—Pontiac

PONTIAC MOTOR DIVISION • GENERAL MOTORS CORPORATION

The GTO hardtop was released in November 1963. This Grenadier Red 1964 is fitted with Custom wheel covers. Exhaust splitters were an extra-cost option. Instead of the standard exhaust pipe exiting under the rear bumper, the splitters located the exhaust behind the rear wheel openings.

Previous page
This ad is what Wangers called "selling the sizzle with the steak." By listing all the options available for the GTO, no other copy was necessary. The GTO sold itself to a performance-starved America.

get the GTO off the ground as an option on the LeMans.

There was only one other hurdle before the GTO could become reality: it had to be sold to Pontiac management. Regardless of how excited Wangers and DeLorean were about the car, without the backing of Pontiac management, the idea of a high-performance street car would remain just that—a dream.

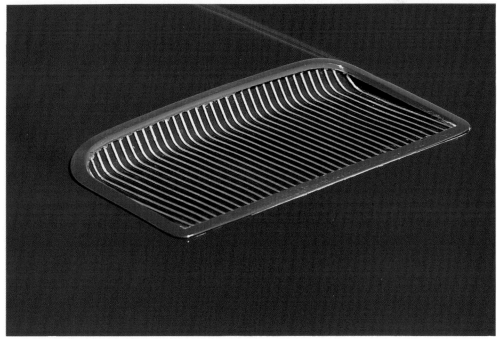

One of the cues that identified the GTO from the LeMans was the twin chromed scoops located on either side of the hood. The pot-metal scoop ornaments were nonfunctional.

While the Hurst floorshifter was standard on all three- and four-speed transmission GTOs, the center console was an extra-cost option.

Previous page
This Silvermist Gray sport coupe is owned by Pontiac Motor Division and is part of the Pontiac Historical Collection. It is equipped with the base 325 hp engine and four-speed transmission.

The GTO's savior would be in the form of Elliot "Pete" Estes, successor to Knudsen as general manager of Pontiac Motor Division. Estes was an engineer and a "car guy." If he could be sold, and if he had the courage to stand up to the corporation once the car was slipped into the hands of the dealer body, the GTO was assured of success. Without his support, it would never see the light of day.

A power top was standard on GTO convertibles. Wire wheel covers were optional.

The GTO Tri-Power was vacuum operated; however, most owners removed the vacuum setup and switched to a mechanical linkage that responded faster to throttle position.

Previous page
The optional engine also displaced 389 ci and was rated at 348 hp. It utilized Pontiac's legendary Tri-Power—three Rochester two-barrel carburetors.

To his credit, Estes stood behind the young Pontiac engineers and the visionary advertising executive. Estes overcame the objections of the sales management team, a group of Pontiac executives entrenched in methods they had used to sell cars since the 1940s. They were certain the car would never sell; dealers would end up eating this colossal failure. The confrontation between the young lions and the old veterans nearly led to fisticuffs, but in the end, Estes pushed the car through the division and to the dealers. The history books will record he was truly the unsung hero of the Pontiac GTO.

Selling the 1964 GTO to a performance-hungry America was no problem. In fact, Pontiac's strategy at first was to introduce the car with a low-key approach, just in case it wasn't the sure-fire success Wangers and DeLorean believed it to be. "Once the car was out

into the hands of the dealers," Wangers recalled, "there was no way the corporation was going to break it down and make the General Manager look bad in the eyes of the dealers."

By January, dealers were taking orders for the GTO, and by the end of the model year, 32,450 copies were roaming the streets, making boulevard fodder of nearly everything on wheels. For the first time, anyone's Walter Mitty fantasies could be fulfilled by simply walking into a Pontiac dealer, plunking down three grand and driving away in a car that was virtually unbeatable.

What was a GTO, and what did it have that no other car offered? While the GTO was essentially a LeMans, sitting on a 115 in. wheelbase, it was a *package*. Checking off the W62 GTO option delivered a 389 ci engine, replacing the LeMans' 326 ci powerplant. It was topped by a Carter AFB four-barrel carburetor, the high-compression heads from the big 421 ci engine and a moderate-lift hydraulic camshaft. The camshaft used a duration of 273 degrees on intake and 289 degrees on exhaust. Lift measured 0.400 in. for intake and 0.410 in. for exhaust. The package was good for 325 hp at 4800 rpm. A chromed air cleaner and valve covers added visual excitement to an already visceral engine.

In standard form, along with the 325 hp 389, the GTO was equipped with a three-speed manual gearbox and Hurst

calling
all sports car
enthusiasts!

Grab This — For Size! Pontiac's All-New

CUSTOM SPORTS STEERING WHEEL

(CODE 524)

Here's a wheel with that rugged sports car flair, combined with distinctive good looks! Handsome, wood-grain styled steering wheel (finger grips all around) . . . bold, stainless steel spokes . . . center horn button. Complements the walnut instrument panel inserts of any Bonneville or Grand Prix interior . . . just "purr-fect" with a 2 + 2 or G.T.O. option. **Available All 7 Pontiac Series—Factory-Installed Only!**

Suggested Retail Price	
$43.04	20 exc. w/Decor
$39.27	(20 with 064) 21-22
$43.04	23 exc. w/Decor or 2 + 2 Sports Option
$28.52	26-28-29 & 23 w/Decor or 2 + 2 Sports Option

The handsome GTO instrument panel was devoid of gauges save for the fuel gauge and speedometer. The only available gauge was a tachometer, located in the far right-hand pod.

Previous page
The Custom Sport wheel looked like wood but wasn't, felt like wood but didn't splinter like wood. Every GTO from 1964 to 1970 could be equipped with a wood-like sport wheel; however, the 1964 was the only four-spoke design.

floorshifter, dual exhausts, GTO emblems on the quarters, trunk lid and front fenders, as well as two chromed, nonfunctional hood scoops. Below deck, the GTO boasted stiffer springs and shocks and a larger front antisway bar. If there was one drawback to the GTO, it was the brakes; they were the same 9.5 in. drums as used with the six-cylinder Tempest. They were admittedly inferior for the tremendous power the GTO possessed under the hood. Ordering the optional metallic linings made a consid-

The woodgrained, four-spoke Custom Sport steering wheel was optional. The horn button was adorned by the Pontiac crest.

The GTO nameplate also appeared on the rear quarter panels. A smaller version of the nameplate was affixed to the rear deck lid.

erable difference in the GTO's stopping power, however. The hotter they got, the better they would work, with little fade.

The legendary Tri-Power was optional for the GTO, with its three Rochester two-barrel carbs and vacuum-controlled linkage. Normal operation was with the center two-holer, but at approximately seventy-percent throttle the two outer carbs would open and produce a banshee-like wail as the 389 wound out to produce 348 hp at 4900 rpm. Under wide-open throttle, the GTO accelerated like a rocket. The driver held on to the wheel and it was all he could do to remember to watch the tach and powershift through the gears.

Wrapped in a lightweight body, even in its most mild-mannered form, the GTO could streak down the quarter mile in the high-fourteens. A Tri-Power version, hooked to the Muncie close-ratio four-speed transmission and 3.90:1 rear axle, could clear the traps in the high-thirteens at a top speed of 108 mph. The 0–60 mph time was in the vicinity of five seconds. There wasn't another car selling at that price that could equal those figures.

The optional 7000 rpm tachometer was located in the far right-hand instrument panel pod. The gauge was rather small and difficult to see.

While the GTO was affordable, it wasn't Spartan. The interior was luxurious for a mid-sized car, with door-to-door carpeting, plush seats, an aluminum-turned dash applique and the unique GTO emblem above the glovebox door. What made the GTO even more exciting was Pontiac's option list, which according to Pontiac Motor Division, was "as long as your arm and twice

Buying the Ultimate 1964 GTO

Imagine for a moment it's 1964, and you've walked into a Pontiac dealer to order a GTO. On the showroom is a Cameo Ivory convertible, but it's equipped with the four-barrel engine and automatic transmission. On the lot are a few other GTOs, all four-barrels, a few with four-speeds, and the salesman tries in vain to push one of these milquetoast models. You refuse, because you know exactly how you want your dream GTO to be dressed out—Grenadier Red with a black interior. You instruct the salesman to break out the order form and you go to work:

Code	Description	Price
2237	LeMans Hardtop Sport Coupe	$2,556.00
382	Gran Turismo Omolagato	295.90
393	Radio—Push Button & Electric Antenna	92.16
404	Lamp, Underhood	3.55
421	Washer & Wipers—W/S	17.27
422	Extensions—Tail Pipe	21.30
452	Tachometer	53.80
471	Lamps—Back-up	12.91
474	Rear Speaker—VerbaPhonic	53.80
501	Power Steering	96.84
502	Power Brakes	42.50
524	Steering Wheel—Custom Sports	39.27
601	Console	48.15
621	Springs—Heavy Duty	3.82
701	Differential—Safe-T-Track	37.66
661	Frame—Heavy Duty	23.35
809	389 V-8 3/2BBL	115.78
009	Transmission—Four-Speed Syncromesh	188.30
Total Price		$3,702.36

You also specified the 3.90 rear axle, since you plan to enter the stock class at the drag strip. After some haggling, the dealer gives you $700 for your 1960 Chevrolet Impala trade-in. You also have a grand in cash for a down payment, leaving a balance of $2,000 to finance for thirty-six months. You can easily handle the payments of $65 per month.

The deal and your credit are approved, and after six long weeks of waiting, your GTO rolls off the hauler at the dealer. After prep and filling out the paperwork, you take the GTO out and start looking for pigeons driving Chevys.

It didn't take long for this emblem to earn a reputation on the street. Most street racers knew better than to tangle with a GTO. "If you don't think this is enough warning," Pontiac noted, "you could always fly the skull and crossbones."

Previous page
The LeMans grille was blacked out and the GTO nameplate was installed.

as hairy." Judicious use of the order book could build a car for high-speed luxury cruising or for just blowing the hubcaps off the competition on the street. Options included air conditioning, a handsome four-spoke "wood" wheel (actually constructed of plastic), tachometer and several radio choices.

The beauty of the GTO was, like the big Pontiac models, the customer could option out a GTO to suit his preferences. A buyer who was strictly performance-minded checked off the high-performance options to package his GTO for drag racing, where the GTO would dominate the B/Stock classes. For those buyers who wanted the boulevard image of driving a GTO but desired creature comforts, there was a plethora of luxury options ranging from power windows to

a power antenna. The ultimate GTO was a combination of all these options. It was possible to literally build a poor-man's Grand Prix from the GTO option list.

The GTO hit the streets and instantly gained recognition as *the* high-performance car. In Detroit, no other manufacturer was prepared to compete against the GTO until the 1964 model year was virtually over. Oldsmobile fielded the 4-4-2, a competent package but underpowered with its 330 ci V-8. Buick assembled the Gran Sport Skylark by dropping in its 401 engine, but Buick lacked the performance image of Pontiac and sales were far behind the GTO. Although Chevrolet had its potent 409 engine, the Chevelle SS still relied on the 327 small-block; however, it was given a shot in the arm by offering the 350 hp Corvette 327. But it wasn't a big-cube engine, and that was part of the GTO's success.

The other car makers were slow to offer alternatives in 1964. Dodge and Plymouth were building special lightweight full-sized cars, but they were limited in production and quite expensive. They were also purpose-built as race cars, and as such were difficult to maintain and their drivability didn't match the GTO. Ford's Fairlane qualified

It didn't take long for GTOs to hit the drag strips, competing and winning in B/Stock. The Pampered Papoose driven by Howard Maseles was sponsored by Packer Pontiac.

Optional at extra cost was a manifold vacuum gauge mounted on the center console. It was available with manual or automatic transmissions.

as a mid-sized car, but the hottest engine offered was the code K 271 hp 289 ci engine. The top performance engine in the new Mustang was the 225 hp 289. The days of high-horsepower pony cars were still a few years away.

To indicate just how good a package the GTO could be, *Car and Driver* made a comparison of the GTO to its namesake, the Ferrari GTO. Using two GTOs prepared by Royal Pontiac, Pontiac's

The chrome-flashed Deluxe wheel cover was optional and featured ten cooling slots surrounding the center ornament. The 7.50x14 in. US Royal Tiger Paws were standard on all 1964 GTOs.

The Custom wheel cover was a three-piece affair with eight cooling slots in the wheel cover, a retaining band and a diecast, three-ear spinner ornament.

backdoor performance dealer in Royal Oak, Michigan, *Car and Driver* wrote that in their opinion the Pontiac GTO did everything the Ferrari could do for a lot less money. "We made a very bold statement with that story," Jim Wangers recalled. "Here we took the darling of the sports car set, the Ferrari, and put it up against something as gauche as a Pon-

tiac. The whole thing was just great image-building press for Pontiac."

The GTO captured the imagination of America. Although overshadowed by the fabulous Mustang, the introduction of the 1964 GTO opened the door for affordable performance. It appealed to the very market Wangers was in touch with: young buyers who wanted the looks and image the GTO provided. The GTO became much like the Corvette in that it was a rolling personal statement.

The tremendous success achieved by the GTO also meant Wangers' vision had been correct. The GTO carried out its mission, transferring Pontiac's image from the racetrack to the street. Its future and the continued strength of Pontiac as a builder of high-performance cars was ensured.

The fuel filler door was located in the center of the taillamp panel, which was trimmed in Marimba Red.

GTO interiors were offered in either Black, Dark Blue, Light Saddle, Dark Aqua, Medium Red or the Parchment scheme shown here with Custom Sport steering wheel. A variation of the fender emblem appeared on the instrument panel just above the glovebox door.

Royal Pontiac

The Performance Dealership

The story of Royal Pontiac reaches back to the late 1950s, when Ace Wilson, Jr., purchased a Pontiac franchise in Royal Oak, Michigan, a suburb on Woodward Avenue halfway between Detroit and Pontiac. Wilson's new Pontiac store was located on North Main Street, not far from Jim Wangers' home in Royal Oak.

Wangers, already established as an advocate of high performance, had been pushing for a network of Pontiac dealers across the country who would become performance dealers, specializing in sales and service of Pontiac Hot Chiefs. Wangers was turned down several times, but his persistence finally paid off. Frank Bridge, Pontiac's general sales manager, eventually agreed to allow Wangers to find one dealer who was willing to be a guinea pig. If the dealer would agree to stock special cars and special parts and get involved in special activities—read drag racing—Bridge promised to find a way of supporting it. The catch was, the connection had to be covert. "I don't want anyone to know it," Bridge told Wangers.

Wangers hooked up with Wilson and things began to happen. "Wilson liked racing," Wangers recalled. "He liked performance, he was a relatively new Pontiac dealer and he thought this was a swinging idea."

Of the two GTOs prepared by Royal for the Car and Driver *road test, only this Grenadier Red sport coupe survives.*

Within six months, Royal established a reputation as the dealer that stocked the fastest cars, had the service technicians that knew how to work on them and a parts department stocked with an assortment of aftermarket and factory performance parts. Wangers took the Royal name before the national press in 1960 when he piloted *Hot Chief Number 1* to the Stock Eliminator title at the NHRA Nationals in Detroit.

Wilson realized the vast potential in the sales and service of high-performance Pontiacs. "In this day and age of professional drag strip racers," stated Royal's 1963 brochure, "car dealers who sponsor Super Stocks are a dime a dozen. At Royal Pontiac, there's a difference. Most dealers who sponsor these hot jobs at the drag strip are content to sit back and wait. They figure a winner or even reasonable success at the strip will mean that all the local enthusiasts will "knock down the doors" to do business at their dealership. This just doesn't happen. At Royal, we go a step further. A successful Super Stocker at the strip is only the beginning. We want to pass our

experience on to you. We want to satisfy your performance needs and problems. We are prepared to offer all the Pontiac factory options plus a custom performance tune-up that is guaranteed to outperform any equivalent Pontiac in showroom stock condition. This treatment is called the 'Royal Bobcat' tune-up package."

It was this philosophy that set Royal Pontiac apart from the mainstream of dealers who weren't versed in the performance market or were apprehensive about the profitability of racing, building and selling special high-performance cars. But racing was just part of the Royal story.

"One of the first things I convinced Ace Wilson to do was to package a car that incorporated some of the special services and the special parts that he was putting into these cars and that's how the Royal Bobcat was born," Wangers recalled. "The Bobcat was created in 1961 off of a Catalina, and it's funny how we arrived at the name Bobcat. Back in those days Pontiac was putting their nameplates on their cars in big, separate

Royal's switch to GTOs was complete by 1965, and they campaigned a pair of Bobcats across the Midwest and the East. The tiger theme was a natural tie-in with the Bobcat package, and Hurst was a major player in supplying shifters and wheels for the cars. Notice the driver in the foreground wearing a tiger suit.

letters with little holes drilled in the sheetmetal. They had model names like Catalina, Ventura and Bonneville. Out of the words Bonneville and Catalina, we came up with the name Bobcat and the letters fit into the same number of holes that Catalina did."

The Bobcat was a packaged performance car, utilizing many of the performance options offered by Pontiac. Starting with the 389 Tri-Power, Royal used the factory's free-flowing exhaust manifolds and dual exhausts, aluminum wheels with the integral drums, four-speed manual gearbox and limited-slip rear. Royal then made special modifications to the car to make it a Bobcat. The distributor curve was reworked, as were

44

Jim Wangers in his trademark white baseball cap checks his mirror while racing the 1962 Hot Chief. Wangers cleaned house in this car, with a best of 12.38 seconds at 116.23 mph. The beautiful red and gold Poncho weighed in at a svelte 3,600 lb., thanks to extensive use of factory lightweight aluminum body components. The 421 was shifted at 6000 rpm and cranked out over 450 hp. It was the most successful Pontiac Royal had ever built.

the carburetor jets. The vacuum carburetor linkage was scrapped for a mechanical setup, and less restrictive mufflers were installed.

To visually set the Bobcat apart, all Catalina nameplates were removed, special paint was applied and the Bobcat nameplate was installed. "It was the first, really packaged supercar," recalled Wangers.

Royal began taking cues from both Pontiac and the aftermarket, and by 1963 they were reworking camshaft timing,

The official membership decal of the Royal Racing Team. Additional decals were available for 50¢.

Previous page
Shrouded in controversy, the Royal Bobcat GTO that blew the collective minds of the sophisticated staff of Car and Driver *has been fingered as a ringer because of its stock-nonstock status. Insiders like Wangers will swear the GTO was equipped with the stock 389 engine. Others believe the 389 was pulled and the bruising 421 HO with over 376 hp installed.*

changing compression ratios and making adjustments to the valvetrain to increase rpm.

It was the emergence of the GTO that ended the short reign of the Bobcat. Much that Wangers had learned in building the Bobcat package he related to the GTO. "When Pontiac finally created the one symbol of what Pontiac was all about in a total package called the GTO, there wasn't any room for a Royal Bobcat. So the Royal Bobcat

The Royal Team toured the country, leaving Detroit on Friday nights and pulling back into town the following week. It was hard work, recalled Milt Schornack, especially when he had a pile of work to face after racing the GTOs all weekend. Royal received tremendous exposure, thanks to the racing team and the numerous magazine articles written about the Bobcat-equipped GTOs.

became a tuning package or a performance package for the GTO, the 2+2 and later the Firebird."

When the GTO arrived on the scene, Royal began experimenting with the GTO, using the tricks they had learned over the years to juice the big Pontiac engine. The distributors were recurved, thin head gaskets were installed to boost compression, the carburetors were rejetted and the lifters were restricted by installing special fiber lock nuts that reduced lifter pump-up and allowed another 500 rpm. This became the Royal Bobcat package, and it could be installed in a GTO by Royal, or shipped as a kit with all necessary parts and instructions for installation by the customer.

The Royal Bobcat package on a GTO was identified by a decal that was applied to the C-pillar. Pontiac fans were also urged to send $3 and join the Royal Racing Team. Membership included a special window decal, price sheets for parts and services and a newsletter. To own a GTO with the Bobcat package, a Royal Racing Team decal on the windshield and a Royal license plate frame was to be one of the "swingingest" dudes on the street.

With the urging of Wangers, who was a "consultant" to Royal, the top car

48

The Car and Driver 1964 GTO launches with Milt Schornack at the wheel. The late Bill Sherman, who had owned the GTO since late 1964, brought the car out of storage several years ago with the help of Schornack. Schornack once campaigned the GTO at nostalgic drag-racing events across the country.

The Mystery Driver wearing the tiger suit would appear everywhere the Royal Racing Team went. Spectators were urged to race the Mystery Tiger and try to beat him in one of the Royal GTOs. The Mystery Tiger promotion came to a close when the costume was doffed to reveal George Hurst himself, although Hurst didn't always play the part.

When the "GTO vs. GTO" article appeared in the March 1964 issue of Car and Driver, *it created a storm of controversy. In the magazine's opinion, the Pontiac GTO was easily the equal of the Ferrari GTO. After the maga- zine hit the stands in late January 1964, GTO sales began to skyrocket. Editor David E. Davis still believes the article guaranteed the success of both the GTO and* Car and Driver.

magazines like *Hot Rod, Car Craft* and *Super Stock* beat a path to Royal to road test Bobcat GTOs and write articles on how Milt Schornack could supertune the GTO engine for more power and faster acceleration. It was not unusual to see pictures of Schornack bent over a Sun distributor, carefully setting the advance curve, or Royal mechanic Dave Warren cracking gears on the drag strip.

Because of the success of Royal Pontiac, there was considerable communication between Schornack and Pontiac Engineering. Parts would travel back and forth, and Schornack would experiment with setups and report back to Engineering on the results. One of the earliest experiments conducted by Royal that eventually appeared in production GTOs was cold-air induction, which Pontiac named Ram Air. Ram Air was introduced as an accessory package in 1965 after Royal had perfected the setup on the 1964 and 1965 GTOs.

Ace Wilson sold the performance arm of the dealership in 1969 to George (brother of John Z.) DeLorean's Leader Automotive. Royal Pontiac was eventually sold by Wilson, and a special era in Pontiac performance was over.

Milt Schornack nails second gear in a 1966 Royal Bobcat GTO. Schornack worked closely with many national magazines, preparing cars and doing the driving at local tracks like Motor City and Ubly. One of the most successful promotions was the GeeTO Tiger that appeared on the cover of the December 1965 issue of Car Craft.

Every Royal-equipped GTO received this decal, which was placed on the C-pillar of 1964 models. Later on, the decal could be ordered through the mail, and many a GTO that was neither a Bobcat nor which had been purchased from Royal wore this badge of honor.

Milt Schornack behind the wheel of the Car and Driver *Royal Bobcat GTO. Since the car was uncovered several years ago, Schornack has driven and displayed the GTO at shows across the country. He has retained much of the car's original appearance; however, it runs much stronger than it did on the street in 1964.*

The Mysterious *Car and Driver* Royal Bobcat

Perhaps one of the most famous Royal Bobcats was this Grenadier Red 1964, built on November 2, 1963, and eventually shipped to Royal on November 8. What happened to the car during that six-day period is open for conjecture; however, it most likely spent a few days next door at the Pontiac Engineering garage before finding its way to Royal Oak. Equipped with the 348 hp Tri-Power and four-speed transmission, the GTO was given the "Royal Treatment" and then delivered to Jim Wangers, who turned it—and an identical GTO painted blue—over to *Car and Driver* magazine. *Car and Driver* wrung both cars out at Daytona, spinning a rod in the red car and using the blue one for the remainder of the tests.

The Royal Bobcat GTOs accelerated from 0–60 mph in 4.6 seconds and turned the quarter mile in the low-thirteens. *Car and Driver* made no bones that the cars were tweaked by Royal, and pronounced the Pontiac GTO to be the equal of its Ferrari namesake in its March 1964 issue, which elicited howls of protest from the magazine's European-oriented readers, but provided Pontiac with reams of copy and great PR. It was after the *Car and Driver* test that GTO sales went ballistic.

What has remained a bone of contention to this day is what happened to the two GTOs during their stay at Pontiac Engineering. Some who were involved in servicing or driving the cars after they returned from Florida swear the two were equipped not with 389s but the thumping 421 HO (High Output), a behemoth that delivered 370 hp and was virtually impossible to distinguish from a 389.

The blue GTO was allegedly destroyed in a fire some years ago. The red car remains, and is now in the hands of Milt Schornack, who became the wizard of Royal in the mid-1960s, not long after the Grenadier Red 1964 GTO had made its triumphant return from road-test immortality. Schornack once campaigned the GTO at nostalgia drag races, turning low-elevens thanks to a vintage 421 HO and modified suspension.

The Car and Driver *Royal Bobcat* is today equipped with a 421 HO engine. Rumors continue to fly as to whether the GTO tested by Car and Driver *was a ringer or legitimately powered by a stock 389 with Royal supertuning.*

Royal used the 1964 Bobcat for various performance experiments, including a cold-air induction system that utilized three tubes fitted from the firewall above the heater box routed to a specially modified air cleaner. A plate now covers the holes Schornack cut over a quarter century ago.

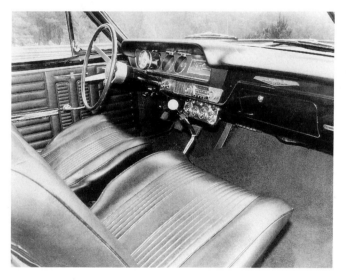

Schornack installed a vintage Sun tach and underhood gauges for drag racing. The Bobcat was campaigned locally for several months after its road test in Florida for Car and Driver.

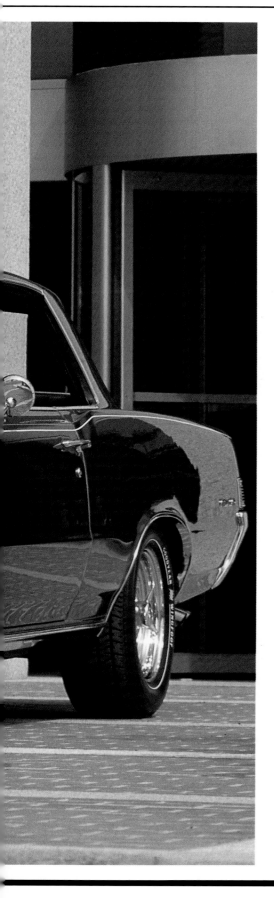

1965 GTO

America Discovers the Tiger

When Humble Oil began their ad campaign in 1962 urging Americans to buy Esso gasoline and "put a Tiger in your tank," advertising agencies began picking up on the tiger theme and applied it to push a multitude of products. Soon the striped beasts were everywhere. The word tiger had worked itself into the lexicon of the day, and every young man wanted to be a tiger, or at least wrap himself in that swinging image.

Pontiac had also used the tiger theme in several Tempest ads in 1963, but it didn't actually spread across the product line, nor did Pontiac aggressively image the Tempest that way. And while Pontiac didn't start out to promote the GTO as a tiger, it didn't take long for Wangers to recognize a good thing when he saw it, and the tiger concept slowly crept into some of the 1964 GTO advertising. "The GTO began to gather the image of the tiger," Wangers explained. "And quite honestly, this wasn't necessarily some-

thing that we went out front to promote. It just kind of happened."

The tiger theme began to snowball thanks to US Royal, which supplied tires for many GM products, and had produced the redline tire for the 1964 GTO. The redlines contributed to the GTO's capability to endlessly burn rubber, not because the car had such a tremendous amount of torque but because the skinny 7.75x14 in. tires had such a small footprint on the ground. For 1965, these redlines were dubbed Tiger Paws and US Royal launched a massive TV and print advertising campaign. After all, the name Tiger Paw was far more appealing than Super–Safety 800, the model designation for the four-ply bias-belted tire.

The GTO was a benefactor of the US Royal campaign. "We really kind of fell into it," Wangers said. "It was a label that grew onto the car because the tires were original equipment and we were the only car to offer the Tiger Paw. It was a logical conclusion: what has a tiger paw on it but a tiger?"

Pontiac constructed a major advertising campaign capitalizing on the tiger theme, starting at the dealer level, with black-and-gold striped paper covering the showroom windows. Added to this

This 1965 Teal Turquoise GTO is well known in the GTO hobby. Owned by Chuck Roberts since 1968, this GTO sports a set of Grand Prix parking lamps in the grille and Cragar SS wheels.

The GTO owner could also modify the underhood to suit his tastes. The use of chrome was very popular, and although Pontiac chromed the valve covers and air cleaner lid, there was plenty more virgin metal for the owner to chromeplate. The Ram Air tub (part of the over-the-counter cold-air accessory package) replaced the air cleaner bases and sealed to the underhood using a thick rubber gasket.

were tiger tails that hung from the fuel filler door in the bumper or emerging from the hood and draped across the fender. Television ads depicted a growling tiger leaping into the engine bay of a GTO. Pontiac magazine advertising proclaimed, "You don't know what a real tiger is until you hear this GeeTO Tiger growl!"

The Wide Track Pontiac Tiger campaign swept the nation, along with men's GTO cologne, GTO shoes and the "GeeTO Tiger," a three-minute song with the California surfer sound that was little more than a musical commercial for the GTO. On the flip side was a test drive of the GTO, in which the listener imagined himself riding shotgun while the announcer took a GTO through its paces on the test track. Imagination was precisely what it took, because in reality a stock GTO could hardly perform as the record indicated (the entire recording was done in a studio). Available from Pontiac for fifty cents, the record was also used to tie in a special promotion with Hurst. Advertisements by Hurst appeared in national car magazines like *Hot Rod* announcing a contest in which anyone who listened to the "GeeTO Tiger" recording, correctly counted the number of times the word tiger was used and explained "why I would like to own the original GeeTO Tiger," could send in their answer and be eligible to win the Grand Prize—a 1965 GTO with special Tiger Gold paint, gold-anodized Hurst wheels and a gold-plated Hurst shifter.

All of this promotion transformed the GTO's image far beyond its true street performance capabilities. Pontiac knew the hydraulic-lifter 389 couldn't outgun a Super Stock Plymouth or a Z-11 Chevrolet and avoided any type of comparison with these cars, which just two years before had been the only game in town. "We knew the only way we were going to survive was to take this car and equate

Peeking out from beneath the open scoop ornament is the chrome lid of a Tri-Power air cleaner. The optional cold-air package included a spare ornament that was opened by the owner and a tub that sealed to the underhood. The blast of cold air was said to be good for extra horsepower under hard acceleration.

The heart of the GTO was its engine, and the Tri-Power was Pontiac's high-performance jewel. It was docile at low speeds, possessed plenty of torque and didn't require a lot of maintenance. Rated at 360 hp, the Tri-Power could propel the GTO through the quarter in the low- to mid-fourteens straight off the showroom floor.

Previous page
The original GeeTO Tiger giveaway car still exists and is in good condition. The Hurst wheels and gold-plated shifter are still intact.

The Hurst shifter was standard equipment on every GTO built.

A popular showroom item was the tiger tail attached to the fuel filler door. The Tiger theme was used in the showrooms and in magazine and television advertising.

it more into a lifestyle," Wangers recalled. This was one of the reasons options like a dual four-barrel induction setup was scrapped, although the new single-scoop hood, which was actually planned for 1966, was placed on the 1965 GTO in anticipation of the canceled dual-quad option.

Pontiac gave the Tempest line a facelift in 1965, changing the headlamps from horizontal to vertical, much like the large Pontiacs had received beginning in 1963. The split-grille theme was retained and a large Pontiac crest was added between the deep-set grilles. For the GTO, the grilles were blacked out. The GTO nameplate seemed to float in the black left-hand grille, making it instantly recognizable from the more pedestrian Tempest and LeMans.

The flanks were virtually the same as on the 1964, as was the greenhouse. The rear was revised, featuring eight thin bars that ran across the back, stretching between the taillamp bezels. The GTO nameplate remained on the rear quarter, and the wedge-shaped 6.5 Litre emblem continued on the front fenders behind the wheel opening.

Inside, the seats were reupholstered, with the seat center inserts ornamented by diagonal bars and the Pontiac crest embossed in the center of the seatback. On the door panels, a smaller version of the fender emblem was attached near the window crank. The center console was nearly identical to the 1964, however, the instrument panel was completely redesigned. A larger pad hooded the top of the instrument panel, and a passenger grab bar was placed directly above the glovebox door. The gauge panel retained the four-pod design of previous years. The standard gauge arrangement included a fuel gauge and speedometer, with telltale lamps for temperature, amps and oil pressure. A clock was optional.

A host of new options were offered for the 1965 GTO, including a Rally cluster. This gauge cluster placed the fuel gauge and battery telltale lamp in the left pod. In the second pod from the left was the 120 mph speedometer, odometer and a semi-furled checkered flag to

It was possible to load up the GTO with virtually every interior luxury such as air conditioning, power windows and tilt steering wheel. Combined with performance options like Tri-Power and a four-speed transmission, it was possible to build a true Grand Touring automobile.

Another example of what made the GTO special from other performance cars was the instrument package layout. While other manufacturers used a large, horizontal sweep speedometer and tiny, tacked-on gauges, the GTO's Rally cluster was housed in four large pods that were easy to read and looked like they belonged in a European sports car.

CAR and DRIVER   MAY, 1965

60   61

Previous page
Two young ladies and a 1965 GTO convertible were the stars in one particular Pontiac television spot, out for a Sunday drive in the country. The commercial ends as the GTO returns at dusk to the city and the announcer coos, "It's the swingingest!" The 1965 GTO in Montero Red.

reinforce the rally theme. In the third pod was an 8000 rpm tachometer with a 250 degree sweep. It was much larger and easier to read than the small, 90 degree tach offered in 1964. In the fourth, far right-hand pod was a water temperature and oil pressure gauge. All characters and graduations were white on black dials, and a wood applique decorated the face of the gauge panel.

Other new interior options for 1965 included an AM-FM radio and three-spoke Custom Sport steering wheel. For the first time, a wheel option was offered for the GTO. The silver-textured 14x6 in. Rally wheel was constructed of stamped steel and featured six cooling slots and a chromed center cap.

Under the new hood was a revised version of the 389 ci engine, sporting a new intake-manifold design with revised runners and ports. The cylinder-head passages were also new, however, intake and exhaust valves were still measured at 1.92 and 1.66 in., respectively. Camshaft profile was unchanged from the 1964 engine. The standard engine still utilized a Carter AFB four-barrel topped by a redesigned chrome air cleaner with louvers in the cleaner's circumference, appearing quite similar to the Corvette. Horsepower for the base engine was upped to 335 at 5000 rpm, with 431 lb-ft of torque at 3200 rpm.

The optional Tri-Power engine also featured the new intake-manifold-runner design, and shared the cylinder

Pontiac quickly learned that they had a tiger by the tail with the GTO, and by the time of this ad in the May 1965 issue of Car and Driver *magazine, the GTO was now the GeeTO Tiger with tiger tail streaming from the hood. Tagged to the ad was the release of "GeeTO Tiger," a special record offered by Pontiac for fifty cents. The record cover pictured a tiger skin adorning the hood of a yellow GTO.*

heads and block, 10.75:1 pistons, Arma-Steel connecting rods and cast pearlitic malleable-iron crankshaft with the base engine. Tri-Power engines mated to the two-speed automatic transmission continued to use vacuum-controlled secondaries, but stick-shift models now featured mechanical linkages for the outer carburetors. The camshaft timing was a tad higher, at 288 degrees duration for intake and 302 degrees duration exhaust. In Tri-Power configuration, the

GTO was rated at 360 hp at 5200 rpm and delivered 424 lb-ft at 3600 rpm. Cast-iron exhaust manifolds dumped the spent gases through dual exhausts with reverse-flow mufflers and resonators.

Four transmissions were available in 1965, starting with a two-speed automatic with either standard column mount or optional console location. Three manual gearboxes were on the order sheet—a three-speed with floor-mounted shifter, and two four-speeds, one close-ratio with a 2.20:1 first gear, and a wide-ratio with a 2.56:1 first gear. All manual boxes were stirred by a Hurst shifter; a center console was optional with the stick shifts. Rear-axle ratios ranged from an economical 3.08:1 up to gut-wrenching 4.33:1 cogs that could be ordered with any transmission and required the extra-cost heavy-duty radiator, power brakes, metallic brake linings and limited-slip rear options.

The suspension was unchanged from 1964, with independent front suspension using unequal-length upper and lower control arms, coil springs, hydraulic shock absorbers and antisway bar. Around back, the four-link rear was used with a live axle, coil springs and hydraulic shock absorbers. Manual steering was slow, with a ratio of 24:1 and a hefty four turns lock to lock. Power assist was faster with a 17:1 ratio.

The weakest link in the GTO package—the brakes—was unchanged from 1964. The metallic linings were again offered; however, in an effort to improve the GTO's braking capabilities, an aluminum front drum option was now on the order sheet. The finned aluminum units were designed to dissipate heat more efficiently and improve braking.

At 3,700 lb., the GTO was no lightweight, but it was 500–600 lb. lighter than full-sized high-performance cars. In pure stock configuration, the 360 hp GTO could turn the quarter in 14.5 seconds at 100 mph. Dropping the exhausts, advancing the timing and bolting on a set of slicks dropped that to 14.06 at 102 mph. As the late Roger Huntington observed, "the quarter-mile times should win the B/Stock class on a good many dragstrips around the country on a given Sunday afternoon."

Because of the tremendous success enjoyed by Pontiac in 1965, with the GTO in particular and the entire product

line in general, the division won the *Motor Trend* Car of the Year award for the entire product line-up. It was one of the last public accolades Pete Estes would field as general manager of Pontiac Motor Division. In June of 1965, Estes was promoted to general manager of Chevrolet and John Z. DeLorean was

The Pontiac-Hurst relationship ran deep. It was unusual for Hurst not to use a Pontiac product in their mid-1960s advertising. To become a Hurst Hustler, all one needed to do was purchase a set of Hurst wheels and send in the membership form. Along with a jacket patch and a membership card came three Hurst Hustler emblems that the owner could proudly install on his car.

elevated to the top spot at Pontiac. The last member of the Knudsen-Estes-DeLorean triumvirate that would rule over Pontiac's successful reign as America's performance car builder was in the driver's seat. The number-three sales position firmly belonged to Pontiac, and with the brilliant young DeLorean at the helm, the future gleamed. DeLorean was attuned to the youth market and understood what it took to market cars like the GTO to the eighteen- to twenty-five-year-old market, which was coming into its own as a huge consumer base. Wangers continued to monitor the trends on the street and telegraph them to DeLorean. He recognized what image and profile accomplished, and that marketing was as important as styling and engineering.

"We put the GTO and its image in the drive-in and we put it in the record machine and we put it in the minds of

What did you expect Pontiac to put on a tiger?

Ordinary tires?

A tiger's entitled to something special:
A set of tiger paws.
And that's exactly what Pontiac went out and got for it.
The tiger, of course, is Pontiac's new GTO. The wildest thing in Detroit. The one that's getting the raves in the road and track magazines.
The tiger's paw is the new U.S. Royal Super-Safety 800. The one that's been picked by Pontiac as standard equipment for the GTO.

Here's what the tiger's paw has done, in special tests for safety and durability:
100 miles at 120 miles per hour without a failure.
17,000 miles at 83 miles per hour, 16 hours a day, without a failure. (Of course, you could expect to get much more mileage under normal driving conditions.)
It has a construction that's taken 300° temperature build-ups without flinching. And that's well above what it's ever likely to run into, even after

a whole day's driving on the turnpike on a hot summer's day with the whole family in the car and the trunk loaded with luggage. (Whew!)
The tiger's paw is sure-footed at high speeds. It corners nimbly and quietly. It gives you a nice sense of stability when you're taking a curve.
If you do a lot of turnpike driving, then you ought to have a set of tiger paws under you.
You'll find them at U.S. Royal tire dealers. Rarin' to go.

Hurst and the GTO

The relationship between George Hurst and Pontiac was firmly established in the early 1960s. Pontiac was the first to offer Hurst's stout three-speed floorshifter, and Estes and Wangers had urged Hurst to develop a four-speed shifter, which he did in 1961. Pontiac immediately put it in their order book. When the GTO arrived in 1964, it was equipped with the Hurst lever, and every manual gearbox GTO built until 1974 was stirred with a Hurst stick.

When Hurst decided to build aftermarket wheels, he constructed them with the same bulletproof engineering that went into his shifters. In the early 1960s, aftermarket wheels were prone to breakage because in the manufacturers' zeal for light weight or styling, lateral load capabilities were less than adequate, and many wheels failed, often causing accidents. George Hurst chose to build an unbreakable wheel.

Hurst built his wheel center out of forged aluminum alloy with heavy-duty steel rims. The rims featured a load-distributing stabilizer plate welded to the rim, and by riveting *and* welding the center section to the rim, the wheel was virtually

unbreakable. Dubbed The Dazzler by Hurst because of its zinc diachromate coloration, the Hurst wheel could be personalized by choosing one of twenty-four different combinations of beauty ring finish, rim bead design and center spoke finish. The Hurst wheel wasn't cheap, priced at $69.50 less lug nuts in the Hurst catalog, but then Hurst was selling safety, construction and styling. The wheels were assigned individual serial numbers for theft protection, and Hurst issued an unconditional guarantee against wheel failure because of faulty design or manufacture.

The Hurst wheel was introduced to the public, tied into the GTO. Because of the Name the Tiger contest conducted by Hurst, Pontiac and Petersen Publications, publishers of *Hot Rod* and *Motor Trend*, the GTO was chosen to pace the *Motor Trend* Riverside 500, and the wheel was introduced at a large press bash in Los Angeles on January 5, 1965, mounted on several GTOs, including one dressed out as the pace car for the race.

Although the wheel was superbly built (it was certified for race use by the NHRA), very handsome and highly advertised by Hurst, the wheel was one of Hurst's few marketing failures.

To many owners, the GTO is also an opportunity to express one's personal statement. Some GTO owners have taken their favorite components from various years and combined them. This particular 1965 interior sports a 1964 Custom Sport wheel and 1967 seats, door and quarter trim panels.

Previous page
Part of what made the GTO stand out from its rivals was the execution of the interior. The driver's seating position, the instrumentation and the overall ergonomics were second only to the Corvette.

The rear seat was roomy and comfortable, however, legroom was cramped for adults.

The 1965 GTO had a taut, aggressive stance. Heavy-duty springs and shocks were standard, as was a front antisway bar. The split-grille styling was a Pontiac trademark that had originated in 1959.

The words GTO 6.5 Litre also appeared on door panels for the first time in 1965.

young people,'' Wangers recollected with pride. "We began to equate the fact that a car was much like a suit of clothes or a pair of shoes. It was the kind of thing that you personified yourself with. And very quickly, almost overnight, there were young guys who were driving a GTO because the GTO had suddenly become accepted much the same as the Corvette had been. The GeeTO Tiger campaign and its success was really one of the most fun periods that any manufacturer went through."

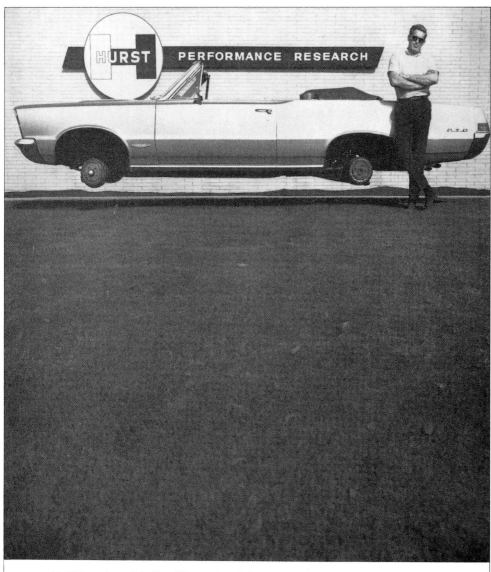

The product announcement for the new Hurst wheel was unusual in that it didn't show the product. All that's pictured is this 1965 GTO convertible floating in air, awaiting its new set of Hurst wheels.

The 1965 GTO in Burgundy. The bubble-styled hood scoop was first planned for 1966 but then moved up a year in anticipation of a dual four-barrel carburetor option. The option was canceled, but the hood was retained for 1965.

For 1965, a grab bar was installed above the glovebox next to the GTO nameplate.

Back in the mid-1960s, a Hurst-equipped emblem was a badge of honor to be worn by musclecars sporting Hurst equipment.

Tied in to the other GTO ads hyping the GTO Tiger and the record was this promotion, put together by Petersen Publishing Company, Hurst and Pontiac. Grand prize was a loaded GTO, equipped with Hurst wheels and a gold-plated shifter. To enter, all one needed to do was count the number of words in the song "GeeTO Tiger" and include a reason for wanting to own the original GeeTO Tiger.

The 1965 GTO received minor styling changes. The quad headlamps were revised from horizontal to vertical, and the grilles were deep set and blacked out. The GTO emblem appeared in the left-hand grille.

The GTO nameplate adorned the quarter panels and the deck lid. A single pinstripe ran the length of the upper beltline from headlamp to taillamp.

Next page
Riding on a 115 in. wheelbase, the 1965 GTO was a nimble-handling, quick-accelerating package that was hard to beat on the street or strip.

We call it GTO. Purists call it names. You'll call it fantastic.

You can get a set of five big, full-color action shots of the GTO and 2 + 2—suitable for framing—see details below.

GTO means *Gran Turismo Omologato*. In Italian, that means about twenty thousand bucks. The way we say it is easier to pronounce and it costs less besides. For a better definition, you have to ask the owners of Pontiac GTOs. They say it means a beautiful car with a swift, smooth 389-cubic inch engine, suspension that makes it handle like our ads say it will, and brakes that stop it right here and now. Why would a car like this make the purists mad? Maybe we should raise the price.

Pontiac will send you a set of five huge 26" x 11½" full-color reproductions of the famous Wide-Track Tigers in action just like the one above—along with a complete set of specs and tune-up tips—and they're suitable for framing. Send 25¢ to cover handling and mailing to Wide-Track Tigers, P. O. Box 888F, 196 Wide-Track Blvd., Pontiac, Michigan. *(No stereos shown.)*

Quick Wide-Track Tigers—Pontiac GTO and 2 + 2

The relationship between Car and Driver *and the GTO continued beyond the infamous 1964 road test that elevated the GTO to Ferrari status, in the eyes of* Car and Driver. *This ad was Pontiac's rebuttal to the many letters the magazine received taking them to task for their editorial blasphemy against the Italian sports car.*

Ram Air, Royal Pontiac and the GTO

The idea of tamping cold air into a high-performance engine had already been well proven on the drag strip; Pontiac racers had installed scoops on the hoods of their 1962 Super Duty Catalinas. When the GTO was introduced, testing was already under way on developing a cold-air package for the street. Because of the design of the 1964 GTO's hood-scoop ornaments, which flanked each side of the hood line and were more scalloped than scooped, a cowl-induction setup, similar to that used in NASCAR, was tested and abandoned.

With the proposed dual-quad setup for the 1965 GTO, a new scoop design was devised, placing the bubble at the hood centerline and capping the opening with a pot-metal ornament retained by three speednuts. This hood would be standard on all GTOs. Dual-quad cars would be available with a cold-air package, consisting of a metal tub or "pan" installed on the carburetors, taking the place of the air-cleaner base. The outer edges of the tub would curl upward and be lined with a thick rubber gasket that, when the hood was closed, would seal out the hot underhood air. The solid ornament would be replaced by an open unit that allowed outside air to be "rammed" into the carburetors under wide-open throttle to increase horsepower.

When the dual-quad option was canceled, a decision was made to leave the hood on the car with the closed ornament installed. It was, however, not the end of the cold-air package. Thanks to testing conducted by Royal Pontiac and Pontiac Engineering, a new air-scoop accessory package was released on August 17, 1965. Available to dealers to sell over the counter, the $49.50 package (part number 984716) was designed to fit the Tri-Power induction setup and consisted of the tub, gasket, a closed scoop ornament and instructions on removing the rear section of the forward hood bracing and opening the replacement ornament. The design and construction of the components was similar to the ill-fated dual-quad cold-air package.

While it would be several more years before becoming available as a production option and officially designated Ram Air, the 1965 air scoop package was the first cold-air induction system for the GTO.

Standard equipment on all 1965 GTOs was the 7.75x14 in. US Royal bias-belt redline tire. If the optional Deluxe, Custom or wire wheel cover or the Rally wheel was not ordered, the basic hubcap was installed. Many buyers pitched the factory wheel covers for a set of Cragars or chrome reversed wheels.

The Custom Spinner wheel disc was an extra-cost item and featured six cooling slots and the words Pontiac Motor Division in the center of the three-eared spinner.

Around back, the GTO had a set of louvered taillamps, trimmed by bright eyebrows and the name Pontiac spelled out in large block letters. The chrome exhaust tips were optional.

1966 GTO

The Juggernaut Rolls On

When the 1966 GTO was introduced in September 1965, DeLorean's stewardship as Pontiac general manager was only a few months old. The 1966 model year would prove to be pivotal in the history of the GTO for several reasons. Most significantly, the GTO matured from an option package based on the LeMans to a separate series with its own 242 model designation. Thanks to the resounding success Pontiac had enjoyed with the GTO in 1964 and 1965, the future of the GTO was ensured for at least the next five model years. Sales of the 1964 GTO had tallied 32,450 units and the 1965 GTO had surpassed Pontiac's projection of 50,000 units by a total of 75,352 cars. With the tremendous success of the GTO in the showroom, Pontiac penciled in sales projections in the 80,000 range for 1966.

Another factor in the GTO's elevation to series status was the climate within General Motors. GM management had come around to the concept of the musclecar, and the engine displacement ceiling for mid-sized cars was raised to 400 ci. Buick, Oldsmobile and Chevrolet were given the corporate nod to aggressively field their own versions of the GTO. Oldsmobile's 4-4-2, which had been released in the tail end of the 1964 model year, had grown into a 400 ci contender in 1965, and for 1966 offered a three two-barrel induction system, its first since the J-2 option of the late 1950s. Buick's Gran Sport was repackaged with the 401 and upgraded options; however, at 340 hp, small exhaust valves and no specific performance camshaft, it still was no match for the GTO. Sister division Chevrolet was the biggest in-house threat to the GTO. The SS396 Chevelle was offered in three horsepower versions—the base 325 hp, 360 hp and a thumping 375 hp engine that was available on special order.

Ford and Chrysler weren't sitting on their hands while the GTO and other GM musclecar programs were gathering strength. Ford's weakness was their lack of a large-displacement engine to drop into the redesigned 1966 Fairlane and Mercury Comet. The GT and GTA were added to the Fairlane line-up, equipped

GTO stands for *Gran Turismo Omologato*. You've probably heard of it. A Pontiac in a saber-toothed tiger skin. The deceptively beautiful body comes in convertible, sports coupe, and hardtop configurations. With pinstriping. On a heavy-duty suspension system that thinks it's married to the ground. Bucket seats and carpeting. Wood-grained dash. Redlines or whitewalls at no extra cost. Chromed 335-hp 4 barrel under the hood. Fully-synchronized 3-speed on the column. Or order a heavy-duty all-synchro 3-speed or 4-speed with Hurst floor shifter. Or 2-speed auto. Or the 360-hp 3 2-BBL. There's a catalog full of options. See if you can get your Pontiac dealer to cough one up. That's the GTO/2+2 performance catalog. You'll recognize it. It vibrates.

Speak softly and carry a GTO

On the high banks at the GM proving grounds, this 1966 GTO barreling by was one of the last speed-oriented ads to be run by Pontiac. New corporate guidelines issued by GM for 1967 forbade these types of ads from appearing in the future.

with the venerable 390 ci FE engine that produced 335 hp. Mercury's Cyclone GT was a carbon copy of the Fairlane GT. At the tail end of the model year, a few of these cars received the 425 hp, 427 ci engine, but it was produced in limited numbers, mostly to enhance the prod-uct line's image. Combined sales of the Fairlane GT and Cyclone GT were a disappointment to Ford, barely breaking the 53,000 unit mark.

Chrysler was in a much stronger position to counter the success of the GTO, and they rolled out the heavy artillery in 1966 in the form of the street Hemi. Dodge also released the new fastback Charger in January of 1966. Although the majority of Chargers were sold with the more mundane 318 and 361 two-barrel engines, both Dodge and Plymouth offered the 325 hp 383 ci engine and the pavement-melting 426 Hemi. Interestingly enough, the Hemi-powered Plymouth Satellite, with 425 hp—65 more than the Tri-Power GTO—only turned the quarter a few tenths quicker than a Royal-prepared GTO, although *Popular Hot Rodding* did record 13.25 seconds at 109.9 mph in a 1966 Hemi Satellite.

All this competition did little to slow the GTO's momentum. At the end of the model year, Pontiac's cash register rang to the tune of 96,946 units as the GTO sales juggernaut rolled on. The Wide Track Tiger was simply too entrenched in the minds of young, performance-minded enthusiasts, and Wangers' genius in promoting the GTO's image was a major contributing factor in the GTO holding back the wave of fledgling competitors.

Much of the GTO's appeal in 1966 can be attributed to Pontiac's handsome restyling effort. Although still riding the same 115 in. wheelbase, all the GM intermediates were reskinned for 1966, and the GTO seemed to benefit the most from the restyling. In fact, it looked more like the full-sized Grand Prix, and it attracted buyers who were drawn to the Grand Prix's styling but resisted the high sticker price and the dimensions of the larger model.

Pontiac again expanded the GTO's option list in 1966, and upgraded the car's interior appointments. According to Wangers: "A maturer performance market emerged as a significant factor, and we felt that perhaps some people might be turned off by the Grand Prix or the Bonneville as being just too big. We thought they may be looking for some kind of personal sophistication in a little smaller package."

When the sales figures for the 1965 and 1966 Grand Prix are examined, a case can be made that the GTO possibly did purloin some potential customers from the GP. Sales of the 1965 Grand Prix totaled 56,881, while 1966 GP sales turned down to 36,757 (excluding chassis sales, which totaled 643 in 1965 and 553 in 1966). Whether the GTO is directly responsible for the decline in 1966 GP

Options like the three-spoke Custom Sport steering wheel and tilt steering column were again available. The instrument panel fascia was covered in real wood veneer.

The diecast GTO emblem was located on the front fenders. A smaller version of the emblem appeared on the door panels.

sales is conjectural; however, it is interesting to note that GTO sales went up 21,594 units in 1966 while Grand Prix sales went down 21,124 units. How significant the GTO was to the decline in GP sales will never be fully ascertained.

The restyling of the 1966 GTO started at the front. The thematic Pontiac split-grille style was retained, but the grilles were plastic like the GP and deep set, with the parking-turn signal lamps

Standard in the GTO was this 389 ci engine, rated at 335 hp. Under the chrome-louvered air cleaner was a Carter AFB four-barrel carburetor.

incorporated into the grille, also like the GP. The Pontiac crest was moved to the hood, and the air scoop bubble and ornament were identical to 1965. Although the flanks were devoid of chrome trim, a bright rocker panel molding extended from the rear of the front-wheel opening to the front of the rear-wheel opening. Brightwork also trimmed the wheel openings. A single, thin pinstripe traced the upper beltline. The 6.5 Litre emblem was retained on the trailing edge of the lower front fenders and the GTO nameplate was affixed to the quarter panels. A smaller GTO nameplate was attached to the deck lid. The taillamp panel was cleaned up, with the name Pontiac spelled out in block letters and thin, bright eyebrows trimming the taillamp louvers again, similar to the Grand Prix.

The rooftop was redesigned, with curved side glass and the sail panels extended back in a semi-fastback effect; the rear glass was more vertically inset into the C-pillars. As in previous years, a hardtop and sport coupe were offered in 1966, along with a convertible.

The standard wheels were stamped steel and adorned by a simple hubcap with the words Pontiac Motor Division spelled out. Deluxe, Custom and wire wheel covers were offered optionally, as was the 14x6 in. Rally wheel. The Rally wheel was similar to the 1965 version, but the center cap was now painted black. As expected, US Royal 7.75x14 in.

Three Options That Never Were

There were three options considered for the 1966 model year that were never released.

Pontiac's beautiful aluminum eight-lug wheel with integral hub and drum had been an extremely popular option on the big cars, and development work had been ongoing for a version of the eight-lug for the intermediate models. This wheel was constructed of cast iron, utilized the same hub and drum assembly and was retained by eight chrome-plated socket-head Allen bolts threaded into the brake drum. It was to be offered on all Tempest, LeMans and GTO models in an attempt to improve the series' woeful braking system. By using twenty-four radial cooling fins, the gain in heat dissipation over the separate iron drum would provide better braking characteristics and longer brake-lining life. It was canceled just prior to production because the wheel was too heavy and too costly to produce.

DeLorean was impressed by the sophistication of European sport sedans, and wanted to meld some of the engineering philosophy from the Continent into Pontiac's design. In 1966–1967, the overhead-cam six-cylinder Tempest-LeMans Sprint was as close as an American car maker came to what BMW and Mercedes were building. DeLorean had also toyed with a radial tire option in 1966, even to the point of naming Michelin as an OE (original equipment) supplier. American tire manufacturers had not yet perfected their version of the radial tire, which was popular in Europe. DeLorean recognized the radial tire's superior ride and handling characteristics, and wanted them for the GTO. Pressure from American OE tire companies forced the cancellation of the option before 1966 production began.

Another option DeLorean had favored for several years was The Tiger Button. An under-the-dash handle would open baffles in the mufflers, reducing back pressure and thus improving performance and increasing the exhaust note. The Tiger Button was kicked around for several years before it was finally released as the Vacuum Operated Exhaust in the beginning of the 1970 model year. The option was short-lived; Pontiac canceled it less than two months after the 1970 models had been released.

The cold-air package was again offered as an over-the-counter package. However, in February 1966, Pontiac released the 360 hp XS option, which included a higher-lift camshaft, stiffer valve springs with dampers and the air cleaner tub and extra scoop ornament packed in the trunk for dealer installation.

A thin chrome bar outlined the trailing edge of the deck lid and the quarter panels. A single pinstripe ran along the upper beltline from the end of the quarter panel to the headlamp bezel.

redline Tiger Paw tires were standard. Whitewalls were available on request.

Inside, the GTO's interior was completely restyled. The dash pad was larger and extended from door to door, with a deep overhang above the instrument panel. The grab bar over the glovebox was redone, and the instrument panel fascia was enlarged and covered by a real wood applique.

The four-pod gauge layout was retained from previous years, and stan-

The GTO was completely restyled for 1966. The Coke-bottle flair of the rear quarter panels, begun with the 1963 Grand Prix, is very prominent in this profile view of a Montero Red convertible.

M&H Race Master slicks were popular at the drags in the mid-sixties. This Royal-prepared 1966 with Tri-Power could still light 'em up off the line, even with sticky M&H rubber.

The wire wheel disc option featured a two-eared spinner and looked like a real wire wheel.

Royal Pontiac continued to build and sell their Bobcat-equipped GTOs in 1966. The Bobcat decal, which appeared on the C-pillars on 1964–1965, was now affixed to the front fenders, just behind the bumper wrap-around.

A new option for all A-body Pontiac models was red plastic fender liners. The fender liners were constructed from heavy-gauge plastic and molded to fit inside the front and rear wheelhouses and were retained by screws. They improved the looks of the GTO and kept salt and dirt out of the wheelhouse. The Rally wheel was mostly unchanged from 1966. The center cap, chromed in 1965, was now painted matte black.

The vertical headlamp theme was continued from 1965. The grilles, however, were revised and were constructed of plastic, a first for Pontiac. The plastic grilles also appeared on the 1966 Grand Prix.

The driving lights for the GTO were mounted within the grilles.

dard instrumentation was a combination of telltale lamps, a fuel gauge and speedometer. An optional Rally clock, placed in the far right-hand pod, was available only with the standard gauge cluster. The Rally gauge cluster was carried over from 1965. The left-hand pod contained the fuel gauge and the battery telltale lamp. The left center pod housed the 120 mph speedometer and an odometer. An 8000 rpm tachometer with 5200 rpm redline was in the right-center pod, and the water temperature and oil pressure gauges resided in the far right-hand pod. The alphanumeric characters on the gauges were white on a green field. Accessory switches, such as power top, rear speaker fader or power antenna, were located above the gauge cluster, attached to the lower side of the instrument panel ledge. Controls and switches for wipers, headlamps, ignition and cigar lighter were below the gauges on the cluster fascia. The standard steering wheel was a solid, two-spoke design, and could be upgraded by the three-spoke Custom Sport wheel option, which was unchanged from the 1965 model.

The bucket seats were redesigned, with more padding and featuring horizontally rib-patterned upholstery. Two new seat options included a reclining

Starring with the Monkees in the hit TV show was a specially designed 1966 GTO, created by California customizer Dean Jeffries.

Extensions were added to the front and rear fenders. Dean Jeffries trial-fits the stock left-hand GTO grille to the new front end taking shape. The stock grilles were used along with the drivetrain and instrument panel.

The Monkeemobile

Consistent with Jim Wangers' aggressive marketing efforts, the GTO appeared on a number of television shows in 1966. Pontiac sponsored the popular "My Three Sons," and a variety of Pontiac products were always prominent in many scenes. The character Maj. Tony Nelson in the "I Dream Of Jeannie" TV show also drove a GTO convertible.

Perhaps one of the most famous cars on TV in 1966 was the Monkeemobile, which transported the rock group The Monkees both on their TV show and at live appearances around the country. The brainchild of Wangers, the Monkeemobile was the creation of Los Angeles car customizer Dean Jeffries. Pontiac supplied Jeffries with a 1966 GTO convertible as a base. The car was equipped with the standard 335 hp engine and automatic transmission. Jeffries cut away the floor and trunk pan and altered the rear suspension, installing semi-elliptical springs and reinstalling a new floor. He retained the basic taillamp design; however, a center compartment was fabricated to house a drag chute.

The front and rear sheet metal were lengthened, and a new nose was designed utilizing the stock grilles. A nonfunctional GMC 671 blower was bolted onto the 389 and a custom interior with four-bucket seats was installed, with another seat in the open trunk. Since Pontiac had picked up the bill for Jeffries' work, they viewed it appropriate that the GTO emblems appear on the fenders and the GTO nameplate remain in the front grille. The show's producers, however, felt it would be difficult to attract other car makers to purchase commercial time, so the GTO nameplate on the grille was removed.

Two Monkeemobiles were eventually built. One went on tour with the band and, according to Jeffries, was left in Australia. The other was used for the television show and is today in the hands of a private collector. It occasionally is displayed at major automotive events.

The Monkeemobile started life as a 1966 GTO convertible equipped with the standard 335 hp engine and automatic transmission. The trunk and floor pans were modified, and the rear suspension was changed from four-link coil to semi-elliptical springs.

passenger seat and headrests, in keeping with the more luxurious upgrade of the overall interior. The door and quarter trim panels echoed the rib pattern of the seats, and the GTO emblem was mounted in the center of the door panels. A host of power and luxury accessories was offered in 1966, including AM-FM radio, tilt steering column, power driver's seat and power windows. The GTO office was considerably more posh in 1966.

While the GTO's exterior and interior were totally redesigned for 1966, the drivetrain and underpinnings were virtually a carbon copy of 1965; the only changes being a new cylinder head with the same valve diameters as 1965, and an enlargement of the center carburetor on Tri-Power engines.

An even-odd pattern of alternating styling and engineering cycles had begun in 1965 and would continue through 1971. In odd-numbered years, the drivetrains would be revised while in even-numbered years, major styling changes would take place. Consequently, the 1965 GTO received new drivetrains, while the body was only given a facelift. In 1966, the body was restyled, while the drivetrain was carried over. This cycle would hold true in 1967 (new engine and transmission, cosmetic styling changes); 1968 (major restyling, drivetrain retained); 1969 (new engine options, styling facelift); 1970 (same engines, new body style); and 1971 (new engines, cosmetic facelift).

One addition to the GTO engine line-up was quietly released in February of 1966. Designated XS (denoting the engine code), this was a factory-built Tri-Power Ram Air package. The over-the-counter, cold-air package that had been released in 1965 was again offered in 1966; however, the XS option went beyond just a carburetor air cleaner tub and open scoop element. The XS option also included a new camshaft (part number 9785744) and stiffer valve springs that used a single spring with an inner spiral flat metal damper instead of the usual inner and outer valve spring arrangement. The 744 camshaft had the same .406 in. lift as the Tri-Power camshaft, but the lobe profiles were different, with intake duration of 301 degrees and exhaust duration of 313 degrees, and an overlap of 76 degrees. The 744 cam would become part of the factory-installed Ram Air package offered from

At the drags in the mid-sixties, GTOs ran in B/Stock. All it took for a 360 hp Tri-Power Goat to turn mid- to high-twelves was some minor engine work, open headers and a set of slicks.

One of the first Pro-Stock drag cars was Clint Logan's Legend, based out of Colorado. Logan's GTO was all-Pontiac, and that included Poncho power under the hood.

Not all GTOs came with bucket seats and four speeds, as evidenced by this GTO convertible equipped with bench seat and automatic transmission on the column.

Previous page
The GTO interior was also redesigned for 1966. The instrument panel fascia was enlarged, but the traditional four-pod cluster was retained. Standard transmission was a three-speed manual with the shifter on the steering column. Few GTOs were so equipped. Most came with the Hurst floor-shifter and four-speed gearbox.

1967 to the middle of the 1969 model year.

A set of mandatory options was required with the XS option. The buyer had to accept the M21 close-ratio, four-speed transmission, 4.33:1 rear gearing, limited-slip rear, heavy-duty fan and metallic brake linings. The XS engine was capable of propelling the two-ton 1966 GTO through the quarter mile in 13.91 seconds at more than 100 mph, about 0.2 second and 3 mph quicker than the standard Tri-Power.

The release of the XS option received little fanfare and, according to Pontiac historian Pete McCarthy, only 190 XS engines were built; it's estimated that approximately 185 GTOs received the XS option. Pontiac Engineering also experimented with a four-barrel version of the cold-air induction package for the 1966 GTO, using a smaller pan fitted over the Carter AFB carburetor. Although it was abandoned before the 1966 model year began, it, and the XS option, pointed the way for future GTO Ram Air engines.

The GTO had come a long way in just three years, selling more than 200,000 units and dominating its market niche. Next to the Ford Mustang, the Pontiac GTO had been the most successful new

The GTO nameplate was on the quarter panels and deck lid. The nameplate consisted of chrome letters faced with black on a chrome bar. The deck-lid nameplate was smaller than the ones that appeared on the quarters.

car ever launched by an American car maker. But internal and external forces beyond the control of John DeLorean or Jim Wangers were about to converge and have a profound effect on how the GTO was equipped, imaged and marketed. The GTO had reached its zenith as the dominant marque in the musclecar field, and the phenomenal success of 1966 would never again be duplicated.

The 1966 GTO, here in Fontaine Blue with Black vinyl top, was an excellent road car. The suspension was firm but not harsh.

Thanks to the new Strato bucket seats, tilt column and six-way power seat, any driver could find a comfortable seating position.

The bubble-style scoop was placed in the centerline of the hood and was nonfunctional on standard and Tri-Power GTOs. The ornament could be opened in conjunction with the over-the-counter cold-air package.

Buying a 1966 GTO

It's safe to say the GTO attracted a diverse range of buyers in 1966; not all GTO buyers were drag racers or street-performance enthusiasts. The market was expanded to include people who might want to buy a GTO for the element of performance or image, and who also wanted a personal car with a little more sophistication and a touch of luxury.

It was DeLorean's goal to image Pontiac as the BMW of America. Sagacious use of the order book could produce a luxurious, high-performance American sport sedan that rivaled the best European Grand Touring cars. After all, isn't that what GTO stood for?

Code	Description	Price
24217	GTO Hardtop Coupe	$2,847.00
062	Protection Group	50.66
071	Mirror Group	13.21
SPS	Paint—Special Color—Tiger Gold	83.20
802	Engine—389 3/2 BBL	113.33
782	Transmission—Automatic	194.84
CC	Tires—Redline 7.75x14 premium	NC
582	Air Conditioner—Custom	343.20
651	Brake Drums—H.D. Aluminum Front	49.08
472	Console	47.13
SVT	Cordova Top—White Code 291	84.26
422	Deck Lid Release—Remote Control	12.64
731	Differential—Safe-T-Track	36.86
448	Instrument Panel—Rally Gauge Cluster	84.26
522	Liners—Fender—Red	26.33
502	Power Brakes—Wonder Touch	41.60
564	Power Bucket Seat—L.H.	69.51
501	Power Steering—Wonder Touch	94.79
551	Power Windows	100.05
345	Radio—Push Button AM/FM & Electric Antenna	162.88
352	Rear Speaker—Verba-Phonic	52.66
621	Ride and Handling Package	3.74
574	Seats—Reclining with RH & LH Head Rests	84.26
471	Steering Wheel—Custom Sports	38.44
504	Tilt Steering Column	42.13
671	Transistor Ignition	73.67
452	Wheel Discs—Wire	69.51
Total Price		$4,819.24

The 1967 GTO in Regimental Red with White vinyl top. Exterior styling was little changed from 1966.

1967 GTO

The Great One

By the middle of the 1966 model year, James Roche, the chairman of General Motors, had already been doing a slow burn about Pontiac's GeeTO Tiger and Wide Track Tigers advertising campaign. He simply didn't like it, and every magazine ad he read and every TV spot he watched just added to his anger.

Unaware of Roche's displeasure with the Tiger, the people at Pontiac were delighted with the success of the campaign. "We had taken the Tiger theme, which came right out of the GTO, and spread it over the whole line," Wangers recounted. "All of the Pontiacs were promoted around the Tiger image. That was when we really reached our maturity in terms of recognizing the value of the GTO as an entire image builder for the division."

Unfortunately, that argument failed to cut any wood with Roche: he ordered the Tiger be returned to its cage. Pontiac needed to find a new theme for 1967.

While Wangers and Pontiac's advertising agency worked to develop a new campaign for the GTO, Pontiac engineering was also faced with challenges from the fourteenth floor of the GM building. Bowing to insurance and auto safety groups, GM president Ed Cole passed the word that all multiple-carburetion options were to be discontinued before the end of the 1966 model year. The only exception was Corvette, which was slated for a tri-carb option on the 427 engine in 1967. Most affected would be Pontiac and its Tri-Power performance option.

The Pontiac Tri-Power had symbolized the division's top-of-the-line performance option since it had been introduced in 1957. Although the dual-quad Super Duty may have displaced the Tri-Power in terms of sheer thunder, on the street where reputations were made, the Tri-Power was king. Losing it now could have been considered a fatal blow to the GTO's image. But DeLorean and Bill Collins already had a more than suitable successor ready. They believed with the right hardware, GTO enthusiasts would soon forget multiple carburetion. Wangers remembered the obstacles placed in Pontiac's way in the spring of 1966: "It made things more difficult. It didn't hurt, we didn't put our heads in the sand

This pre-production 1967 GTO shows some interesting variations. The Rally wheels have nonstock center caps and the wheels are color-keyed to the body. The rear quarter nameplate is a decal, which wouldn't be used until 1968.

When Is a Goat Not a Goat?

With The Great One theme on the screen and in print, the GTO for 1967 took on a new air of sophistication. Pontiac positioned the GTO to still appeal to the street enthusiasts, but older buyers, professionals and women were targeted as potential customers. One theme Wangers was never able to sell to GM management was the name that still endears itself to the GTO—The Goat. Wangers put together an ad showing a young man standing in his driveway, a pail under his arm, posing with his freshly washed bright red GTO. The ad was titled, "A Boy and His Goat," and by submitting it to the corporation for approval, Wangers, who always had one ear to the pavement, was to discover just how out of touch GM management was with the language and the culture of high-performance enthusiasts.

"At that time, they (GM) had already initiated a corporate committee for all of the divisions to submit their advertising and get approval on everything before we could run it," Wangers recalled. "They were sort of policing the division to make sure we didn't break any of their policies."

Wangers felt the "Boy and His Goat" ad met the criteria. "The ad suggested that everyone ought to have a GTO in order to complete their life cycle," Wangers said. "The ad was very much in line with the pride of ownership image. We felt we had

been very successful in capturing that and thought this was an ad that set itself completely within the framework of what the corporation wanted and did for us what we wanted."

The corporate committee rejected the ad based on its perception of what the word goat defined. "The guys downtown told us a goat is the butt of a joke or the butt end of a mistake," Wangers commented. "And they said they certainly understood it enough to know they wouldn't approve it."

Wangers put together a study that quoted enthusiasts in the field, and assembled magazine articles that referenced the GTO as The Goat, and presented it to the committee, explaining, "You've got to give us the benefit of the doubt here, that we know what we're doing. The word Goat is an accepted nickname of the GTO in the field. The people who are living with this car and love and respect it have assumed that the word GTO stands for Goat. Allow us the professionalism of knowing our market. That's why we're successful."

The committee refused the appeal, responding that GM was not going to allow Pontiac to demean the name of their car by referring to it as a goat. Pontiac no longer had the freedom to image and market its products without corporate approval of all advertising. It was the end of a grand era of Tigers, and Wide Tracking would never be the same again.

The GTO emblem was moved from the fender to the rocker trim panel, which was higher and bolder than 1966.

and die and cry. We just rolled up our sleeves a little further and dug in a little deeper."

Wangers' first responsibility was to set the tone for the 1967 GTO introduction. For the public to forget the Tiger, he needed a theme that would set a new direction for the GTO. "We took liberty with the initials GTO and came up with TGO—The Great One." Drawing on the GTO's image with the "kids on the street" and the reputation the GTO had earned as the premier musclecar, The Great One campaign was built around the 1967 model.

With the theme intact, there was one more hurdle to jump, this one also imposed by the corporation. The Federal Trade Commission, under increasing pressure from insurance lobbies and safety groups spearheaded by Ralph Nader, had advised car makers that high-performance models should not be advertised in ways that "promote racing or aggressive street driving." Always sensitive to government intervention, GM management distributed guidelines advising how the divisions could advertise their high-performance models. GM didn't want to see cars with dust flying, wheels spinning, leaning into curves or exiting curves at high speed. Ideally, the cars were to be presented in static reposes. They could be shown in motion; however, the motion used was

not to suggest or promote "aggressive driving."

Wangers and the D'Arcy advertising staff developed a series of magazine ads depicting the 1967 GTO in a neutral studio environment, either touting its good looks, plethora of options or engine line-up. For television spots, actor Paul Richards was hired as Pontiac spokesman. Richards was cool and sophisticated—like John DeLorean—and smoothly delivered the new message about The Great One. As he walked around a GTO convertible in a darkened arena, the camera caressed the quarter panel's profile, then snapped to the grille emblem, wheel, hood and the interior. All the while Richards was making the message clear that the GTO was the Ultimate Driving Machine: "if you don't know

The 360 hp Ram Air engine. The Ram Air took over where the HO left off and added a more radical camshaft and stiffer valve springs. The only rear axle ratio offered was 4.33:1.

Previous page
The optional 360 hp HO 400 ci engine featured an open-element air cleaner, free-flowing cast-iron exhaust headers and high-lift camshaft.

what that means, then you're excused," Richards explained. "But if, when you see this car, you're seized with an uncontrollable urge to plant yourself behind the wheel and head for the wide-open spaces, then we're talking to you."

The Wide Track theme was still the foundation for Pontiac's main image, and for 1967, buyers were urged to "Ride the Wide Track Winning Streak." One TV commercial depicted two young ladies out for a cruise in a 1967 GTO convertible. The same composition had also been used in 1965 and 1966, and through the use of upbeat music, the idea was presented that driving a GTO was for pretty, sophisticated people. The message was simple: you could become sophisticated and attract females if you, too, drove a GTO.

While the battles for image and themes were going on, the solu-

tion to the end of the Tri-Power was much easier to find. Bill Collins and Pontiac Engineering had been ready for the Tri-Power's demise, and were ready to discard the Carter AFB as well in favor of a new series of Rochester Quadra-Jets. The new Q-Jets flowed more air than the old AFBs, and with a venturi area of 9.4 sq-in, the new Q-Jet would soon have Pontiac fans forgetting about the legendary Tri-Power.

For 1967, there were four engine choices, all now displacing 400 ci. This was the first time the 389 had been punched out since 1959. To achieve the new displacement, bore diameter was drilled out from 0.406 to 0.412 in.; the stroke remained constant at 3.75 in. The cylinder head was redesigned for improved volumetric flow. Part of its efficiency was achieved by moving the chamber to the center of the bore, thus permitting larger 2.11 in. intake and 1.77 in. exhaust valve diameters. The intake-port design flowed significantly better than previous heads, and also boasted screw-in rocker-arm studs and stamped-steel valve guides. The dual-plane intake manifold was redesigned to accept the Quadra-Jet and was plumbed for future emissions equipment, as was the 1967 head, which featured exhaust-port air-injection holes. Interestingly enough, port dimensions were identical to 1966, and quite a number of Pontiac enthusiasts took to bolting the 1966 Tri-Power

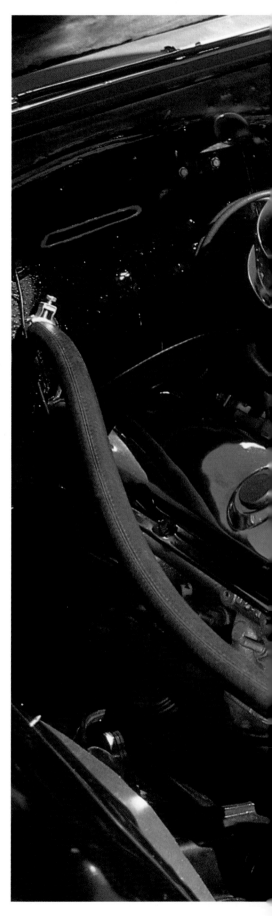

onto the 1967 engine. Some legends just die hard, it seemed.

The base 400 was rated at 335 hp at 5000 rpm. This engine was quite similar to the standard 1966 GTO engine, and utilized the same air cleaner, camshaft profile, valve springs and exhaust manifolds.

Optional at no cost was a low-compression, small-valve 255 hp 400 that was offered only with automatic transmission. It was the first time a nonperformance engine was installed in the GTO. Its introduction into the line-up was the result of the Marketing Department insisting on a low-compression engine available for the buyer who wanted the GTO image but not the horsepower or the GTO's unquenchable thirst for gas.

Next step up the engine option ladder was the new 360 hp 400 HO. The HO featured an open-element air cleaner, a slightly bumpier camshaft and cast-iron exhaust manifolds that were similar to the classic "long branch" headers from the 1962 Super Duty. These new headers separated the exhaust pulses beyond the

The changing of the guard took place in 1967, as Pontiac discontinued the legendary Tri-Power. After ten years as the division's top-performance engine option, the potent trio of Rochester two-barrel carburetors gave way to the new Rochester Quadra-Jet carburetor. Both are shown with their Ram Air tubs in the Pontiac Engineering garage.

The base engine was rated at 335 hp and displaced 400 ci.

ports and allowed the engine to exhale with less restriction.

At the top rung of the ladder was the Ram Air engine, also rated at a tongue-in-cheek 360 hp. All the usual Ram Air goodies were there like the open scoop ornament and the foam-lined tub around the carburetor, but now the four-barrel Q-Jet breathed through the HO's open element and exhaled freely thanks to the HO's exhaust headers. Inside, the Ram Air was a carbon copy of the 1966 XS

The Rally clock was optional and available only with standard instrumentation. The Rally gauge cluster, which included an in-dash tachometer, didn't allow room for a clock in the gauge cluster. Pontiac had planned to release a second version of the Rally gauge cluster, which would have placed the tach on the hood and the other gauges in the dash, along with a clock. The second Rally gauge cluster was canceled before production began, although a few have been found in 1967 GTOs.

The luxurious interior appointments for a mid-sized car placed the GTO above many of its competitors in the musclecar field. Many buyers wanted a comfortable, mid-sized high-performance car, and the GTO suited their needs.

engine, right down to the 744 cam and stiff valve springs and dampers. Toward the end of the model year, the 670 cylinder head was replaced by the 97 head, which used a special set of valves and taller valve springs.

The Ram Air engine was offered only with 4.33:1 rear gears and was a real handful on the street. Put it on the drag strip in street trim and closed exhaust and The Great One could pull the quarter in 14.11 seconds at 100 mph. Breathe on it just a little by advancing the timing, loosening the belts and bolting on a set of cheaters and times would drop to 13.72 seconds. That was almost 0.5 second faster than the 1966 Tri-Power GTO.

Mated to the new 400 engine was a new transmission option, the three-speed Turbo Hydra-Matic, replacing the

The Pontiac-Hurst relationship was still going strong in 1967. Although this plate was never installed by Pontiac on a GTO, many owners who purchased Hurst wheels or were just proud that their GTOs were equipped with Hurst shifters screwed a set of Hurst badges on their cars.

A solid-walnut gearshift knob was optional on the four-speed shifter only.

two-speed Powerglide that had been in use since 1964. The M40 Turbo Hydra-Matic was a strong, gutsy transmission that could handle the torque and shock of the powerful GTO engine. An automatic transmission was favored not only by the older, more sophisticated buyer, but also by the drag racer, who knew the automatic tranny would make him more consistent in the quarter mile.

When the console option was ordered with the Turbo Hydra-Matic, the Hurst Dual Gate shifter was standard equipment. Introduced in the early 1960s, the Dual Gate was picked up by Pontiac for use in 1967 as original equipment. The Dual Gate allowed the driver to leave the shifter in drive, permitting the transmission to shift at the factory's predetermined points. If he wanted to shift for himself, the driver slipped the lever into the right gate and slapped the lever forward. A positive latching mechanism prevented missed shifts, and it was virtually impossible to whack the lever into neutral and grenade the engine. Hurst claimed their new Dual Gate would "switch a lot of manual-shift lovers over to automatic." They were right. For the first time in GTO production history, automatic transmission-equipped models outsold the stick-shift versions by roughly 3,000 units.

The remainder of the drivetrain options and rear-axle ratios were essentially carried over from 1966, although the base three-speed manual transmission shift lever was moved from the steering column to the floor.

The exterior styling of the 1967 GTO was mostly unchanged from 1966, but cosmetic touchups were applied to the grilles, which received a handsome chrome mesh. The rocker panel was pulled up to cover the lower edge of the door, and the GTO emblem was dropped to the bottom of the fender and mounted in the bright rocker molding. A twin pin-stripe highlighted the upper beltline. Around back, the bumper was redesigned, as was the trailing edge of the deck lid, providing a flat horizon across the rear. The taillamps were changed, now placed in two stacks of two on each side and recessed into the panel. The GTO nameplate remained in its usual location on the quarter panels and the deck lid.

Several new options appeared in 1967, including the Rally II wheel. The five-spoke wheel featured red lug nuts and a chrome-trimmed center cap with the letters PMD encased in a clear lens. The Rally wheel introduced in 1965 was still available, now designated Rally I. For improved stopping power, Delco Morraine front disc brakes were available. These four-piston units were offered with or without power assist.

Mechanically, there was little revision to the GTO's suspension or chassis in 1967. A relocated cross-member was used for the Turbo Hydra-Matic, and a new, dual-cylinder master brake system was standard equipment.

As always, every manual gearbox in 1967 GTOs was stirred by the famous Hurst shifter. The optional console was restyled in 1967 and had a woodgrained vinyl applique that matched the instrument panel fascia.

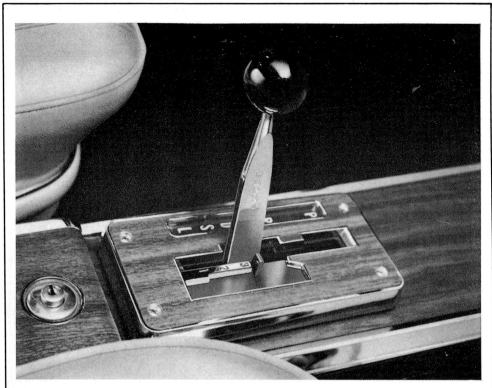

Wouldn't you know Hurst would introduce its new automatic control

wrapped in a '67 GTO?

It's only proper. Hurst has been in GTOs since the first GTO was born. Now that they've kicked loose the Great One for '67, with a new engine, drive train components and a 3-speed Turbo-Hydramatic, Hurst is in there with something new of its own. A console-mounted Dual Gate control that's going to switch a lot of manual-shift lovers over to automatic.

The reason is simple. Because the manual side of the Hurst automatic control is for *real*. This is no merchandising gimmick that promises you manual shift control, but in reality makes you guess your way through the automatic gears. The new Turbo-Hydro is a gutty, performance-prone transmission that's as home on a race track as it is on the highway. And controlling it can

be as precise as handling a fully synchronized manual transmission. The Dual Gate gives you that control with its positive latching mechanism that takes the guesswork out of gear-changing, going up or down. It eliminates any possibility of missing a gear, or accidentally hitting neutral and blowing an engine.

You're in complete control. You've got the automatic side when you feel shiftless and all the advantages of the manual side when you want to let it happen.

Soon you'll be able to buy Hurst automatic controls (along with all the other Hurst products) at your speed shop. Right now, though, you'll have to buy a Pontiac to get one. Write for details. Hurst Performance Products, Dept. 61C, Warminster, Pa. 18974.

34   CAR and DRIVER

Only 759 GTOs were equipped with the notchback bench seat and four-speed shifter. The Hurst T-handle was not standard equipment in 1967.

The GTO received a new transmission in 1967, the M40 Turbo Hydra-Matic, along with a new floorshifter for the M40, the Hurst Dual Gate. The Dual Gate, also known as the His and Hers, allowed the driver to either shift through the three-speed transmission or leave it in drive and let the transmission shift itself. It proved to be a popular option. For the first time, automatic transmission sales outstripped manual gearboxes. The stick-shift GTO would never outsell the automatic version again.

Few changes were made to the GTO's interior. The upholstery pattern was revised on seat and door panel surfaces, and a notchback bench seat was now offered at no extra cost. The dash pad was restyled, and a woodgrained plastic applique faced the instrument cluster fascia. The optional console was also covered in a woodgrained applique. The steering column was re-engineered to meet new federal safety regulations that required the column to collapse in a front-end collision, reducing the chance of injury to the driver. The standard steering wheel was a three-spoke design with a brushed-metal center cap and the horn buttons located in the spokes. Optional was the three-spoke Custom Sport wheel, unchanged from 1966 with the exception of a slightly revised horn bezel and cap.

Standard instrumentation was identical in appearance and placement for 1967. The Rally gauge cluster was again offered, and it too was a carbon copy of 1966; however, the oil pressure gauge was changed to peg at 80 psi, up from 60 psi in 1966.

Pontiac also released a new tachometer in 1967. Unlike most factory tachs, which were usually buried by the driver's knee or bolted to the console, this tach was right in the line of sight, mounted on the hood. This novel idea had been toyed with since 1965, and when released at the start of the 1967

The Rally gauge cluster was virtually unchanged from 1966 with the exception of an 80 lb. oil gauge.

Previous page
The rear styling was cleaned up for 1967. The taillamps were stacked four per side, and the deck line ran horizontally across the rear of the car.

The pancake-style air cleaner had first been introduced in 1965 and was continued through 1967. It was quite similar to the Corvette air cleaner.

model year, it was to be dealer installed only. Less than a month later, the hood-mounted tach became a regular production option and one of the most talked about new options in Detroit.

With sales of 81,722 units, The Great One held its own against the rising flood of competition in the marketplace. Only Lincoln and Cadillac weren't fielding some kind of musclecar in 1967. At Chrysler, both Plymouth and Dodge introduced their versions of the GTO. The Plymouth GTX carried the same basic dimensions as the GTO, and was powered by the 375 hp 440 ci engine. Dodge's entry was the Coronet R/T, also

114

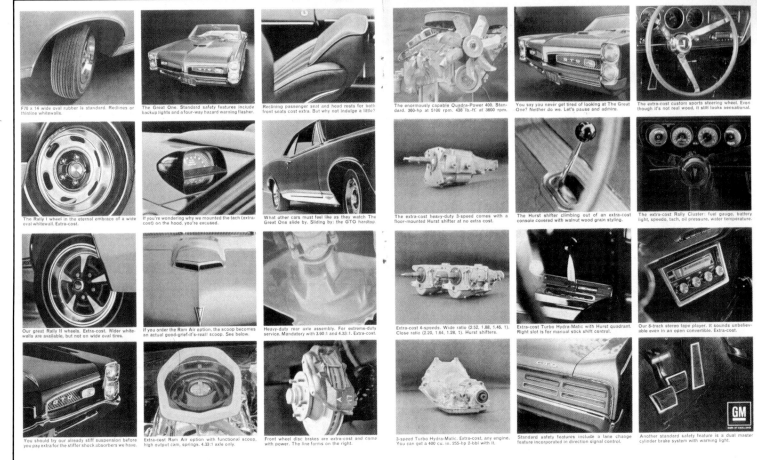

F70 x 14 wide oval rubber is standard. Redlines or thinline whitewalls.

The Great One. Standard safety features include backup lights and a four-way hazard warning flasher.

Reclining passenger seat and head rests for both front seats cost extra. But why not indulge a little?

The enormously capable Quadra-Power 400. Standard. 360-hp at 5100 rpm. 438 lb.-ft. at 3800 rpm.

You say you never get tired of looking at The Great One? Neither do we. Let's pause and admire.

The extra-cost custom sports steering wheel. Even though it's not real wood, it still looks sensational.

The Rally I wheel in the eternal embrace of a wide oval whitewall. Extra-cost.

If you're wondering why we mounted the tach (extra-cost) on the hood, you're excused.

What other cars must feel like as they watch The Great One slide by. Sliding by: the GTO hardtop.

The extra-cost heavy-duty 3-speed comes with a floor-mounted Hurst shifter at no extra cost.

The Hurst shifter climbing out of an extra-cost console covered with walnut wood grain styling.

The extra-cost Rally Cluster: fuel gauge, battery light, speedo, tach, oil pressure, water temperature.

Our great Rally II wheels. Extra-cost. Wider whitewalls are available, but not on wide oval tires.

If you order the Ram Air option, the scoop becomes an actual good-grief-it's-real! scoop. See below.

Heavy-duty rear axle assembly. For extreme-duty service. Mandatory with 3.90:1 and 4.33:1. Extra-cost.

Extra-cost 4-speeds. Wide ratio (2.52, 1.88, 1.46, 1). Close ratio (2.20, 1.64, 1.28, 1). Hurst shifters.

Extra-cost Turbo Hydra-Matic with Hurst quadrant. Right slot is for manual stick shift control.

Our 8-track stereo tape player. It sounds unbelievable even in an open convertible. Extra-cost.

You should try our already stiff suspension before you pay extra for the stiffer shock absorbers we have.

Extra-cost Ram Air option with functional scoop, high output cam, springs. 4.33:1 axle only.

Front wheel disc brakes are extra-cost and come with power. The line forms on the right.

3-speed Turbo Hydra-Matic. Extra-cost, any engine. You can get a 400 cu. in. 255-hp 2-bbl with it.

Standard safety features include a lane change feature incorporated in direction signal control.

Another standard safety feature is a dual master cylinder brake system with warning light.

Pontiac GTO

Now you know what makes The Great One great.

---

powered by the 375 hp 440. Both the GTX and the R/T could be powered by the 425 hp street Hemi. Chrysler was still a year away from finding the formula that would launch the success of the Pentastar performance program. The hardware was more than adequate, but Chrysler was to look long and hard at how Pontiac marketed the GTO and then apply those techniques with great success.

Ford continued their Fairlane GT and GTA, while Mercury stayed with the Cyclone GT. Both were basically unchanged, still powered by the 335 hp 390 engine and in a holding pattern until 1968, when they would be restyled and a new 428 ci engine would be offered in an attempt to make them more competitive with the GTO.

Corporate rivals Chevelle and Cutlass 4-4-2 grew stronger in 1967 as their programs initiated in 1965 came to market.

The SS396 Chevelle was the GTO's fiercest competitor, posting sales of 63,006 units, down from 72,272 in 1966. The 4-4-2 grew hair in 1967 with the addition of the W30 package, a cold-air package that included hand-selected engine parts, big cam with heavy-duty valve springs, fiberglass inner fenders and trunk-mounted battery. Rated at 360 hp, the W30 4-4-2 was a bruising, 13.8 second musclecar that was not kind to the GTO. Fortunately for Pontiac, it was a well-kept secret. Total 4-4-2 sales were 24,833 units, of which only a handful were W30s. The Buick Gran Sport trailed far behind, still lacking an image and an engine; sales were dismal at 13,813. It wouldn't be until 1970 that the 455 Stage 1 Gran Sport would gain a reputation as a torque monster.

The Great One also met new competition from within its own family. Pontiac fielded the Firebird, their own version of

Beginning in 1967, Pontiac changed the way they presented and sold the GTO. Corporate guidelines now forbade the use of action photography and other suggestions of aggressive driving. To counter these prohibitions, Jim Wangers assembled all the major components that made "The Great One great" into one two-page advertisement. The tiger of 1966 was quickly fading away.

Hurst wheels were offered in two finishes—gold and silver. Many Pontiac dealers would install Hurst wheels on new GTOs for their customers.

the Mustang-Camaro ponycar. The Firebird was offered in five different packages, using lessons learned from the GTO. The mild versions were powered by either a six-cylinder or a 326 V-8; however, two Firebirds were stepping on The Great One's shoes. Both were

equipped with the 400 ci engine and both were rated at 325 hp, with one version equipped with Ram Air. The Firebird's horsepower figures were altered because the Firebird was 500 lb. lighter than the GTO, and although the F-bird's 400 was just as powerful as the heavier GTO, it was forbidden to break GM's policy of 1 hp for every 10 lb. of curb weight. There was another reason for underrating the Ram Air Firebird's horsepower rating, and it had to do with image. If the GTO was The Great One, flagship of the Pontiac performance fleet, it could not be outpowered by the new Firebird. On the street or strip, however, the 325 hp Firebird was capable of embarrassing its big brother.

The diecast GTO nameplates still appeared on the quarter panels. The upper beltline pinstripe now consisted of two paint lines.

The plastic grilles first introduced in 1966 were restyled. It was now a two-piece affair, with a handsome chrome mesh insert.

Although the GTO faced increased competition, it retained a panache and style all its own, and that was the key to its continued strong sales. Other manufacturers screwed together high-performance cars that looked like GTOs

and ran like GTOs—but they weren't anything like the Pontiac GTO. Years later, Pontiac would field a GTO ad titled, "Others have caught on, but they haven't caught up." That ad was more than just advertising hype. It was a statement that rang true on the street, at the drive-ins and the drag strips across America. Dedicated men like Pete Estes, John DeLorean and Jim Wangers had poured their very souls into the GTO; it was one of the reasons no other car had its unique character.

Some of the strong styling cues that made the Pontiac GTO unmistakable on the road were the stacked vertical headlamps, the split-grille theme and the massive front bumpers.

Previous page
The 1967 GTO convertible in Signet Gold. The GTO grille nameplate featured chrome letters, filled with white paint and riding on a chrome bar. It was unchanged from 1964 to 1967.

The GTO's interior received only minor revisions for 1967. The instrument panel fascia was now covered in a woodgrained vinyl, the turn-signal indicator was split and the seat, door panel and quarter trim panel upholstery was restyled. Seatback locks were also new for 1967.

Red fender liners were first offered in 1966. Constructed of heavy-gauge plastic, the liners were molded to fit into the wheelhouses. The option was discontinued after 1967, since only 1,334 were sold on GTOs. The new five-spoke Rally II wheel was mounted on F70x14 in. redline tires. The styling for the new Rally II wheel was reminiscent of the Porsche road wheel, with its five cooling slots and recessed lug pockets.

The optional power antenna was available with both AM and AM-FM radios. It was mounted on the right-hand quarter panel.

Previous page
The 1967 GTO convertible in Tyrol Blue. In
the second year of a two-year styling cycle,
the 1967 GTO rode on a 115 in. wheelbase.
The classic Pontiac styling cues of split grilles
and Coke-bottle quarter-panel styling are
evident.

Rear styling was simplistic, and that was part
of its appeal. Pontiac had moved away from
excessive trim, lots of chrome and other styling tricks. The functional looks set the GTO
apart on the street.

128

The hood-mounted tachometer was a new option in 1967. Although it was first a dealer-installed option, within two months of production it became a factory-installed option.

It was lighted at night, controlled by the headlamps switch along with the instrument panel lamps.

Buying a 1967 GTO

The serious drag racer could put together a very competitive C/Stocker with the Ram Air GTO. If anything was working against the GTO, it was the price—assembling a hot Ram Air Goat resulted in a pretty stiff sticker. There was enough potential in the package, however, to build a street stocker that would go 12.4s, and in 1967, that was about 0.4 second *below* the NHRA C/Stock record.

Code	Description	Price
24207	GTO Sports Coupe	$3,029.00
75–	400 Ram Air Engine	263.30
781	Transmission, Three-Speed Automatic	226.44
731	Differential, Safe-T-Track, Heavy Duty	63.19
514	Fan—H.D. 7–Blade Fan and Clutch	3.05
584	Heater Deletion (Credit)	–71.76
681	Radiator—Heavy Duty	14.74
664	Regulator—Transistorized Voltage	10.53
634	Shocks—Super Lift Rear	39.50
671	Ignition—Capacitor Discharge System	104.26
622	Springs & Shocks—Heavy Duty	3.74
661	Frame—Heavy Duty	22.86
Total Price		$3,708.85

A drag racer ordering his 1967 GTO would do without options like a console or power accessories; they added weight, and weight is the enemy of the drag racer. Disc brakes also wouldn't be on the order sheet. They stop better, but they drag the wheels which slows the car. A Great One setup for the strip must also be a light one.

Production Figures

Production Figures by Body Style

Year	Body Style	Production
1964	Coupe	7,384
1964	Hardtop	18,422
1964	Convertible	6,644
Total		32,450
1965	Coupe	8,319
1965	Hardtop	55,722
1965	Convertible	11,311
Total		75,352
1966	Coupe	10,363
1966	Hardtop	73,785
1966	Convertible	12,798
Total		96,946
1967	Coupe	7,029
1967	Hardtop	65,176
1967	Convertible	9,517
Total		81,722

Production Figures by Transmission

Year	Transmission	Production
1964	Manual	NA
1964	Automatic	NA
1965	Manual	56,378
1965	Automatic	18,974
1966	Manual	61,279
1966	Automatic	35,667
1967	Manual	39,128
1967	Automatic	42,594

Production Figures by Engine

Year	Engine	Production
1964	389 3x2	8,245
1964	389 4bbl	24,205
1965	389 3x2	20,547
1965	389 4bbl	54,805
1966	389 3x2	19,045
1966	389 4bbl	77,901
1967	400 RA	751
1967	400 HO	13,827
1967	400 2bbl	2,967
1967	400 std	64,177

Production Figures for 1967 L67 Ram Air Engines

Block Code	Production
Manual	
XS	538
YR (California)	64
Total	602
Automatic	
XP	159
Total	761*

Includes 10 service blocks.

SHELBY MUSTANG

Hertz Rent A Car promotional photograph from 1968 to announce the arrival of the new Shelby GT 350 model available for rental.

Acknowledgments

No book of this nature is created by one person. Because I have long been intrigued by the uniqueness of Mustangs, this study of the 1965-1970 Shelby began for me as a photographic exercise. I enjoyed the details, and Donald Farr of Dobbs Publications, then editor of *Mustang Monthly*, gave me my first encouragement to keep at it. Putting words on paper came with the deal, so Donald is again to thank for keeping me primed (of course I must accept all blame for the quality of the text). To Larry Dobbs, who gave me the only real job I've ever had (my mother always dreamed I'd work in an office), I offer gratitude for his confidence and willingness to approach the world of Mustangs and Shelbys in exciting ways.

I would like to point out several people who have offered support beyond the call of duty: Dan Gerber, a fountain of information from his days as both an independent racer and a Shelby team member; the late Lee Cigler of Billings, Montana, whose infectious enthusiasm touched all Mustang and Shelby fans; Earl Davis, whose technical wizardry and tutoring over the years has proved invaluable; Don and Tot Buck from New Orleans, folks with a constantly positive outlook, who love to see the Shelbys at speed; Rob Reaser, my associate at *Mustang Monthly*, whose dependable efforts allowed me the mental space for this book; Bruce Weiss of Melbourne, Florida, a closet perfectionist with a constantly helping hand; Rick Kopec, co-director of the Shelby American Automobile Club (SAAC), for his carefully researched *Shelby American World Registry* (c/o SAAC, PO Box 681, Sharon, CT 06069) as well as his ongoing efforts to keep the world of Shelby alive and kicking; Paul Zazarine at Dobbs Publications for aiming me into this project; Bob Perkins of Juneau, Wisconsin, for his unending contribution of knowledge to the hobby and for steering my camera toward many fine automobiles; and Michael Dregni at Motorbooks International, for his patience and wisdom.

Over the past ten years, many car owners, club members, automotive journalists, restorers, and parts vendors have helped to shape my ideas regarding the evolution of the Shelby Mustangs and the state of today's Shelby scene. The cars are the core of both a significant international hobby and a thriving mini-world of business. I owe a debt of gratitude to everyone I've met in my years on the trail of Mustangs and Shelbys, especially Drew Alcazar, Bob Aliberto, John Craft, Lauren Jonas Fix, Pete Geisler, Ray Hamilton, Walt Hane, Jerry Heasley, Peter Klutt, Melvin Little, Scott McNair, Paul Newitt, Jan Orme, Richard Porter, Frank Reynolds, and Tom Wilson.

A special thanks must go to the car owners. Without their willing cooperation there would be no photographs, there would be no book. Many thanks to Debbie Ames, Steve Ames, Bill Anziani, Bill Blank, Grant Blohm, Dick Bridges, Jim Bridges, Don Buck, Gary Burke, Gary Childress, Judy Cigler, Lyle Cigler, Mack Darr, Frank Davis, Ken Eber, Cliff Ernst, Bob Estes, Paul Fix, Rich Florence, Shannon Florence, Dan Foiles, Brian Freeman, Gilbert Funk, Carl Gocksch, Mickey Graphia, Bob Hoover, John Jackson, Bob Jennings, Carol Jennings, Wayne Johnson, Colleen Kopec, Rick Kopec, Bruce Larson, Dan Lawless, Tommy Moore, Jim Osborn, Bob Perkins, Corky Reynolds, Frank Reynolds, Perry Rushing, Adam Scheps, Carroll Shelby, Bob Spedale, Jack Staples, Ron Starnes, Bob Steinberg, Bob Thrower, Owen Tomlinson, Tom Van Wagner, Robert Vance, John Brad Wagner, Bruce Weiss, Karen Weiss, Mike Williams, Pete Wolff, and Steve Yates. If I have omitted any deserving person from these rosters, I blame it on the fumes and apologize in advance.

This book is for everyone who has skinned a knuckle working on a Shelby, and has experienced the goose bumps while listening to, watching, riding in, or driving a Shelby Mustang.

—*Tom Corcoran*

Introduction:
Cobra Meets Mustang

The Shelby Is Born

Entrepreneurs feed on dreams of success. They see vacancies in the marketplace, and work to create products to meet those consumer needs. That kind of pioneering requires a blend of risk, knowledge, experience, hope for profit, confidence in methods and, for sanity's sake, a sense of fun. Carroll Shelby, with the Cobra roadsters, had that blend. His successes led to further collaboration with Ford Motor Company, in a project to promote the hot new 1964½ Mustang.

The story of Shelby's entry into automobile manufacturing has been told in hundreds of magazine articles and two

The 1964½ Mustang, with its long hood, short trunk, bucket seats, and floor-mounted shifter, was introduced on April 17, 1964. The eye-catching cars were featured on the covers of Time and Newsweek, and Ford dealers racked up sales records from the first week onward. Hailed as an all-American sports car, the Mustang was available by early summer with the 271hp High Performance 289ci engine. But Ford felt the Mustang's overall image needed a strong boost to carry it into the 1965 sales season. As events developed, the astounding and raucous Shelby GT-350 would provide the victories and the headlines that Ford's marketers wanted.

dozen books. It is such a modern-day little guy, big guy fable—the gutsy and foresighted individual in partnership with one of the largest corporations in the world—that it has taken on the trappings of legend. The story will be retold well into the future, with embellishments as well as omissions, with new information and diehard fictions. I hope to present it simply and correctly.

In the Beginning, There Was the Cobra

No automotive history begins on the first day of production. The Mustang was introduced to America on April 17, 1964, and its origins precede that date by several years. The Shelby GT-350s commenced production in the first months of 1965, but their history easily predates that of the standard Mustang. During the mid-to-late-1950s, Shelby enjoyed a remarkable competitive driving career, with three national championships in sports cars, a spot on the Aston Martin team, and significant victories in Europe that included a 1959 win at the 24 Hours of Le Mans. During those years, he established a memorable image: a lanky Texas chicken farmer in overalls and cowboy hat. He would scratch his head, say, "Aw, shucks" (or something spicier), and then go out and win a race.

BUY IT!.....OR WATCH IT GO BY!

Buy It! Or Watch It Go By! Inspired by an enthusiast magazine advertisement, the author sent away for one of the first Shelby AC Cobra brochures. The roadster's $5,995 price tag was stratospheric for a twenty-year-old, but the brochure remained a keeper. Ironically, in Ford's initial promotional efforts for the 1993 Mustang Cobra, with its 5.0liter GT-40 engine package, no mention of Carroll Shelby was made to link the Cobra name to its origins.

After the race, he would "Shucks" some more, but he was no country fool.

Shelby astutely recognized that although they were agile, most European sports cars lacked the raw torque available in small American engines. He knew that combining proper handling with abundant, lightweight power would create a winner. Unfortunately, when he tried to act upon those first ideas (in a proposal said to involve General Motors' eight-cylinder Corvette engine and chassis), his efforts were stymied. Others laughed at his ideas, and he did not have the hard cash to pursue his plan. Still, the concept remained on his mind.

Not long after the Le Mans pinnacle, health problems forced Shelby into retirement. A coronary condition that would lead to numerous bypass operations (and, finally, a 1991 heart transplant at Cedars-Sinai Hospital in Los Angeles), caused the doctors to disqualify him from competition. This setback did nothing to quench his

Carroll Shelby's personal automobile collection includes the first 260ci AC Cobra and this 427 Cobra. This big-block roadster was among the undetermined number of 427 Cobras originally built with 428ci engines.

spirit. He found several business opportunities in California, but still wanted to build that small pocket of horsepower.

In 1960, after learning that Ford had developed a 221ci V-8, he kicked into high gear. He mentally pictured that engine in something like an Austin-Healey, a car weighing 2,500lb or less. After a few months of investigative legwork, some help from friend and future associate Lew Spencer, a few prospective designs, and some shuffling of ideas, Shelby finally put it together. In 1961, he convinced both AC Cars in England and Ford Motor Company in Detroit that he could combine the AC chassis and Ford's small-block engine to create a world-class sports car.

The Cobra was born. Shelby pulled it off with the thinnest of budgets, a great sense of how to deal with the automotive media, and occasional sleights of hand. But he made it work. Not only did his boardroom and telephone tap dances turn executives into believers and reporters into supporters, but Shelby leapt past his goal and took his enterprise years into the future, into realms of production and racing conquest no one imagined at the start. The 260 Cobras (with performance versions of the 260ci Fairlane engine), 289 Cobras, Cobra Daytona Coupes, King Co-

bras, 427 Cobras, and selected Ford GT-40s forged their marks on the automotive world.

One should never imagine that Shelby lost his eye for the long term. His sense of doing business always stressed survival, and the only sure way to ensure longevity is either to make money or to make the money people happy. The "Cobra-Mustang" deal out of which the Shelby Mustang was born is proof of Shelby's success. In the beginning, it was the man who went hat-in-hand to Ford to propose the AC Cobra. Several years later, in 1964, it was Ford who went to the man. The corporation saw Shelby as the individual best suited to spark the Mustang image.

Carroll Shelby delivered enough excitement and adventure in the 1960s to secure elevated status in the history of both American and worldwide automobile manufacturing. He created ideas, cars, and teams. A fighter, a thinker, a winner, and a champion, Shelby did the job. The legend deserves to grow, and will expand with the passing of time.

Shelby and the Mustang

Introduced in April 1964 with floor-mounted shifters and bucket seats, the Ford Mustang appealed to a broad cross section of the public. Stylish and sized for a personal touch, the cars appealed to sporty minded buyers of all ages. They could be delivered as economical six-cylinders with minimal options. Or they could be eight-cylinder automatics with deluxe interiors, perhaps with air conditioning or a center console. For special enthusiasts, Mustangs were available with four-speed transmissions and 271hp High Performance (or "Hi-Po") engines.

One year after that April 1964 debut, Ford introduced the Mustang GT package with its stiff suspension, dual exhausts, and front disc brakes. The combination of a Hi-Po 289ci V-8, the GT option package, and a four-speed transmission offered a genuine sports package. To purchase such a vehicle, someone had to have both desire for extra performance and additional dollars to pay for the options.

Naturally, with each step up the ladder of Mustang style and power, the cost of a car increased. Fewer buyers stepped forward. The Shelby Mustang, at the top rung of that ladder, effectively converted a snappy boulevard touring car into a gutsy, stiff, loud, and incredibly fast street-legal race car. The price was premium and the product was primitive. So when Carroll Shelby, in the summer of 1965, positioned the first GT-350s, the folks placing orders must have been a rare bunch, indeed.

It is fairly well known that as time passed, Ford Motor Company exerted increasing influence on the makeup, design, and marketing of the Shelby Mustangs. Over that period of approximately five years, Shelby became disenchanted with his project. For him, the concept became diluted and sour. He thought that the cars had become oversized, overproduced, and out of his control. It is a salute to his initial conception that no matter how Shelby perceived the situation and despite Ford's attempts to make the vehicles luxurious and easily marketable, the cars remained distinctive to the end. Of course, the end came in late 1969, by Shelby's request.

Even before then, Ford and Shelby fans knew how special and distinctive the cars were. Many realized that with governmental regulations and insurance industry pressures mounting, Detroit was unlikely ever to produce another factory race car. Some may have hoped that the Shelbys would be "worth something" down the

Mix a Mustang with a Cobra . . . When the December 1964 Hot Rod *hit the newsstands, the Shelby GT-350 project was still in development. Yet, this ad proves Ford's eagerness to blend the Shelby image with the Mustang name. This early offering of Cobra brand speed equipment also promoted the Fastback that had been introduced to the Mustang line in September.*

road. Surely, few suspected that the uniqueness of the factory-built hot rods, the mystique of the Ferrari-beating company from California, and the enduring respect for Carroll Shelby would elevate prices so astoundingly. The Shelby's value at the beginning was founded on power, looks, and ability to win. Their value today is derived from the fact that nothing like them has appeared since.

1965 Shelby GT-350

Built for the Track.
Sold for the Street

The Shelby GT-350, a high-performance version of the smash hit 1964½ and 1965 Mustangs, was created to help Ford beat the competition in dealer showrooms. The GT-350 racing models whipped opponents everywhere else, too.

Detroit always has valued its charade of industrial espionage, the endless insider talk that fires up market strategy and stokes the flames of product development. In mid-1964, Ford knew it had a winner with the Mustang. Its bucket seats, floor-mounted shifter, long hood, and personal size had won so many admirers that the hardtops and convertibles set sales records from the first introductory hoopla. But planners recognized that sales of a "one-trick pony" could suffer when other manufacturers introduced similar vehicles. They had heard the rumors and seen the "spy" photos. Barracudas were in the stores; the

Created by Shelby American engineers from a 271hp Mustang Fastback, the 1965 Shelby Mustang offered enthusiasts a tough, loud racing vehicle straight from a Ford dealer's showroom. Its modified suspension, engine, and interior were not immediately obvious, but the twin Guardsman Blue Le Mans racing stripes announced the GT-350 as something other than a standard Mustang.

Camaros and Firebirds were on the way. Market position was sure to be threatened, and the Mustang's success, a huge corporate victory, needed to be preserved.

That August, with assembly plants phased out of 1964½ Mustang production and already building the 1965 Mustangs with alternators instead of generators, different engine and color choices, and trim changes, the marketers were faced with a new round of promotion. Checkered flags seemed an exciting theme.

Starting With a Blank Slate

Ford's ongoing projects with Carroll Shelby, the established Cobra 289 production run, the winning race programs involving small-block Cobras, Daytona Coupes, and King Cobras, and the 427 Cobras on the verge of production, made it natural for the company to approach the man who had working knowledge. Ford wanted an upgraded Mustang with power, flash, and, if possible, immediate racing victories. By then, Shelby had seen almost four years of wrestling with production headaches, bending, molding, and adapting to the racing rules of various sanctioning bodies, and making incredibly quick and perceptive decisions. Survival had forced him to master cost effectiveness, public relations,

and plain old going faster in straight lines and corners. He got the call.

The blank slate would be the Mustang Fastback, the "2 + 2" model new to the Mustang lineup with the introduction of the 1965 models. To qualify the GT-350 for SCCA B/Production competition, a process called homologation, Shelby American would have to produce at least 100 cars before the end of 1964.

Beginning in June that year, Ford had offered its High Performance 271hp 289ci engine in the Mustang. Shelby felt that a street version would be needed to sell 100 cars, so, with a powerful engine already covered by Ford factory warranty, Shelby elected to go easy on the powerplant and to concentrate on modifying the Mustang's handling characteristics to accommodate both racing and street situations. Within the safety envelope, street comforts would be secondary to performance. Of course, the cars built specifically for competition would be hard-core and expensive. But the racing project would evolve without being bogged down by slowly moving inventory.

To create the Shelby suspension, Shelby American engineer Ken Miles went to work with two Mustang hardtops. Testing took place at Willow Springs Raceway, where Miles and Bob Bondurant combined the tricks of their driving experience with the existing unibody and various parts already available from Ford. It was understood that using such components would tap a dependable source, facilitate ordering and inventory, and contribute to the bottom line. Miles eventually determined that if Ford's San Jose assembly plant could furnish Fastbacks with Detroit Locker units in Ford 9in rear ends, close-ratio Borg Warner T-10 close-ratio synchronized four-speed transmissions, 9.5in front disc brakes and station wagon rear drum brakes with metallic linings, plus the heavy-duty firewall-to-shock tower V-shaped brace installed on Mustangs destined for export, Shelby could finish the job in Venice, California. As *Motor Trend* pointed out in its first road test of the car, "The words here are: control, limit, locate, stiffen, and snub."

The San Jose cars would be Wimbledon White with black standard Mustang

Clean and mean from the rear, the first-edition Shelby carried detailing right down to the GT-350 badge on the taillight panel. The 1965 GT-350s used a stock Ford Mustang gas cap, though later models would sport Shelby-unique designs.

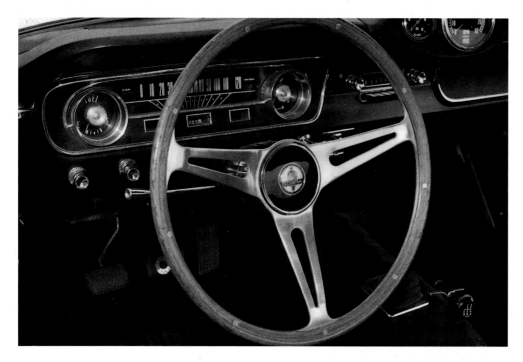

While a Falcon-type instrument cluster domi-
nates the driver's forward view, the custom
wood steering wheel and Cobra logo center cap
promise more adventurous action. Early cars

received 16in-diameter steering wheels, though
most got 15in models. The stock Mustang four-
speed shifter handle and knob ride atop a Borg-
Warner T-10 transmission.

spare tire mounted on the fiberglass deck
that had replaced the rear seat; and 3in-
wide Ray Brown competition seat belts.

The 271hp Hi-Po engine received only
external changes. A 715cfm Holley four-
barrel carburetor was mounted upon a
cast-aluminum Cobra Hi-Riser intake manifold. Cast-aluminum Cobra-lettered valve
covers and an extra-capacity cast-aluminum Cobra-lettered oil pan replaced the
stock pieces, and tubular steel Tri-Y exhaust headers led to 2in-diameter Glaspak
mufflers and exhaust pipes that exited just
ahead of the rear wheels. Still, these simple
external changes boosted power, and
Shelby advertised his version of the 289ci
High Performance engine as having 306hp.
For the advantage of weight transfer, batteries were shifted to trunk mountings; due
to complaints of fumes and corrosion, this
modification was discontinued about halfway through 1965 production. Goodyear's
7.75x15 High Performance Blue Dot tires
were mounted on the standard steel
wheels or the optional Cragar-built wheels
with CS center caps.

Additional modifications included the
addition of the following:
• Twin axle limiting cables connecting the
rear axle to frame rail-mounted eyebolts
• Driveshaft safety loop affixed to the
underside of the front seat belt mounting
holes
• Transverse engine compartment "Monte
Carlo" bar from shock tower to shock tower
• Dash-mounted horn toggle to replace
the one lost in swapping steering wheels
• Fiberglass hood with a working air scoop
and Klik pin retainers
• Guardsman Blue GT-350 lower body
stripes
• Mustang tri-color bar/running horse
fender emblem mounted on the left side of
the grille mesh.

The Production Line Rolls

The street GT-350s produced by
Shelby American caused a stir in the dealer

interiors, and 5.5x15in argent steel wheels
as produced for Ford by Kelsey-Hayes.
Assembly would delete hoods, hood
latches, the "pony and corral" grille bars,
Ford and Mustang identifying badges, rear
seats, radios, and exhaust systems.

After the first three prototype fastbacks
were delivered, built, and approved early
in the model year, Shelby American ordered from San Jose enough partially completed, or "knockdown," Mustangs to satisfy both the 100-car homologation rule
and the company's anticipated need for
racing models. The transformations began.
Some changes were quick and clean, while
lowering the front upper control arms (for
lower center of gravity and to optimize
camber changes) or removing the rear

axles to install override traction bars were
labor intensive. The front suspensions were
reassembled using new 1in anti-sway bars,
Koni shock absorbers (also added at the
rear), and special idler and Pitman arms for
improved response and, with a power
steering ratio in the steering gear box, less
lock-to-lock travel.

The Shelby interior retained the early
Mustang's (Falcon style) instrument cluster,
standard upholstery, standard door panels,
and black carpet. It then received a wood-
rimmed Cobra steering wheel (16in steering wheels on the first batch of cars, and
15in wheels on subsequent Shelbys); an
instrument pod at the center of the dashpad, housing a CS custom-logo Delco
tachometer and an oil-pressure gauge; a

The Le Mans up-and-over stripes, ornament-free grille area, side stripes, GT-350 designation, *and side-exit exhausts proclaimed the new Shelby Mustang's demeanor.*

Cast of Characters

Klaus Arning: Ford Motor Company suspension engineer, who assisted in design of initial GT-350 suspension.

Pete Brock: Shelby American designer, who created "G.T. 350" lower body panel stripes. Shelby's first employee.

Chuck Cantwell: Shelby American GT-350 project engineer. Team driver.

Peyton Cramer: Shelby American general manager, who proposed and closed the deal with Hertz Corporation for the sale of 1,002 1966 GT-350H models. Partner with Carroll Shelby in Hi-Performance Motors, Inc., 1150 South La Brea, Los Angeles.

Al Dowd: Early Shelby American employee. Partner in Hi-Performance Motors, Inc. Managed race teams.

Ken Miles: Shelby American competition director. Engineer and primary development test driver for Shelby GT-350. Won B/Production class at the first race entered by a Shelby GT-350 (5R002), the SCCA Nationals at Fort Worth, Texas, February 14, 1965. Killed August 1966 while testing Prototype J-chassis GT-40 at Riverside.

Jerry Schwartz: Shelby American fabricator and race mechanic. In charge of R-Model construction.

Lew Spencer: Shelby American team driver (Cobras, Tiger, Daytona Coupe). Partner in Hi-Performance Motors, Inc. Shelby American competition sales manager who oversaw the Race Assistance Program. Trans Am team manager, 1967-1969. Returned to Shelby's employ from early 1980s until early 1990s.

Jerry Titus: Shelby American team driver, who won 1965 SCCA B/Production championship in SFM5R001.

The 260 Cobra Impact: Reactions from the Automotive Media

"For those wishing to cause consternation in the hairy big-bore production ranks, the line forms on the right."
—*Sports Car Graphic*, May 1962.

" . . . the airblast at high speeds tends to bend the windshield right back."
—*Car Life*, 1962.

" . . . the AC Cobra attained higher performance figures than any other production automobile we have tested. And it did it with the 'street' engine."
—*Car and Driver*, March 1963.

"Lest there be any doubt as to the effectiveness of the Cobra, be it known that the Miles car had blown an oil hose early in the race, spent time having it replaced, came back to the pits to wait around some more while a flat tire was changed, and still managed to beat Dick Lang's Sting Ray, Tony Denman's Corvette roadster, two more Sting Rays and Al Rogers' ailing Morgan SS."
—*Sports Car Graphic*, December 1963, regarding that year's SCCA GT Class U.S. Road Racing Championship race at Mid-Ohio. Miles came in second to Bob Holbert's Cobra.

In keeping with SCCA competition rules, all 1965 Shelby Mustangs were two-seaters. A fiberglass deck replaced the rear seat, and Shelby American mounted the spare tire on the deck. The naugahyde spare tire cover at left was standard for the GT-350.

Shelby American riveted its own Vehicle Identification Number plate over Ford's inner left fender VIN stamping. The code on this car is SFM5S266; SFM indicates Shelby Ford Mustang, the 5 is the final digit for model year 1965; the S means a street version (as opposed to R for a racing Shelby), and 266 is the consecutive unit number.

1965 Shelby GT-350 Color Chart

Exterior color: Wimbledon White, 1964½–1971 Mustang code M. All GT-350s had Guardsman Blue lower body stripes.
Interior color: Black standard Mustang upholstery and door panels.

Le Mans stripes: Guardsman Blue (Mustang code F). Fewer than 200 cars were shipped from Shelby American with Le Mans stripes; of those, fewer than twenty-five had base steel wheels. Ford dealers were responsible for the application of many additional sets of Le Mans stripes.

GT-350 Engine Specifications

Displacement	289ci ohv V-8
Bore	4in
Stroke	2.87in
Compression ratio	10.5:1
Horsepower	306 at 6000rpm
Horsepower per cubic inch	1.06
Torque	329lb-ft at 4200rpm
Carburetor	Holley 715cfm

GT-350 Body and Frame

Unitized body	Bolt-on front fenders
Wheelbase	108.0in
Track, front	56.0in
Track, rear	56.0in
Overall length	181.6in
Overall width	68.2in
Overall height	52.2in
Curb weight	2,800lb

Ford and Shelby Vehicle Identification Numbers

Because the 1965 Mustang Fastbacks destined for Shelby American came from San Jose with the same engines, their eleven-place 5R09Kxxxxxx VINs were similar. The 5 was for 1965, R designated the San Jose plant, 09 was the fastback body style, K signified the High Performance 289ci engine, and the final six digits pinpointed an individual car's sequence on the assembly line. Mustang VINs were stamped on the inner fenders and on most K-code engine blocks.

Shelby American, as a bona fide manufacturer, assigned its own numbers to each completed GT-350. The VIN form was SFM5Sxxx, with the first three letters for Shelby Ford Mustang, the 5 indicating the 1965 model year, the S for street model (or an R for race model), and three consecutive unit numbers. Shelby stamped their VIN on an aluminum plate attached to the driver's side inner fender (atop the Ford VIN) and on the passenger's side inner fender. On cars 004 through 034, the fifth space in the VIN (for an R or an S) was left blank. After 034 had been completed, the company realized the need for separate designations; prototype cars 001, 002, and 003 were assigned official VINs late in the model year, so the R and the S appear in their codes.

1965 GT-350 Production

Street prototype:	1
Competition prototype:	2
Competition Shelbys:	34
Base price: $5,995.00	
Street models:	516
Base price: $4,547.00	
Drag racing models:	9
Total:	562
Source: 1987 *Shelby American World Registry*.	

The Shelby Mustang interior featured a genuine wood steering wheel, the Falcon-style instrument cluster, a dashpad-mounted gauge pod, special Ray Brown 3in seat belts, standard black Mustang upholstery, and the stock Mustang four-speed shifter. Note the stock radio in Shelby 5S266.

The 1965 Shelby grille was the Mustang unit without the chromed pony and wing bars, but with the running horse and vertical tri-color bar emblem found on Mustang front fenders. The stock Mustang hood latch mechanism was removed, and Klik pins through chromed posts secured the fiberglass hoods.

Shelby American was a bona fide manufacturer; thus, their Vehicle Identification Numbers took precedence over Ford's numbers. To cover the factory-stamped Ford VIN, Shelby American riveted its own identification plate at the top inner fender. This remarkable restoration includes vintage heater hoses, the proper fuel pump (with early-style fuel filter), open-letter Cobra valve covers, Koni shocks, and Tri-Y headers. The Monte Carlo bar between the inner fenders and the U-shaped "export" brace connecting the top center firewall to the shock towers strengthened the forward section and helped maintain front end alignment under stress. Ford specified the "export" brace for Mustangs ordered to be shipped out of the country. Presumably, the roads of Europe and South America would put unusual strain on the Mustang unibody.

These days, a winning concours restoration requires incredible details. The new old stock radiator hose and original spark plug wiring are among this car's finer points.

network and production leapt beyond the original target of 100 cars. By March 1965, the small company outgrew its Venice plant and moved to a converted North American Aviation factory on West Imperial Highway, adjacent to the Los Angeles International Airport. The Shelbys also brought much ink to the automotive magazines, and, perhaps too often, caught the attention of law enforcement.

One primary reason for the 1965 Shelby's instant and continuing reputation as a genuine performer is that the only modification Shelby American made strictly for effect was the paint stripe scheme. In most opinions, the eye-catching stripes were tasteful and mindful of the world-class Ford race cars of the day. But every change ordered from Ford and installed by Carroll Shelby's factory personnel during the 1965 model year related directly to improved road-course performance and durability.

Even after all the planning, ordering, and designing, Shelby American remained flexible and open to change. The steering wheels were downsized, then changed. The battery was returned to the engine compartment after problems arose. The hood design was changed to provide steel bracing for the fiberglass. And, toward the end of the model year, California-, Florida-, and New Jersey-bound GT-350s needed rear-exit exhaust systems. Whether brought about by customer input, legal problems, parts availability, or improved performance, changes were swift and positive.

Carroll Shelby worked off a gut philosophy centered on torque, fun, g-forces, and potential profit. Having great employees was also a key. The designers, test drivers, team managers, fabricators, transport drivers, and office employees made up a genuine team. With that help, plus his grass roots manufacturing expertise and ability to charm the automotive media, Shelby was the man for the moment. The 1965 Shelby Mustang proved it.

No matter what Ford thought it needed, Shelby produced the car he wanted. In the beginning, demand for 1965 Shelbys had to grow to match production. The situation quickly turned and, for a while, demand outpaced output. Subsequent years' changes would lead us to believe that Shelby's first version of the specialty Mustang might have been too rough-and-ready for the majority of Ford dealers to market. Today, those premier

To add to the real world performance feel as well as genuine utility, Shelby American installed a custom-crafted dash gauge pod on the 1965 GT-350. The CS logo oil-pressure gauge and tachometer (actually a Delco unit) helped keep costs low because the Falcon-style instrument cluster could remain as installed by the factory.

A shock tower-to-shock tower brace, called a Monte Carlo bar, crosses above the forward section of the Shelby-modified High Performance 289hp engine. Ford's Hi-Po, available in 271hp form in the Mustangs, departed Shelby American now rated at 306hp. Note the fan shroud and missing battery.

Standard for the GT-350 were the heavy-duty station wagon 5.5x15in argent-painted steel wheels with chromed lug nuts. The wheels were subcontracted to Kelsey Hayes and delivered to Ford's San Jose Mustang plant to be installed on the Fastbacks destined for Shelby American.

models are most highly prized. Who was right? Who can say?

The project was right, and no one will argue that fact.

In the beginning, Shelby American mounted the Autolite battery in the right side of the trunk. After receiving owner complaints about fumes and corrosion, the company installed the now-rare Cobra vent caps shown here—but complaints continued. The final forty percent of 1965 GT-350 production found the batteries in the standard underhood location.

Cragar worked from an existing design to accommodate Shelby specs for an optional 6x15in two-piece wheel. Chromed steel rims surrounded aluminum centers with chromed CS logo center caps. The G.T.350 lower side stripes were Guardsman Blue, a 1964½ Mustang exterior color.

"We recommend it as a sure cure for all strains of boredom."

"When you start the [1965 GT-350] engine, you're first impressed with a raucous note from the twin exhausts. They're actually louder *inside* the car, because there's no insulation or undercoating.

"The GT-350, in fact, develops so much cornering force that the idiot light came on and the gauge wavered (it has both) on several occasions due to oil surge in the sump.

"Our best was just under 17mpg when driving at steady legal speeds on freeways. The low, 11.2, came during performance testing. Average for our 900-mile test was 14 mpg."
—*Motor Trend*, May 1965

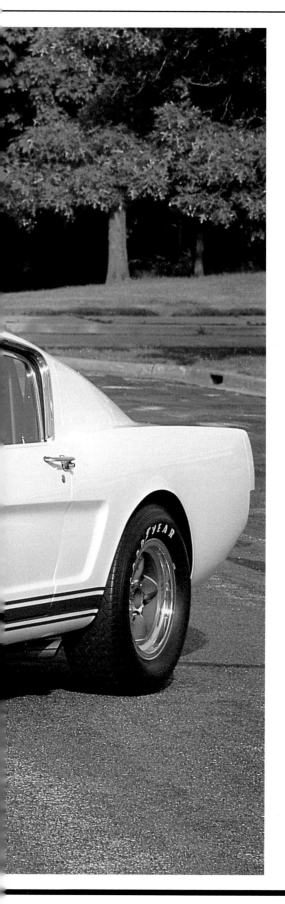

Shelby GT-350 Competition Models

It's Who's Up Front that Counts

Ford initially failed to convince the SCCA to qualify the Mustang for production class competition. In a second approach, Carroll Shelby became the messenger. After talking shop with John Bishop, executive director of the SCCA, Shelby got the go-ahead for a two-seated sports racer. In order for the cars to qualify as "production" models, Shelby agreed that no fewer than 100 would be built before January 1965. And, based on those limited production cars, the racing version could have either a modified engine or a modified suspension. While the SCCA may have doubted Shelby's ability to build 100 spe-

The real reason for the Shelby GT-350 was to win headlines and boost the image of the 1965 Mustang. While the regular 1965 Shelby was a formidable performance vehicle, the workhorses meant for competition were the thirty-six racing or R-Models built specially by Shelby American for SCCA B/Production battles across the country. Among the weight-shaving measures incorporated in the Shelby R-Models was the elimination of the front bumper and the replacement of the steel valance with a fiberglass front apron. Openings in the apron allowed additional engine cooling, plus the ducting of air to the front brakes. To allow tire clearance, the front fender edges were flattened and the bottom front corner trimmed.

cialty automobiles in a matter of months, it was the Green light Ford needed.

The Shelby Success Formula

Step one was to turn a Mustang Fastback into a production sports car, the "street" Shelby GT-350 with its essentially unmodified and Ford-warranted 289ci Hi-Po engine and its highly modified Shelby American-designed suspension. That car would be reasonably priced and reasonably functional for highway use.

Step two was to build 100 of the cars, a few for racing but the majority for dealer showrooms. Shelby American's Cobra manufacturing facility in Venice, California, would be adapted for that process and, eventually, selected dealerships across the nation would sell the cars.

Step three called for the creation of a race car in compliance with the SCCA's edict regarding the modification of either the engine or suspension. That was easy. By changing a Mustang into a street Shelby, the suspension already was optimized; that left the door open for Shelby American to internally modify the race car engines. Only weeks into production, when the SCCA's representatives inspected the Shelby American plant, they found 100 white fastbacks with blue stripe schemes.

IT'S WHAT'S UP FRONT THAT COUNTS!

When you take half a Mustang and half a Cobra, power it with 306 Ford horses and call it the G.T. 350, you end up with a pile driving powerhouse from Shelby-American that's unbeatable anywhere...on the street or in competition. Take the SCCA Pomona ABC Production race on June 20...first overall. Take Elkhart Lake on the same weekend...first in B, fourth overall (the first three, all A Production, were Cobras). Let's take a look at just a small part of the record.

Kent	Titus	1st overall
Cumberland	Johnson	1st in Bp
Lime Rock	Johnson	1st in Bp
	Donahue	2nd in Bp
	Krinner	3rd in Bp
	Owens	4th in Bp
Willow Springs	Cantwell	1st in Bp
Mid-Ohio	Johnson	1st overall
Dallas	Miles	1st in Bp

G.T. 350 STREET VERSION SPECIFICATIONS Shelby-American prepared 289 cubic inch O.H.V. Cobra V-8 engine equipped with special high riser aluminum manifold, center pivot float four barrel carburetor, hand built tubular "tuned" exhaust system featuring straight through glass-packed mufflers, finned Cobra aluminum valve covers, extra capacity finned and baffled aluminum oil pan; fully synchronized Borg Warner special Sebring close ratio four speed transmission; computer designed competition suspension geometry; one inch diameter front anti-roll bar; fully stabilized, torque controlled rear axle; 6½" wide wheels mounted with Goodyear "High Performance-Blue Dot" tires; Kelsey Hayes front disc brakes; wide drum rear brakes with metallic linings; competition adjustable shock absorbers; integrally-designed functional hood air scoop; competition instrumentation including tachometer; racing steering wheel; rear quarter panel windows; rear brake air scoop; competition seat belts; 19:1 quick ratio steering.

G.T. 350 COMPETITION VERSION Additions to the street version include: Fiberglass front lower apron panel; engine oil cooler; large capacity water radiator; front and rear brake cooling assemblies; 34 gallon fuel tank, quick fill cap; electric fuel pump; large diameter exhaust pipes; five magnesium bolt-on 7" x 15" wheels, revised wheel openings; interior safety group including roll bar; full Shelby-American competition prepared and dyno-tuned engine; every car track-tested at Willow Springs before delivery.

The racing community learned in the November 7, 1964, issue of *Competition Press and Autoweek* that the "Cobra-Mustang" racing effort had been approved for B/Production in 1965.

While the more numerous street Shelbys allowed the marque to be homologated by the SCCA, the competition, or R-Model GT-350s, wrote the headlines. The gunsmoke and tire rubber Ford wanted for its Mustang image campaign, the victories noted at regional tracks and in the national press, and the brain-rattling reputation of the Shelby cars came directly from the race cars. The R-Models came directly from the minds and wrenches of successful competitors and mechanics versed in optimizing the 289ci engines. The GT-350 victories would come from both Cobra team veterans and regional independents.

"It's What's Up Front That Counts!" This vintage advertisement showing Shelby's R-Model in action appeared in the fall of 1965. It was, pure and simple, an ad for the Shelby GT-350 (as opposed to other promotions that linked the Shelby and Mustang names). By the end of the racing season, the cars would dominate SCCA B/Production, and Jerry Titus would win that year's championship runoff, the American Road Race of Champions, at Daytona. The text of this ad mentions that in some races, the only cars capable of beating a GT-350 were A/Production Cobras.

If San Jose's knockdown models destined to be street GT-350s were devoid of certain parts, the Mustangs headed for R-Model status were downright bare. They were expressly built with the goal of eliminating excess weight. Many things were deleted: steel hoods, hood latches, grille bars, Mustang badges, rear seats, radios, exhaust system, sound deadener, seam sealer and undercoating, window regulators, side glass, backlight, gas tank, door panels, headliner, heater/defroster system, and carpet. The R-Models reached Shelby American at fighting weight. Furthermore, at Shelby American, a lightweight fiberglass apron, ducted for brake and engine cooling, replaced the front bumper, the rear bumper was removed, and thin aluminum panels were riveted over the holes created when the heavy C-pillar air extractor vents were removed.

To replace the missing back and side Carlite glass, pull-up Plexiglas side windows in aluminum frames were installed in the doors and a molded Plexiglas rear window filled the space, saved weight and, with a slot at its forward edge, provided additional ventilation to the interior. All told, nearly 500lb were eliminated in the building of Shelby competition models.

The High Performance 289ci Mustang engines were removed from the R-Models-to-be and dismantled at Shelby American. The heads went to Valley Head Service for porting and polishing, internal components were balanced, and reassembly was done to blueprint specifications. Each four-barrel competition engine received a camshaft that pushed the power curve toward the top end, a fully degreed harmonic balancer, and a 7qt Aviad oil pan, which required a custom-made anti-sway bar.

To keep the engines alive, Shelby modified the oiling system and installed an oversized radiator; an oil cooler was positioned low and just aft of the radiator. A spun-aluminum plenum directed air from

The R-Models could be ordered through the dealer network, though their $6,000 price tag kept many mid-1960s purchasers on the sidelines. In June 1965, Shelby 5R104 was delivered directly to Ford dealer Mack Yates in St. Louis, Missouri, who campaigned his GT-350 with much success throughout the Midwest. For a number of the earlier R-Models, including the one in this photograph, the custom production process included enlarging the rear wheel openings. Perhaps to avoid a rule technicality, this was done in a manner that left the openings looking close to stock. Eventually, a challenge ended the modification, and later R-Models simply had the fender lip rolled and flattened for clearance.

the stock hood scoop to the 715cfm center-pivot Holley. A dual-plane high-rise aluminum intake manifold, large tube headers, a Stewart-Warner electric fuel pump, and a straight pipe exhaust system topped off the performance R-Model changes. Finally, each R-Model engine was tuned on a dynomometer. Horsepower readings generally registered in the neighborhood of 350.

To deal with the realities of racing, the R-Model GT-350s also received slightly flared and re-radiused wheel openings, 34gal baffled gas tanks (actually two stock Mustang tanks welded together, then painted black), quick-release gas caps fitted with splash collars, gutted dash panels equipped with six CS analog gauges, two lightweight and snug racing seats, 3in competition harnesses, and a four-point rollcage for both rigidity and driver safety.

In spite of the Le Mans and lower body stripes common to the street and race GT-350s, an R-Model, with its Goodyear Blue Streak 6.00/9.30x15 racing tires, fiberglass rear window and front valance, and American Racing's aftermarket GT model five-spoke 7x15in magnesium wheels, looked much meaner than a standard Shelby. To complete the assembly process, each R-Model was tested by Shelby American company drivers at Willow Springs.

A Winner From the Start

All this preparation was done to win races, and proof of the Shelby success formula came with the debut outing of the first prototype R-Model. A winner popped right out of the box in north Texas when Ken Miles captured a B/Production victory at Green Valley Raceway on February 14, 1965. This success at an SCCA national

From the carburetor plenum to the oversized Modine radiator, an R-Model engine compartment indicated a single purpose: the production of horsepower long enough to win the race. SCCA B/Production rules permitted either engine modifications or suspension upgrades, but not both. Because the production Shelbys had beefy suspensions to begin with, Shelby American opted to boost the horsepower and longevity of the High Performance 289ci engines. An engine block adaptor fed the oil cooler mounted just aft of the radiator. This restored Shelby incorporates every known vintage detail, including cylinder heads reworked and polished by Valley Head Service.

event provided exactly the headline Ford had in mind when the Cobra-Mustang project began. With the pedal to the floorboard, the Shelby GT-350 was off on the right foot.

After the first two racing prototypes were built, R-Models began to be distributed to independent racers throughout the United States, Canada, and Europe. Eventually, several would head for Peru, but the main action happened in the United States. According to Shelby American Automobile Club documents, made public in 1992, thirty-six R-Models—including the two prototypes—were built.

In this more modern era, when new car showroom decisions seem to be limited to color choice and stereo quality, it is astounding to think that in 1965 and 1966, a track-ready car could be ordered from and delivered to dozens of Ford dealerships. The prices of the cars generally ranged from $6,500 to $7,150, at least twice the cost of a street Mustang of the era but, in retrospect, fantastic bargains.

Even today, these Shelby R-Models are regarded as serious racing vehicles. To call them jarring is an understatement: When "seat of the pants" is redefined as "where a driver's butt muscles can detect a broken shock or a rock in the road," you know a race car is eager for action. Except in areas of electronic technology and tires, there are few ways today's vintage racers can improve on the old design.

The Shelby formula for success, invented on the spot for perhaps only a season or two worth of Ford Motor Company advertising claims, for boosting the Mustang image, did more than its task. It has stood the test of time.

The R-Models could have received any of four different sized tires. One of those choices was Goodyear Blue Streak 6.00/9.30x15 tires on 7x15in magnesium American Racing wheels.

GT-350 Drag Cars

According to factory paperwork located by SAAC, nine 1965 and four 1966 GT-350s were built specifically for drag racing. Don McCain, a Shelby American sales representative, conceived of the idea to campaign a Shelby GT-350 at West Coast tracks. Racing fabricator and engine builder Bill Stroppe was asked to help create a car that would be legal for National Hot Rod Association competition.

To protect Shelby American from customer complaints about blown engines, all non-factory racers were delivered with the stock Shelby version of the High Performance 289ci engine. But the rest of a drag GT-350 was designed for a single purpose.

The best time registered by one of these factory drag cars was a 12.68 turned by Gus Zuidema at Lebanon Valley, New York.

Drag unit features included:
Gabriel Silver Eagle 50/50 rear shocks (1965)
Koni rear shocks (1966)
9x14 tires on 5x14 steel wheels (1965)
Casler "cheater slicks" on 15in steel wheels (1966)
5.13:1 gear ratio (1965)
4.86:1 gear ratio (1966)
Engine torque strap (1965)
Belanger drag headers
Cure-Ride 90/10 up-lock front shocks
NHRA-approved Cobra scattershield
Hurst Competition-Plus shifter
Driveshaft safety loop
"AFX" rear traction bars
Heater/defroster delete option (1966)
Aluminum carburetor plenum chamber (1966)
Source: *1987 Shelby American World Registry*

A reunion of R-Model Shelby GT-350s at the SAAC 1989 convention in the Pocono Mountains brought together seven of the original thirty-six race cars.

Road-Racing Finesse

"The Shelbys were primitive by today's standards, but were the most fun car I ever drove. If the car wasn't handling right, you could compensate for it in your driving. Throw it into the corner sideways, manhandle it, almost like driving a dirt track car. They had so much torque that you could get away with a lot. They were a fairly forgiving car, although when you made a mistake, it was usually a big one."
—*Dan Gerber*

Another method of shaving weight from the competition Shelbys was to eliminate the Mustang C-pillar air vents and rivet simple aluminum plates over the holes.

A Ford GT-40 leads a pack of R-Model GT-350s through a quickly moving parade lap on Pocono's tri-oval track.

SCCA rules permitted the elimination of bumpers to save weight. The Shelby R-Model gas filler inlet was inside the trunk, so a cover plate replaced the stock Mustang inlet. For quick pit stop access to the R-Model filler, a Klik pin replaced the trunk lid lock mechanism.

160

Only three of the original R-Models are believed to be actively raced in vintage competition. SAAC co-director Rick Kopec enters his Essex Wire GT-350 whenever possible.

Early 1965 GT-350s (perhaps the first 300 units) had trunk-mounted Autolite batteries, but only the R-Models had custom-built 34gal fuel tanks fabricated from two bottom sections of the stock Mustang 16gal tank. Internal baffling helped fuel delivery during high-g action, and the conical splash plenum surrounded a 3in pop-open filler cap. The overflow hose leading from the splash plenum drained through the floor pan; the gas tank vent hose looped upward between the rear window and trunk opening, then forward of the right-side trunk hinge, then inside the upper right rear fender to exit above the right taillight.

Fremont, Michigan, Ford dealer and racing enthusiast Dan Gerber became a successful independent R-Model driver. He would occasionally race as a Shelby team member and, in 1966, qualified for the American Road Race of Champions (ARRC). Note the size of the rear tires and enlarged rear wheel opening on car number 14 (5R099).

Replacing the standard rear glass with a specially molded Plexiglas piece saved 20lb. A 1in opening across its top allowed air to be ducted from the car's interior and blended with the exterior airstream; this was thought to contribute to top speed. Note the rear deck spare tire mounting and a portion of the R-Model rollcage.

R-Model Race Results

All but a handful of the competition Shelbys went to independent racers, and they were responsible for some of the more significant victories and finishes at the time.

In the mid-1960s, the SCCA sponsored regional races throughout the country and, at season's end, held the American Road Race of Champions (ARRC). Only the top three cars in each class from each of the six regions were invited to the ARRC. At the 1965 race at Daytona, ten GT-350s were among the fourteen B/Production cars and two alternates invited. Five of those had won regional championships, and Jerry Titus in the Shelby American team car 5R001 went on to win the national title. Six other R-Models finished in the top ten: Bob Johnson in 5R102, Walt Hane in 5R103, Tom Yeager in 5R094, Marty Krinner in 5R100, Brad Booker in 5R210, and Mark Donohue in 5R105.

The ARRC race, which capped the 1966 season the Sunday after Thanksgiving, saw at least eight GT-350s entered. A red flag stopped the race on the fourth lap when Dan Gerber's 5R099, doing over 100mph, was hit from behind by a Corvette and sent head-on into the pit wall. (Gerber today refers to the incident as setting the World Deceleration Record.) On the restart, it was learned that work had been done to Mark Donohue's 5R105. He was disqualified, along with eventual winner Don Yenko (Corvette), so the 1966 championship went to Walt Hane in 5R103. Also placing in the top six were Fred Van Beuren in 5R108 and Marty Krinner in 5R100.

Eighteen GT-350s were invited to the 1967 ARRC in Daytona. The top four places went to Fred Van Beuren in 5R108, Brad Booker in 5R210, Roger West in 5R538, and Mack Yates in 5R104.

With little support from Ford and with Shelby American gone on to other racing venues, the GT-350s lost ground to the competition in subsequent years.

A mirror under the front suspension provides a view of the 9qt R-Model Aviad oil pan and brake cooling duct. Because the stock crossmember did not clear the special oil pan, each R-Model received a custom-fabricated unit. This steel-tube crossmember, installed during a complete rebuild by Bob Perkins Restoration, was done to exact original specs. The 1in anti-sway bar was standard on all GT-350s, though the inner-fender sound deadener was deleted only for R-Models.

The sturdy R-Model steering wheel presides over the special six-gauge instrument cluster. The race cars also had radio and heater block-off plates and center hump-mounted fire extinguishers. Some had a standard Mustang bucket seat, while others, as shown here, were constructed with a naugahyde-covered lightweight fiberglass racing seat. The glovebox door, carpeting, and complete heater assemblies were deleted.

The stock Mustang side glass and window regulators were replaced with weight-saving aluminum-framed plastic side windows with lift straps. A textured aluminum sheet replaces the inner door panel.

1966 Shelby GT-350

The First Restyling.
Sales Quadruple

The 1966 model year became hectic around Shelby American. There were matters of profitability, some "better ideas" from the Ford hierarchy, an anticipated shortage of vehicles available for Shelby while the Mustang plants readied for a new year's production, numerous problems with supplies, and one big surprise: the Rent-a-Racers. What began as a shot in the dark—the attempt to sell Hertz Corporation a handful of GT-350s for more adventurous and well-heeled clients—became a massive interplay between the rental car company and Shelby American. Production for Hertz would end up accounting for forty-two percent of the year's output.

Ford, with its substantial stake in Shelby American, went into 1966 production with a slightly altered viewpoint. Management had viewed the 1965 Shelby GT-350s as effective "loss leaders," a limited number of loud and gutsy image cars that were not, one by one, profitable. But by being seen in competition, in sales literature, and in showrooms, they had done their job of boosting the Mustang's reputation and keeping Mustang sales at record-setting levels. Still, if the program were to continue and grow, a situation closer to profitability was preferred.

At the same time, dealers saw the potential for increased Shelby sales, if only

a few changes were made. If only they had back seats and were slightly less expensive; if only they were quieter, more comfortable, and multi-colored; if only automatic transmissions were offered; and if only they stood out a little more from the standard Mustangs. To the purists, the rough and raw product was fine; to the masses, a little less rough and a lot less raw were needed.

The dealer requests coincided with the recommendations of Ford executives, who had observed the Shelby American operation and had evaluated methods and cost effectiveness. Planning for the 1966 model year began well before production ceased on the 1965 Shelbys. After much discussion, Detroit Locker rear ends, with their odd clunking sounds, became optional, rather than standard, equipment for 1966 Shelbys. Override traction bar instal-

When the promotional aspect of the previous year's Shelby Mustang succeeded, Ford sensed the possibility of profits for the 1966 models. Efforts were made to appeal to an audience broader than the racing enthusiasts who appreciated the first GT-350s. The most obvious change in dealer showrooms was the availability of color combinations other than Wimbledon White with Guardsman Blue stripes.

lation, deemed too time-consuming and therefore too expensive, was reconsidered. After the supply of those units was exhausted (about one-third of the way through 1966 production), Traction Master underride bars sufficed. The 1in drop of the front upper control arms (resulting in a lowered front end and better handling) also took too much hands-on effort and time. Those two changes, when factored out of the initial Shelby package, were substantial in terms of philosophy as well as performance.

A strange anomaly kicked off the 1966 model year. The Mustang production lines in Metuchen, Dearborn, and San Jose would shut down during approximately the first ten days of August in order to ready themselves for the next year's assembly changes. Because of demand in the distribution and dealer networks, the initial cars off the 1966 lines would necessarily be standard Mustangs. Someone wisely foresaw that Shelby American's supply of partially completed San Jose knockdown models would be interrupted, and Shelby would have few or no cars with which to debut its 1966 GT-350. The solution: As 1965 Mustang production was phased out, 252 chassis—1965 Mustangs intended to be 1966 Shelbys—were shipped from San Jose to the new Shelby American plant in hangars adjacent to the Los Angeles International Airport.

The 252 Wimbledon White carryover vehicles would, in many ways, differ from subsequent 1966 models. They would have some 1965 Mustang characteristics, a good many 1965 Shelby GT-350 details, and many 1966 GT-350 cosmetic changes, including the adaption of the 1966 Mustang grille, Plexiglas C-pillar windows, quarter-panel air scoops, Deluxe Mustang wood-grain-style steering wheel, dash-mounted Cobra tachometer, and Cobra logo GT-350 gas cap.

When the group became completed, the domesticating changes requested by both Ford and its dealer network immediately took effect. Car number 0253 became the first 1966 Shelby based on a 1966 Mustang; it received the first automatic transmission and a true 1966 interior (with updated standard upholstery, inner door panels, and dashpad). Other items found only on the carryover cars were the lowered front upper-control arms, the 1965-style silver painted 15in steel wheels, and Koni shock absorbers (which, along with the Detroit Locker, became a dealer-installed option). Emergency flashers and backup lights first became standard on 1966 Mustangs and so appeared on the post-0252 GT-350s.

All these changes, adaptions to the market, and departures from the race-car nature of the Shelby street models were glimmerings in the crystal ball. The final years of the decade would see a changing Mustang, a more competitive—almost reactionary—pony car market, and the increasing influences of government regula-

"If you get lonesome for Italy, eat spaghetti." Much mileage was gained from the Ford-Ferrari rivalry and Ford's victory with GT-40s at Le Mans. Because of Carroll Shelby's input to the GT-40 program, promotional efforts for his products played on Ford's dominance.

tors and insurance industry pressure. The Shelby, too, would change with the times.

Adding Flash to the 1966 Shelby

To differentiate the 1966 Shelby from its predecessor, the designers at Shelby American took steps to add flash and, beyond the scooped hoods and striping scheme, visually separate the GT-350 from its Mustang Fastback brethren. Most obvious were the triangular Plexiglas C-pillar windows and the functional lower rear quarter-panel scoops that ducted air to the rear brakes. Three basic 1966 Mustang colors—Raven Black, Candyapple Red, and Ivy Green—plus Sapphire Blue (a 1966 Thunderbird color called Bright Blue Metallic) also became available after the first 252 cars were made.

The 14in wheels offered on 1966 models moved a step away from 1965's 15in pure utility (painted steel) and the Cragar/Shelby option. The standard wheel became a painted Magnum 500, and an attractive cast-aluminum ten-spoke wheel became optional. Reminiscent of the 1963½ Falcon Sprint V-8s, the 1966 Shelbys had 9000rpm tachometers centered atop the dashpad.

Engines in the 1966 cars were internally unchanged, with only a mid-year change in valve cover design marking their uniqueness. Late in the production year, Shelby American made available the Paxton supercharger factory option that had been tested as early as car 0425 during the 1965 model year and car 0051 in the first weeks of 1966 production. Car 0051 received the only known factory application of GT-350S (for supercharged) side stripes.

To some, the model changeover represented a first-stage devolution of the Shelby Mustang. Compared to anything else out there, the slightly restyled car was tremendously exciting, eye-catching, and powerful. To the hard-core enthusiasts, the concept, with all its "if only" stipulations, had become diluted. Many did their best to

Advertisement for Shelby Accessories, mail order coupon. Perhaps one reason for the immediate and continuing reputation enjoyed by Shelby products was Carroll Shelby's expertise in visionary marketing techniques. The Cobra speed parts business, with Ford's cooperation, spread nationally. Not one to miss a chance, Shelby also authorized the licensing of a broad selection of ancillary items, from posters to deodorant, and beer glasses to driving gloves.

order 1966 GT-350s with the 1965 Shelby in mind: Wimbledon White with no Le Mans stripes, Detroit Lockers, Koni shocks, and a deleted rear seat. Still, things had changed. There was no going back.

Still, Carroll Shelby was an inventive marketer. In coordination with selected Ford franchised dealers, he aggressively promoted a line of Cobra brand speed equipment, from complete high-rev racing engines and ring and pinion gear sets to chrome air cleaners and oil cooler adapter kits. Shelby Parts and Accessories, working out of the West Imperial Highway plant, advertised for mail order CS/Shelby logo aluminum valve covers, cam and tappet sets, tachometers, intake manifolds, and exhaust headers; one dollar would have bought a respondent the Shelby catalog plus tuning tips and a decal.

Additionally, a subsidiary called Shelby Accessories working out of El Segundo, California, marketed driving gloves, Shelby Cobra logo cuff links, ball

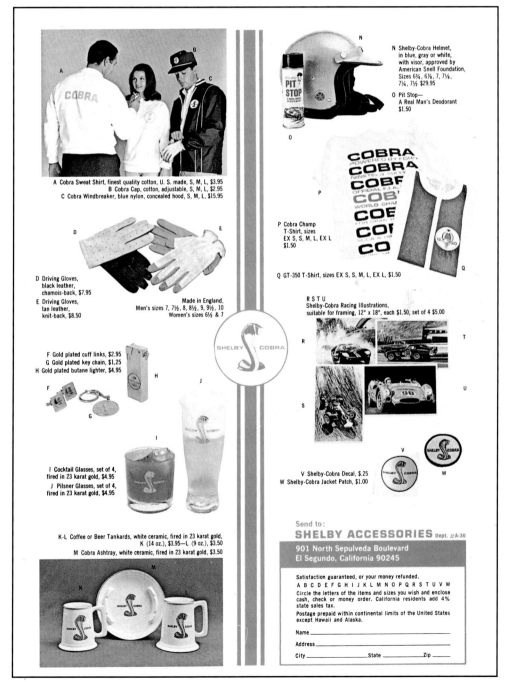

A Cobra Sweat Shirt, finest quality cotton, U. S. made, S, M, L, $3.95
B Cobra Cap, cotton, adjustable, S, M, L, $2.95
C Cobra Windbreaker, blue nylon, concealed hood, S, M, L, $15.95

D Driving Gloves, black leather, chamois-back, $7.95
E Driving Gloves, tan leather, knit-back, $8.50
Made in England. Men's sizes 7, 7½, 8, 8½, 9, 9½, 10 Women's sizes 6½ & 7

F Gold plated cuff links, $2.95
G Gold plated key chain, $1.25
H Gold plated butane lighter, $4.95

I Cocktail Glasses, set of 4, fired in 23 karat gold, $4.95
J Pilsner Glasses, set of 4, fired in 23 karat gold, $4.95

K-L Coffee or Beer Tankards, white ceramic, fired in 23 karat gold, K (14 oz.), $3.95—L (9 oz.), $3.50
M Cobra Ashtray, white ceramic, fired in 23 karat gold, $3.50

N Shelby-Cobra Helmet, in blue, gray or white, with visor, approved by American Snell Foundation, Sizes 6¾, 6⅞, 7, 7⅛, 7¼, 7½ $29.95
O Pit Stop— A Real Man's Deodorant $1.50

P Cobra Champ T-Shirt, sizes EX S, S, M, L, EX L $1.50

Q GT-350 T-Shirt, sizes EX S, S, M, L, EX L, $1.50

R S T U Shelby-Cobra Racing Illustrations, suitable for framing, 12" x 18", each $1.50, set of 4 $5.00

V Shelby-Cobra Decal, $.25
W Shelby-Cobra Jacket Patch, $1.00

Candyapple Red, Raven Black, Ivy Green, and Sapphire Blue 1966 Shelbys all received white side and Le Mans stripes. In 1966, the GT-350 also incorporated a Plexiglas C-pillar window in place of the Mustang's louvered vents.

Previous page
Because Shelby American's production schedule coincided with Ford's model year changeover, a quantity of 1965 Mustang Fastbacks were shipped from the San Jose plant to Shelby American to be made into 1966 Shelbys. The first 252 GT-350s produced for 1966 were made from that carryover 1965 inventory. The 1966 Shelby grille is the 1966 Mustang grille without a center "pony and corral" ornament.

caps, windbreakers, T-shirts, sweatshirts, beer and cocktail glasses, mugs, ashtrays, jacket patches, decals, artists' prints of racing scenes, Snell-approved driving helmets, and the capper, the renowned Pit Stop, "A Real Man's Deodorant!"

For a period of time, Shelby even succeeded in having his accessory product line included in the catalogs of both Sears and J.C. Penney.

Included among the 2,380 Shelbys constructed for 1966 were six convertibles, essentially an end-of-production special order for Carroll Shelby. Produced in six different colors—Springtime Yellow, Candyapple Red, Ivy Green, blue, Wimbledon

White, and pink—they all had stock Mustang air conditioning with underdash evaporators. As can best be determined, all had ten-spoke wheels, except the red convertible which had 14in Magnums. With Vehicle Identification Numbers ending in 2375 through 2380, these were the only Shelby convertibles created during the 1966 production year. Since then, on two occasions, additional groups of convertibles, created essentially from used Mustang convertibles, have received Carroll Shelby's blessings. No matter how they are judged now and in the future, they are not to be confused with the six original, San Jose-sourced K-code convertibles built by Shelby American.

The complex details needed for proper restoration include the correct distributor, plug wires, and heater hoses, and the numerically coded fuel filter.

The interior of an early 1966 carryover car combines 1965 and 1966 characteristics. The 3in seat belts appeared in both years, though the Ray Brown versions were replaced during 1966 production by those of another vendor. The black standard upholstery, door panels, dashpad, glovebox, and standard interior-style GT instrument bezel are from 1965. Later 1966 Shelbys used the standard 1966 Mustang five-gauge bezel. The dashpad-mounted tachometer for 1966 replaced the previous year's gauge pod. The steering wheel in this Shelby is a woodgrain Mustang Deluxe interior component with a Cobra logo insert. Its chromed center cap is from a Fairlane and does not have Ford Mustang lettering. The biggest interior difference from 1965 was the retention of the Mustang rear seat that all but the first few 1966 Shelbys received.

It is the lucky restorer who locates an unused, original Hi-Po air filter.

The Shelby version of Ford's 289ci Hi-Po remained basically unchanged from 1965 and, with the Shelby-specific Hi-Rise Cobra intake manifold and Tri-Y headers, claimed 306hp. Hollow-letter Cobra valve covers are shown here, though a minor running change was later made in valve cover style. The Monte Carlo transverse bar and heavy-duty "export" firewall-to-shock tower brace were standard for both years. Note the orange Koni shocks, standard on this and all carryover cars and optional for the remainder of the 1966 production year. The carryover cars also had black engine blocks, while later 1966 Shelbys had blue engines, and the carryover 1966 GT-350s had 1965-style fuel pumps with integral filter cannisters. Later cars had standard fuel pumps and their in-line filters screwed directly into the Holley carburetors.

Shelby trunks remained basically identical to the Mustang's. Like many early 1966 Shelbys—carryovers and a few regular production cars— this has no taillight panel GT-350 emblem. The spare wheel matches this Shelby's Cragar wheels.

After test-fitting Shelby #6S051 with a proto-type Paxton supercharger, Shelby American made the Paxton available as a factory-installed option for the remainder of the year.

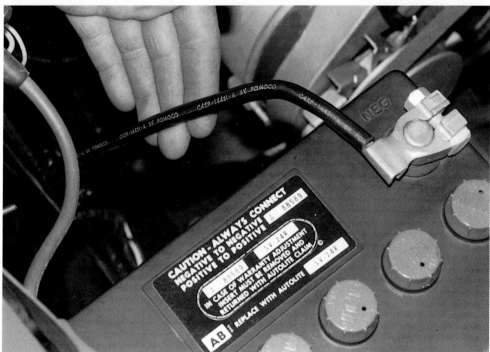

Even the battery and battery cables must have Ford's original part numbers to be correct in today's concours world.

The Cobra logo GT-350 gas cap was standard throughout the 1966 production year.

The Shelby taillight panel emblem was used throughout 1965 but, for some reason, the first 300 or so 1966 GT-350s did not get them. Their installation was resumed, and continued through the end of 1966 production.

In the later months of 1966 production, the 14in Magnum 500 (Motor Wheel), painted gray, with a Cobra/GT-350 logo center cap, became standard. The chromed Magnums were fairly standard for Hertz cars and were found on some regular-production Shelbys.

In addition to Ford's Mustang jacking instructions, the underside of the Shelby deck lid carried a warning label regarding the Detroit Locker differential. Because not all owners were satisfied with the Detroit Locker for daily use, it was made a dealer-installed option for 1966.

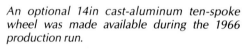

An optional 14in cast-aluminum ten-spoke wheel was made available during the 1966 production run.

The fine touch in restoration requires duplicating the factory's inherent imperfections, such as the undercoat spray on the firewall slopping over to the heater hoses.

The six Shelby convertibles built at the end of the 1966 production run were produced in six different colors. The cars were not made available to the dealership network, but were presented by Shelby American to special employees and associates. They received the standard Shelby fiberglass hoods and side scoops, the grille treatment, racing mirrors, and emblems.

Previous page
While most of the 1966 Shelby convertibles had cast-aluminum ten-spoke wheels and automatic transmissions, this Candyapple Red GT-350 has chromed 14in Magnum 500 wheels and a four-speed. It is, quite simply, one of a kind.

This is not just a Mustang convertible with a racing mirror, hood scoop, and optional Cobra GT-350 wood rim wheel.

The six special convertibles were the only early Shelbys to have had trunks of this size. Note the Cobra logo gas cap and GT-350 taillight panel badge.

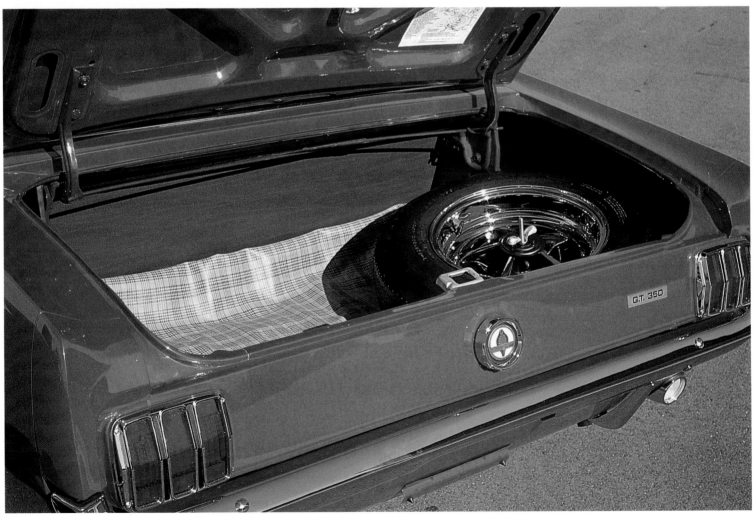

1966 Shelby Color Chart

Color Name	1966 Mustang Color Code	Ditzler Number	DuPont Number
Wimbledon White	M	8378	4480
Raven Black	A	9300	88
Ivy Green	R	43408	4611
Candyapple Red	T	71528	4737
Sapphire Blue	G[1]	13075	4735

[1]1966 Thunderbird Bright Blue Metallic. Not a Mustang color.
1966 Shelby GT-350 interiors were standard black vinyl.

1966 Shelby GT-350 Retail Price List

Shelby GT-350	$4,428.00
High-performance Ford automatic transmission	n/c
Fold-down rear seat	50.00
AM radio	57.50
Alloy wheels	275.00
Rally stripe	62.50
Detroit Locker	141.00
Paxton/Cobra supercharger	670.00

1966 GT-350 Applications, Options, and Exceptions

Lower body stripes: Wimbledon White cars received blue stripes; others received white stripes. Hertz cars received gold stripes (except for several early Wimbledon White-with-blue combinations). Either GT-350 or GT-350H was inset at the lower front fender. All other colors received white stripes.

Le Mans stripes: The over-the-top "rally" stripes, generally dealer-installed, matched the lower body stripes. Most GT-350H cars received Le Mans stripes.

Hoods: Steel-framed fiberglass hoods predominated, with a few mid- and late-production cars receiving all-steel hoods. Attempts to convert to all-steel were plagued with supplier quality control problems.

Wheels and tires: Carryover vehicles received the 1965 choices of silver-painted steel wheels (15x5.5 Ford station wagon units with chrome lug nuts) or 15x6 five-spoke Cragar/Shelby aluminum wheels with chrome CS logo diecast aluminum center caps.

Standard for 1966 was a gray-painted 14in Magnum 500, with 14in aluminum-alloy Shelby ten-spoke wheels optional. Hertz cars received either chromed Magnum 500s or the ten-spoke style with, in most cases, Hertz logo center caps.

Interiors: A single Cobra tachometer replaced the previous year's two-gauge dashpod. The dished Mustang Deluxe woodgrain steering wheel carried a Cobra GT-350 logo in a chromed Fairlane center cap. The 1966 Mustang dashpad, door panels, upholstery pattern, and glovebox appeared after the carryover run of 252 1965-based models.

Traction bars: Shelby American's stock of override bars held through the manufacture of approximately 800 cars. Underride bars predominated after that point.

The standard Mustang upholstery and black-finish instrument bezel and glovebox door do not accurately tell the story. The optional Shelby steering wheel, air conditioning, dash-mounted tachometer, disc brake pedal pad, four-speed shifter, Hi-Po choke lever, and power top switch tell a stronger tale. Note the 00001.0 odometer reading, fresh out of Concours Restorations.

Previous page
The 1966 convertibles' engine compartments differed from the regular GT-350s only in the installation of air conditioning. Only these six special cars received that extra touch directly from the Shelby American factory.

The detailed restoration of the Candyapple Red Shelby convertible included the finer touches of original wiring, starter solenoid, battery, and battery cable.

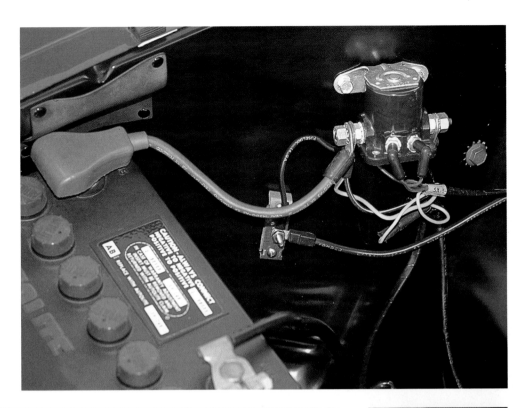

Many production details were ignored by enthusiasts in the beginning. As time goes by and concours efforts intensify, more is being learned about restoration details, regarding obscure driveshaft and differential bare metal finishes, component paint schemes, and paint daub codes. Note the date-coded Ford Motor Company mufflers, properly tagged differential housing, and Koni shocks.

The Cobra brand 9000rpm tachometer for 1966 replaced the dash-mounted 1965-style tachometer and oil-pressure gauge cluster.

Such details as underbody primer, the proper amount of exterior color overspray, the correct Shelby exhaust system, original convertible underbody brace, grommets, wiring, cables, and natural metal finishes must be extensively researched for restoration.

The 1966 Shelby grille was a 1966 Mustang unit without the "pony and corral" chromed center ornament. The standard Mustang fender emblem is positioned to the left side of the "egg crate" aluminum grille. Note the hood latch pin, Monte Carlo bar, and parts of the air conditioning system in the background. This could only be a Shelby convertible.

The ultimate open-air driver's seat, with the optional Shelby steering wheel and its GT-350 center hub, the Cobra tachometer, radio, air conditioning, a disc brake pedal pad, four-speed shifter, racing-style exterior rear view mirror and, out front, the hood scoop in Candyapple Red. This particular convertible is the only car ever produced that could legitimately have all these extras.

The discrete touch of a Cobra-lettered and finned aluminum extra-capacity oil pan adds to the muscle image of the GT-350.

1966 Shelby GT-350H - The Rent-a-Racers

America Takes the Ultimate Test Drive

If it hadn't been for the Hertz Corporation, Shelby American might have only tripled its output in 1966. Instead, with two prototypes and another 1,000 units going to the rental car concern, Shelby more than quadrupled the GT-350 sales tally of 1965.

In a spirited marketing move, Hertz already had formed the Hertz Sports Car Club so presumably adult and responsible renters might add a little spice to their business trips or weekend breaks. For $17 a day or $70 per week (in the New York area), plus 17 cents per mile, anyone with a proven ability to locate the steering wheel and all of the pedals could sign his or her name and drive away.

To most Hertz clients, it amounted to borrowing a personal race car. Naturally, legend grew from certain truths. More than a few of the rental units ventured toward drag strips and road-racing tracks to become, if not always competitors, prime parts donor cars. Some competed and certainly most were abused on the highway. Years later, general concern about the condition, upkeep, and maintenance of the old rental units caused them to suffer in reputation and value. That suffering screeched to a halt in the late 1970s and early 1980s, and the cars are held today in the same high regard as their private original-owner counterparts.

The performance rental concept had begun with Hertz's program to offer customers Corvettes. So when Shelby American General Manager Peyton Cramer, in September 1965, proposed the sale of a limited number of GT-350s, street versions of that year's B/Production champion, Hertz listened. The corporation's next step, a shock to Shelby American, was to indicate its intent to order 100 models to be called GT-350H (for Hertz) and to incorporate certain minor changes for driver convenience and safety. The news sent Shelby planners scrambling, and during that period Peyton Cramer continued with his correspondence and negotiations.

A prototype car was requested by Hertz on October 26 and, on November 2, the rental company ordered a December delivery of 100 black cars with gold (Bronze Powder) stripes. The cars would be

The Hertz Corporation gave many future Shelby owners their first test drives. Available to members of the Hertz Sports Car Club, presumably clients of maturity and financial substance, the special Shelbys could be leased at more than fifty major airport locations, nationwide. The 1,000 vehicles created for Hertz amounted to better than forty percent of Shelby American's 1966 output.

Approximately 800 Hertz cars were black, and the remaining 200 or so received the standard white, red, blue, and green 1966 Shelby colors. All of the black rental cars had gold side and Le Mans stripes. It is thought that a few early white cars had blue striping, and that few of the non-black cars had Le Mans stripes. Of course, with Shelby American, like Ford, exceptions to the norm were common; for Hertz cars, because of production running changes, there simply was no norm. Note the 1966 Shelby gas cap.

priced at $3,547 f.o.b. St. Louis—a central location—plus $45.45 for a Shelby-installed radio. Shelby American also offered Hertz Corporation a guaranteed depreciation rate which, in the end, amounted to a sort of buy-back program.

On November 9, Hertz requested an automatic transmission version prototype.

It was shipped to Hertz headquarters in New York and, by the end of November, the collaboration had ratcheted up another notch: Hertz increased its order to 200 cars.

According to files found in the mid-1980s in Carroll Shelby's storage areas (and related in the 1987 *Shelby American World Registry*), a series of meetings ensued, during which Hertz and Shelby American planned a joint advertising effort for major print media—automotive and otherwise. Hertz capped the deal by promising, if the $300,000 ad effort received approval, to order another 800 1966 Shelbys. The official order, for a total of 1,000 GT-350s, arrived in late December.

By December 21, Shelby American knew that the first 200 units would be black with gold stripes and that the subsequent

800 units would be built in a variety of Shelby's 1966 color options. What had begun as a longshot sales call evolved into what would become forty-two percent of Shelby American's assembly efforts for 1966. And Shelby GT-350s, unknown to the nation twelve months earlier, suddenly would appear at more than fifty airport rental facilities, Hertz Sports Car Club Centers, coast to coast.

Rent-a-Racers

Both Ford and Shelby are noted for having built cars that were exceptions to the norm. Hertz car production saw similar irregularities. In general, the GT-350Hs had chromed versions of the standard 14in 1966 Shelby Magnum 500 with Goodyear

This front fender detail shows the significant differences between the standard Mustang and the Hertz cars. The functional hood scoop, hood tie-down pin and attaching wire, regal gold Le Mans striping, and the Hertz center cap on the chrome Magnum wheel all contribute to the special image Hertz desired.

Blue Streak tires, radios with front fender-mounted antennas, and, after the first eighty-five units were built, automatic transmissions. Records located and evaluated by the Shelby American Automobile Club indicate that a number of Hertz cars were delivered with cast-aluminum ten-spoke wheels and that approximately seventy-five percent of the cars were black with gold stripes. It is believed that, late in the model year, some cars were delivered with Autolite 595cfm four-barrel carburetors.

One significant problem with the rental units was the difficulty customers encountered with unboosted metallic-lined brakes. After much testing, Shelby American began to install MICO "piggyback" master cylinders made by Minnesota Automotive. These boosters, which worked in conjunction with the existing master cylinders, led to their own set of problems due to great inconsistencies in brake pedal pressure from unit to unit.

Shelby American had its hands full in producing 1,000 of these cars. For that reason (and because no one thought at the time that car-by-car details would be needed twenty-five or more years into the future), records of running changes, production line exceptions, and parts installed for assembly line expediency are scattered and confusing. Owners and prospective owners needing details on Hertz car characteristics (the information could be its own book) are encouraged to contact SAAC.

Although there is correspondence that indicates a Shelby/Hertz project was dis-cussed for 1967, the end of 1966 production brought the deal to a close. At that point, the repurchase clause concerning guaranteed depreciation brought pressure on Shelby American and Ford to dispose of the Hertz cars being retired from active rental. As John Craft noted in the September 1990 *Mustang Monthly*, a Ford employee named Marv Neely won a contest (called the Visibility 500) to sell the greatest number of ex-Hertz vehicles. Neely and his colleagues are to be credited with saving numerous GT-350Hs from less-noble circumstances.

In retrospect, the Hertz cars, today referred to as Rent-a-Racers, provided Shelby American with genuine traction in the world of commerce. A deal of that magnitude carries its own legitimacy, and the reputation of the small California-based manufacturer grew beyond the increased exposure and production. It provided a fine chapter in the history of Carroll Shelby's manufacture of automobiles.

Hertz is Number One in the minds of hundreds of current Shelby owners. This placard, probably from the early 1980s, is great for display. Collectors constantly search for true vintage artifacts, such as rental counter price lists, color postcards, and old four-fold brochures. Oddly, Hertz considered the 1966 rental program less than successful. In promoting the air conditioned, automatic transmission GT-350s offered to Hertz Sports Car Club members in 1968, the company offered apologies for having previously offered cars that not "everyone" could drive.

Prior to effective sleuthing in recent years by Shelby enthusiasts, it was thought that one could confirm a Hertz model's identity by checking for a steel hood. Perhaps only 150, if that, actually received an all-steel hood; generally speaking, Hertz cars, like regular 1966 Shelbys, used steel-reinforced fiberglass hoods with the functional Shelby scoop.

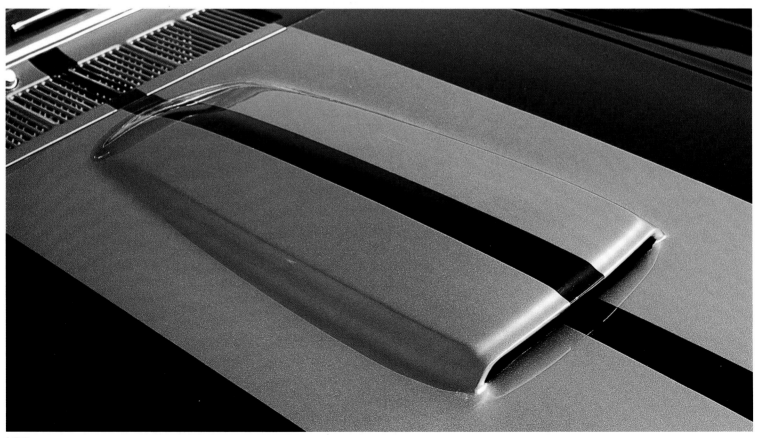

Like regular 1966 Shelbys, the Hertz cars had standard black Mustang upholstery, 3in front seat belts, front disc brakes (note pedal pad), and dash-mounted tachometers. Early GT-350Hs had four-speed transmissions, but over 900 came with an automatic transmission, as shown. All had radios and rear seats. The sticker positioned underneath the radio (also found on the dash pad above the radio) warned rental drivers that the "competition" brakes might require higher-than-normal pedal pressure. A few years ago, the Montana-based owner of this car had Carroll Shelby autograph and date the glovebox door.

Hertz specified unique gold and red corporate decals for the wheel center caps that most, but not all, cars received. The rental company also requested that Shelby American add an H to the side stripe GT-350 designation. Chromed 14in Magnum 500 wheels were most common on the GT-350H models, though cast-aluminum ten-spoke and Cragar/Shelby five-spoke wheels also were found on the 1,000 original Rent-a-Racers.

For a period of time early in Hertz car production, the 1966 Shelby colors Wimbledon White, Ivy Green, Sapphire Blue, and Candyapple Red were used. With the exception of a handful of white cars, the non-Raven Black cars received gold Hertz GT-350H side stripes but no Le Mans stripes.

Road Test: Shelby Mustang GT-350H

"Good things do come for the driver of a GT-350. Its cornering ability is a lovely mixture of the beast getting the better of you and you keeping hold of the tiger's tail."
—*Car and Driver*, May 1966

Acceleration

0-30mph	2.1sec
0-40mph	3.1sec
0-50mph	4.9sec
0-60mph	6.6sec
0-70mph	8.9sec
0-80mph	10.8sec
0-90mph	14.2sec
0-100mph	17.9sec

Standing quarter-mile	93mph in 15.2sec
Top speed, observed	117mph
Temperature	51F
Altitude	83ft above sea level

Engine

Type	Water-cooled V-8, cast-iron block, five main bearings
Bore and stroke	4.00x2.87in
Displacement	289ci; 4727cc
Compression ratio	10.5:1
Valve gear	Pushrod-operated ohv, solid lifters
Power (SAE)	306bhp at 6000rpm
Torque	329lb-ft at 4200rpm
Specific output	1.05bhp per cubic inch
Usable rpm range	800-6000rpm
Electrical system	12volt, 55amp-hr battery
Mileage	6-12mpg
Range on 16gal	96-192 miles

Drivetrain

Transmission	Three-speed automatic
Final drive ratio	3.89:1

Chassis

Platform steel frame, semi-integral steel body	
Wheelbase	108.0in
Track	Front, 57.0in; Rear, 57.0in
Length	181.6in
Width	68.2in
Height	51.2in
Ground clearance	5.3in
Curb weight	2,884lb
Test weight	3,158lb
Weight distribution	52% front, 48% rear
Pounds per bhp (test)	10.9

Suspension

Front	Independent, upper wishbone, lower control arm and drag strut, coil springs, anti-sway bar
Rear	Rigid axle, semi-elliptic leaf springs, trailing arms

Brakes

Front	11.3in Kelsey-Hayes discs
Rear	10x3in drums, 408sq-in swept area

Steering

Type	Recirculating ball
Turns, lock to lock	4
Turning circle	40ft

Tires 7.75x15 Goodyear Blue Streaks

"Incidentally, the 'H' might well stand for 'Homologated' if Shelby—or, for that matter, Hertz—wanted to race the car as a Group 2 sedan; the 1,000 examples Shelby will produce for Hertz fulfill the FIA's minimum production requirement."
Source: *Car and Driver*, May 1966.

1967 Shelby GT-350 and GT-500

New Styling for the Road Cars

Lime Gold became a popular color in 1967, as did the optional Kelsey-Hayes MagStar wheels. This would be the final year that a High Performance 289ci engine would power the GT-350. The unique C-pillar air extractor scoops added a distinctive touch to the Shelby exterior.

With its roof-mounted and quarter-panel air scoops, an extended nose, and an upswept, spoiled tail, the 1967 Shelby looked like no other automobile on the highway. The cars succeeded in evoking the image of the Ford GT-40s which had won Daytona and dominated the 1966 24 Hours of Le Mans. The center grille-mounted high beams, the wide wind-split hood scoop, the roofline, which, unlike the earlier Shelbys, swept to the rear of the trunk, and the wide, clean taillights, helped separate the GT-350s and GT-500s from all others, especially the standard Mustang.

Competition was evolving in the classes that team cars and GT-350 independent racers had dominated in prior years. The headlines had been won, the victories logged, the image created. Much had changed, and much of the philosophy and strategy behind the new cars would come from Ford and its dealer network. Hot off the sales success of 1966, growth became foremost in their plans. The redesigned Mustang presented a slightly larger and heavier car to Shelby American, and that certainly inspired the designers to take the next generation Shelby a step further.

"The Road Cars"

In line with the concept of pleasing a broader segment of the car buying public,

1967 found many of the previous years' rough edges smoothed by additions of luxury touches: the Mustang Deluxe interior, power steering, power brakes, optional air conditioning, and twice as many exterior colors. Even the premier dealer brochure promoted the Shelbys as "The Road Cars." Still, changes such as the GT-500's 428ci engine option, the progressive rate springs, and the standard rollbar (a first for any production car, as were the shoulder harnesses actuated by rollbar-mounted inertia reels) kept the Shelby in a league of its own. Though the power steering system interfered with its 1965-1966 type steel tube headers, the GT-350 retained the race-proven Shelby-tweaked High Performance 289 engine. The more restrictive Mustang Hi-Po manifolds were used, and probably cost some horsepower.

An article in the February 1967 *Car and Driver* gives credit for the fiberglass

Summer Place

What better way to get there—or anywhere—than a
Shelby GT? Pleasure begins the second you turn the key and bring
alive America's answer to Europe's finest GT cars.

Let your Shelby dealer deliver the goods . . .
and save enough to rent a summer place, buy a boat—
or just chuckle all the way to the bank.*

 SHELBY G.T. *350 and 500* **The Road Cars** Powered by *Ford*

Shelby American, Inc., 6501 W. Imperial Highway, Los Angeles 90009

*GT 350: $3995 Manufacturer's suggested retail price. Includes Cobra 289
CID 306 h.p. V-8, dual exhaust, competition-based front and rear suspensions,
4-speed transmission, h.d. rear, full instrumentation, safety bar, exclusive GT
styling. GT 500 with dual quad Cobra 428 CID V-8, just $200 more. Options, ac-
cessories, delivery, dealer preparation, state and local taxes, additional.

"Summer Place" advertisement for 1967
GT-350 and GT-500. The pleasures of highway
driving were promoted for The Road Cars for
1967. Only two years after the Shelby pitch
touted nothing but performance, Ford's eye had
shifted to a broader market. The "good life"
certainly would include an A-frame summer
house and a quick car to get you there.

Next page
This GT-350 has the standard 1967 wheel
covers: 1967 Thunderbird covers with Shelby
center medallions. In addition to Brittany Blue,
shown here, Shelby American also offered
Bronze Metallic, Dark Blue, Raven Black, Candyapple Red, Wimbledon White, Dark Moss
Green, Medium Metallic Gray, Lime Gold, and
Acapulco Blue. Shelby taillights for 1967 were
1967 Cougar units, and the Shelby-specific gas
cap was a pop-open unit.

The 1967 Shelby, with its jutting grille opening, Le Mans stripes, and center-mounted high beams, looked more menacing than its predecessors. It certainly could not be confused with a mere Mustang.

body panels to Chuck McHose, a Ford stylist who worked closely with Shelby American. In addition to helping distinguish the GT-350s and GT-500s from standard and GT model Mustang Fastbacks, the fiberglass pieces saved weight. Though the stock Mustang front bumper was mounted to stock support braces, the fiberglass Shelby hood measured almost 4in longer than a Mustang's.

The pin-secured hood (which also used a standard-type hood latch) mated to a one-piece fiberglass nose that replaced the front fender extensions, grille surround, gravel pan, and lower valance. The grille-mounted high beams were positioned at

the center until it was learned that certain states, including California, had statutes mandating minimum distance between headlights. Cars headed for those states started receiving lights at the outboard edges of the grille. Legend has it that, in Pennsylvania, one lawmaker who had counted on the purchase of a Shelby with inboard lights actually initiated a change in the state law to accommodate his wish.

The fiberglass roof air extractor worked with an interior vent that could be opened or closed, and the first 200 or so 1967 Shelbys had small red running lights installed in the outflow of the C-pillar scoop. Activated by the brake pedal, the lights were deleted from the production run after those, too, were found to conflict with laws in several states. The lower quarter-panel air scoops fed fresh air, on most early cars, to the rear brakes.

At the rear, the spoiler effect of the fiberglass deck lid was matched by fender

extensions, and wide 1967 Cougar taillights were split by a Shelby-specific pop-open gas cap. Special Shelby tailpipe extensions were routed through the partial cutaways in a 1967 Mustang GT-style lower valance. Again, a stock Mustang bumper was used.

Shelby exterior emblems included identical grille and deck lid nameplates, front fender badges, and lower body panel stripes, all specific to either the GT-350 or GT-500. Shelby emblems also appeared on gas caps and wheel centers. The base wheel for 1967 was a 15in steel one with a Shelby logo 1967 Thunderbird wheel cover. The $185 Shelby wheels offered to purchasers of 1967 models were Kelsey-Hayes 15x7 MagStar units (at only $151.74 on one owner's original invoice) and, later in the model year, the 15in ten-spoke cast-aluminum wheel was offered.

The Deluxe Mustang interior, in either black or Parchment vinyl (with a few white interiors produced as well), included an

Shelby taillights for 1967 were 1967 Cougar units, and the Shelby Cobra gas cap, specific to either the GT-350 or GT-500 models, was a pop-open unit.

1967 Shelby Color Chart

Unlike any Mustang, the 1967 Shelby had its original exterior color noted in the Shelby American-assigned VIN. A numeral located seven positions from the left provided the color code. The letter to the right of the color code numeral indicated the color of the Deluxe interior: A indicated black and U indicated either Parchment or white. The first eighty-nine cars produced did not have the interior code in their VINs.

The first five colors were the only ones scheduled for September build by Report II of the 1967 Prototype Program. Red, gray, and Lime Gold began appearing after car 0099; Brittany Blue started appearing with car 0288; and Acapulco Blue was not a scheduled color until the final third of production.

Color Number	Color Name	1967 Mustang Color Code	DuPont Number	Ditzler Number	R-M* Number
1	Bronze Metallic	V	4793	22749	
2	Dark Blue	K	4780	13076	A-1780
3	Raven Black	A	88	9000	
4	Wimbledon White	M	4480	8378	A-1633
5	Dark Moss Green	Y	4788	43567	A-1879
6	Metallic Gray	4**	4733	32520	
7	Lime Gold	I	4790	43576	A-1882
8	Brittany Blue	Q	4813	13619	A-1643
9	Candyapple Red	T	4737	71528	A-1782R
0	Acapulco Blue	D	4857	13357	A-1935

*R-M stands for Rinished-Mason, the brand of paint generally used on Shelbys made in the San Jose plant. Generally, later-model Shelbys were painted with Ditzler.

**Metallic Gray, termed "Special Dark Metallic Gray #1900 (1967 Thunderbird Only)" in the 1967 GT-350 Prototype Program Report II, also has been called Medium Gray Metallic and Dark Gray Metallic. It was the only 1967 Shelby color that was not a Mustang color for that model year.

Early-production 1967 Shelbys were fitted with C-pillar scoop running lights. Due to legal problems in some states, including California, the state of manufacture, the lights were phased out of production after the first 200 or so cars were completed.

"Everybody looks at you" ad for 1967 GT-350 and GT-500. The elements of luxury and prestige are foremost in this appeal to consumers. Along with "zesty" performance, handling, and brakes, the ad pushes safety and comfort. It would seem that winning races has become secondary to winning friends.

Next page
"Big Stuff" print ad for Shelby Parts Company mail order. The Shelby operation continued to market high-performance bolt-on parts for all Ford enthusiasts. Here, the Shelby Parts Company, an offshoot of Shelby American, promotes speed equipment for big-block engines. The ad copy overflowed with imagination: Here was your chance to own a "Le Mans Kinetic Superflow Solid Lifter Camshaft Kit."

8000rpm tachometer, aluminum insets for the dash area and door panels, an "optional" fold-down rear seat, and deluxe lap belts to accompany the harnesses. The unique wood-rimmed steering wheel and a set of underdash gauges for oil pressure and amperes (fitted to an upside-down early Mustang Rally-Pac) topped off the performance touches.

A Winning Compromise

There were old arguments that because the Mustang was upsized for 1967,

the 1967 Shelby, with its power steering and such, had gained too much bulk to be competitive. With fifty-seven percent of its weight on the front wheels, the GT-500 probably was not destined for road-racing glory, but the SCCA rulebook kept the GT-350s from B/Production competition more than any inherent factor.

Certainly, the size of the cars didn't bother the 1967 Mustang hardtops competing in that year's SCCA A/Sedan series and winning the Trans-Am Sedan Manufacturers Championship. (Ironically, when Ford elected to support the Mustang race cars, it turned to Shelby American for behind-the-scenes expertise.) The true rea-

202

203

Ready for drag-strip action, this big-block Wimbledon White GT-500 runs center headlights and 15in cast-aluminum Shelby ten-spoke wheels with slicks mounted at the rear. The 428ci engine was capable of delivering impressive straight-line performance, though road racers felt that the engine's weight diminished overall handling.

son for the Shelby's exclusion went back to its original homologation: The class called for a two-seater, and the 1967 Shelby clearly had four seats.

For 1967, Carroll Shelby was forced to rethink his approach and blend it with Ford's intentions. But once again, Shelby American created and produced an eye-

and ear-catching performance car. Marketed at the lowest price ever offered for a Shelby and promoted as an exciting highway GT touring car, its sales easily topped 3,000 units.

If compromises are to be won or lost, Carroll Shelby certainly won this one. He may have had doubts at the time, but the

1967 Shelby Production Figures

GT-350 1,175 units
GT-500 2,048 units
Total 3,225 units
    There was one GT-500 prototype hardtop, "Little Red," with a twin Paxton supercharged 427ci engine, built for Fred Goodell, a Ford employee who became Shelby American chief engineer. This car was eventually destroyed by Ford to avoid product liability problems. There was also one prototype 1967 GT-500 convertible that eventually became the prototype for the 1968 Shelby convertible. Evidence indicates this car still exists.
    Source: 1987 *Shelby American World Registry.*

1967 SHELBY G.T.350/500
The Road Cars

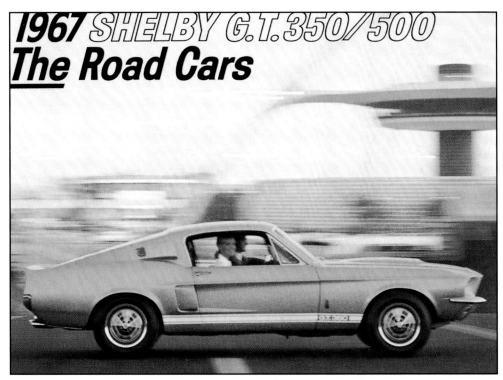

Original showroom brochure for 1967 Shelby. The six-page Shelby dealer showroom brochure targeted the affluent with lifestyle photos of a GT-350 cruising past the Los Angeles International Airport, a GT-500 in a rural, romantic setting with horseback riders, a racetrack setting, and attractive women throughout. Amidst all that, the ad copy highlighted the low price of the car compared to other domestic and imported GT models.

This fresh-looking Brittany Blue GT-500 has 15in ten-spoke wheels and center-mounted high beams, but no Le Mans stripes. The rollbar and inertia reel shoulder harnesses are plainly visible in the uncommon white interior (most were black or Parchment). The rear quarter-panel and C-pillar air scoops strongly suggest Ford's world-class GT-40 race car.

Ford's Police Interceptor 428ci engine puts the squeeze on the GT-500 engine compartment. The twin Holley 650cfm carburetors atop the aluminum medium-rise intake manifold were actuated by a dual-quad progressive linkage with vacuum secondaries. Early cars had no lettering on their aluminum oval air cleaners, but this later version has Cobra above the forward carburetor.

concept shift Ford dictated to make the Shelby more luxurious did not substantially alter the nature of the car. The small- and big-block cars were genuine muscle cars, with responsive handling, quick steering, serious brakes, and a grand heritage. At this stage of the game, the marque was rolling.

Shelby American designed unique GT-350 and GT-500 front fender emblems for 1967, and continued the use of lower body-panel stripes and model designation lettering.

For the 1967 Shelby GT-350 and GT-500, Shelby American, Inc., created a special cover and two ten-page Shelby-specific sections in its adaption of the standard 1967 Mustang owners manual.

1967
SHELBY
G.T. 350/500
OWNERS MANUAL

SHELBY AMERICAN, INC.
6501 W. IMPERIAL HIGHWAY
LOS ANGELES, CALIFORNIA

The headlight housing/fender extension was incorporated into the fiberglass nose and grille surround for 1967. Many cars with outboard high-beam lights, like those on this GT-500, had a letter Z stamped in front of the serial number on the underhood VIN plate. A standard hood latch was used in conjunction with twin securing pins.

208

All 1967 Shelbys received the Mustang Deluxe interior, with special upholstery and molded seatbacks, fold-down rear seats, door panels with brushed-aluminum insets and molded armrests, brushed-aluminum dash trim, and aluminum trim pieces in the lower door area. Both GT-350s and GT-500s also featured the rollbar and integral inertia reel shoulder harnesses, an oil-pressure and ammeter gauge cluster under the center dash, a 1967-only steering wheel, a Shelby insignia (identical to the grille ornament) on the aluminum dash panel above the glovebox, and Shelby American logo inserts on the sill plates.

This rare white interior shows a clean example of the model-designated center horn button on the 1967 steering wheel, air conditioning ducts (also uncommon on 1967 Shelbys), the in-dash 8000rpm tachometer, and Deluxe Mustang aluminum dash trim.

Road Test:1967 Shelby GT-350 and GT-500

Acceleration, GT-350

0-30mph	2.8sec
0-40mph	4.1sec
0-50mph	5.6sec
0-60mph	7.1sec
0-70mph	9.0sec
0-80mph	11.8sec
0-90mph	15.0sec
0-100mph	19.3sec
Standing quarter-mile	91mph in 15.3sec
Top speed, observed	129mph (average, two-way run)

Acceleration, GT-500

0-30mph	2.8sec
0-40mph	4.0sec
0-50mph	4.9sec
0-60mph	6.7sec
0-70mph	8.1sec
0-80mph	11.8sec
0-90mph	15.0sec
0-100mph	16.9sec
Standing quarter-mile	92mph in 14.3sec
Top speed, observed	132mph (average, two-way run)

Engine

Type	V-8, iron block, water-cooled
Head	Cast-iron, removable
Valves	Pushrod/rocker-actuated ohv

GT-350

Max. bhp	306 at 6000rpm
Max. torque	329lb-ft at 4200rpm
Bore	4.005in
Stroke	2.87in
Displacement	289ci; 4727cc
Compression ratio	10.5:1
Induction system	Single Holley four-barrel, 750cfm
Exhaust system	Standard, dual
Electrical system	12-volt, distributor ignition
Fuel consumption	Test, 13mpg; average, 15mpg

GT-500

Max. bhp	355 at 5400rpm
Max. torque	420lb-ft at 3200rpm
Bore	4.13in
Stroke	3.984in
Displacement	428ci; 7015cc
Compression ratio	10.5:1
Induction system	Dual Holley four-barrel, 600cfm
Exhaust system	Standard, dual
Electrical system	12-volt, distributor ignition
Fuel consumption	Test, 9.4mpg; average, 11mpg

Chassis

Frame	Unit, welded
Body	Steel and fiberglass
Front suspension	Unequal arms, coil springs, adjustable tube shocks, anti-sway bar
Rear suspension	Live axle, multi-leaf springs, tube shocks
Tire type and size	Goodyear E70-15

Weights and Measures

Wheelbase	108.0in
Front track	58.0in
Rear track	58.0in
Overall height	51.6in
Overall width	70.9in
Overall length	186.6in
Ground clearance	6.5in
Crankcase	6qt
Cooling system	20qt
Gas tank	18gal
Curb weight, GT-350	2,723lb
Test weight, GT-350	3,048lb
Curb weight, GT-500	3,286lb
Test weight, GT-500	3,576lb

Clutch

Type	Single disc, dry
Diameter	10.5in
Actuation	Mechanical

Transmission

Type	Four-speed, full synchromesh

Ratios

First	2.32:1
Second	1.69:1
Third	1.29:1
Fourth	1.00:1

Brakes

Front	11.3in Kelsey-Hayes discs
Rear	10x3 drums

Differential

GT-350 ratio	3.89:1
GT-500 ratio	3.25:1
Drive axles (type)	Enclosed, semi-floating

Steering

Type	Recirculating ball
Turns, lock to lock	3.5
Turning circle	37ft

The Kelsey-Hayes 15x7 MagStar wheel was a Shelby option for 1967 only. Chromed steel rims surround aluminum center sections and Cobra logo center caps.

It is rare to find original air conditioning on the GT-350 small-block Hi-Po engine. Note the finely detailed power steering pump, date-correct fan belt, and numerous other concours touches.

"How Much Does It Cost?"

Item	Retail List
GT-350	$3,995.00
GT-500	4,195.00
Power disc brakes	64.77
Power steering	84.47
Shoulder harness	50.76
Select-O-Matic transmission	50.00
Air conditioner, Selectaire	356.09
Exhaust emission control system	45.44
Closed crankcase emission system	5.19
Fold-down rear seat	64.77
Deluxe (Shelby) wheels	185.00
Rally stripe	34.95
Paxton supercharger for GT-350	549.00

Source: *Sports Car Graphic*, March 1967.

1968 Shelby GT-350, GT-500, and GT-500KR

The Royal Treatment, and a King of the Road

The 1968 Shelby Cobra took styling to an even wilder realm than its facelifted counterpart of the previous year. From the more massive grille opening with its inset rectangular foglights to the broad, chrome-trimmed taillights, from the luxurious console-equipped interior to the highly visible convertible rollbar, the 1968 GT-350s and GT-500s radiated aggressiveness with a touch of elegance. Whereas the 1967 and 1968 Mustangs were nearly identical, the Shelbys of those years were wholly dissimilar.

At the onset of 1968 production, the two most outstanding changes were the introduction of the convertible model and the shift of production from California to Ionia, Michigan. The convertible actually had been discussed for the 1967 line, and VIN prefixes with a C in the sixth position (instead of the F for Fastback) had been outlined in FoMoCo correspondence. But it was not until the 1968 model year that a customer could obtain an open-air Shelby.

In comparing Shelby sales figures for 1967 and 1968, the increase of 1,225 vehicles coincides remarkably with the total of 1,124 convertibles produced in 1968. The distinctive design of their rollbars certainly added to the convertibles' appeal, and Ford's promotional efforts obviously paid off.

A number of factors led to the shift of final assembly from Shelby American's huge shop near the Los Angeles International Airport to the A. O. Smith Company in Ionia, but the main factor seems to have been Ford's desire to have it that way. Quality control problems with fiberglass body pieces were solved by shifting to a Ford-found source nearer Detroit; Shelby American's plant lease would soon expire in Los Angeles; production numbers (over 3,200 in 1967 and what would become 4,450 in 1968) required a sizable capacity and a proximity to parts; and Ford's Metuchen, New Jersey, plant had become, more than San Jose and Dearborn, the assembly line most easily sourced for the Shelbys-to-be.

In order to continue their approach to expanding consumer acceptance of the Shelby, Ford offered multiple color options. The front-end design changed for 1968, with a more pronounced and rounded grille opening, inset driving lights, and scoops further forward on the hood. Instead of Klik pins, Dzus fasteners helped secure the hood and, again, the stock Mustang front bumper was used. In 1968, Shelby provided GT-350 Fastbacks to Hertz Rent-A-Car, though much fewer than in 1966, and without exterior modifications to identify the cars as Hertz models.

The rear treatments seemed to change only slightly from 1967 to 1968, but actually were substantially different. The argent panel is a fiberglass section to which 1965 Thunderbird three-bulb taillights with sequential turn indicators and a Shelby pop-open gas cap were attached. The entire tail panel then was affixed to the existing taillight panel with screws and sealer. Note the rear quarter-panel reflector assembly required for added safety on all 1968 models.

This evolution of Shelby manufacturing required a change in the company structure as well. Shelby American, Inc., remained a corporate entity, but its operations were split into three companies. Shelby Automotive, Inc., in Livonia, Michigan, coordinated the manufacture and sale

of production cars; the Shelby Parts Company, in Torrance, California (which eventually moved to the Detroit area and became Shelby Autosports) handled the manufacture, purchase, and sale of Shelby aftermarket parts and accessories; and the Shelby Racing Company, in Torrance, continued and expanded racing activities.

King of the Road

Several changes in Ford's engine offerings affected the 1968 Shelby. The discontinuation of the stalwart 271hp 289ci Hi-Po (which Shelby had coaxed to the 306hp level) meant that GT-350s received a four-barrel 302ci engine. The engineers had hoped to start the year with a cast-aluminum intake manifold, but encountered trouble in passing emissions tests. The early

cars received cast-iron manifolds; they were later recalled to be refitted, though many owners neglected to take part in the swap program. Rated at 250hp, the engine marked a performance reduction out of keeping with the Shelby image. The 428ci engines that had powered the previous year's GT-500s were continued in that line. Their high-rise aluminum intake manifolds were matched with 715cfm Holley carburetors, and were rated at 335hp. Toploader four-speed close-ratio transmissions were used with both engines, while C-4 automatics went to GT-350s and C-6 automatics were installed in big-block cars.

The most remarkable (and most easily promoted) engine change came after the model year was two-thirds gone: Ford introduced, in the highly touted 1968½ Mustang Cobra Jet GT and the Shelby

"King of the Road," a wonderfully reworked version of the 428 engine. The cars were launched into the realm of straight-line wildness. The Cobra Jet included revised 427 low-riser heads with expanded porting, stronger connecting rods and crankshaft, a dual-plane intake manifold, the 735cfm Holley four-barrel carburetor, and a Ram Air intake setup. Additionally, the Cobra Jets received heavy-duty front and rear shocks (four-speed cars got staggered rear shocks), front power disc brakes, power steering, and larger-capacity rear drum brakes.

It is said that the name "King of the Road" (which led to the GT-500KR designation for the late 1968 big-block Shelbys) was slated for a General Motors product. Ford got wind of the rumor, and swiped the name outright.

Oddly, Ford elected to go low-key on promoting the increased power of the Cobra Jet. Perhaps to escape the wrath of the safety-minded public and the insurance industry, the company downscaled the Cobra Jet engine horsepower rating by about twenty percent. The claim of 335hp simply wasn't correct.

The true tip-off to the nature of the 1968 Shelby could be found in the Deluxe

In 1968, for the first time, a Shelby convertible model was offered, and, for the second year, Ford promoted a premium image with the Mustang Deluxe interior in all Shelbys. The 1968 luxury interior had been redesigned to incorporate woodgrain panels. All Shelbys received a center console with oil-pressure and ammeter gauges. The Paxton supercharger was available for GT-350s and, with this installation, a fuel-pressure gauge would be mounted below the oil-pressure gauge (left side), and a manifold-boost gauge below the ammeter. This four-speed GT-350 features an optional eight-track tape player.

Cobra GT-350 and GT-500KR Special Features

- Two engine choices: GT 350, 250hp 302ci V-8; GT 500KR, 335hp 428ci V-8.
- High-velocity, high-volume Cobra intake manifold.
- Advanced design cathedral float four-barrel carburetor.
- Dual exhausts.
- Low-restriction custom paper-element diecast-aluminum air cleaner.
- Diecast-aluminum Cobra rocker covers, chromed filler cap, dipstick.
- High-rate front coil spring.
- High-capacity heavy-duty adjustable shock absorbers, front and rear.
- .94in-diameter front stabilizer bar.
- Crisp 16.0:1 steering ratio with power assist.
- Heavy-duty four-leaf rear springs.
- Anti-windup rear spring dampers for sure acceleration.
- Heavy-duty rear axle.
- Power-assisted floating caliper front disc brakes.
- Heavy-duty rear drum brakes.
- Four-ply polyglass Goodyear high-performance tires.
- 6in rim width 15in safety wheels.
- Inertia-reel shoulder harnesses and seat belts for front seat passengers (seat belts in rear).
- Integral overhead safety bar in all models.
- Safety-sequence wide taillights.
- Front marker lights.
- Rear quarter reflectors.
- Rectangular foglights.
- Dual master brake cylinder with proportioning valve and low pressure warning light.
- Collapsible steering column and safety padded center steering wheel.
- Fully unitized chassis and body.

Styling Appointments

Exterior: Precision-molded custom fiberglass hood and front assembly incorporates dual air intake scoops, functional louvered extractors. Custom self-retained push-and-turn hood locks. Rectangular foglights mounted in grille opening. Le Mans-type air extractors on rear quarters of Fastback roof. Brake air scoops set in lower quarters. Precision-molded custom fiberglass trunk deck lid with integral air spoiler. GT stripe on lower rocker panels.

Interior: Deluxe all-vinyl interior with bucket seats, full-loop pile carpeting, matching custom-styled console with padded armrest-glovebox, walnut-grained appliques on instrument panel and door panels. Full instrumentation; 8000rpm tachometer; 140mph speedometer; oil-pressure, ammeter, water temperature, and fuel gauges; electric clock. Optional folding rear seat with retractable safety luggage retaining bar (Fastback only), tie-down loops on safety bar (convertible only).

Source: Full-page advertisement for Shelby Automotive, Inc., in *Car Life*, June 1968.

In 1968, four-speed GT-350s, with their 302-4V engines, were required to run anti-smog equipment (like all GT-500s), while GT-350s with automatic transmissions ran a simpler crank-case ventilation system. All 1968 GT-350 and GT-500 Shelbys used the Cobra-lettered oval air cleaner and finned aluminum valve covers. The later GT-500KRs used Ram Air induction.

1968 Shelby Color Chart

Like the Mustang (and unlike any previous Shelby), the 1968 Shelby had a Ford warranty/data plate riveted adjacent to the driver's door latch. Colors were noted by a letter code. Interior color codes also were noted on the data plate; 1968 Shelbys offered 6A or 6AA for black vinyl, and 6F or 6FA for Medium Saddle vinyl. Both were available with any exterior color, as were black or white convertible tops. The GT side stripe was blue on a white exterior, and white on all others.

Color Code	Color Name	DuPont Number	Ditzler Number
A	Raven Black	88	9300
D	Acapulco Blue	4857	13357
I	Lime Gold	4790	43576
M	Wimbledon White	4480	8378
R	Highland Green	4869	43644
T	Candyapple Red	4737	71528
W	Fleet Yellow		
X	Dark Blue Metallic		
Y	Gold Metallic	4874	22833

1968 Shelby Production

GT-350 Fastbacks	1,253
GT-350 Convertibles	404
GT-500 Fastbacks	1,140
GT-500 Convertibles	402
GT-500KR Fastbacks	933
GT-500KR Convertibles	318
Total:	4,450

Source: 1978 *Shelby American World Registry.*

The lifestyle image building continued from 1967, and Shelby convertible rollbars even had D-rings for surfboard attachment. This GT-350 has the Marchal 656/322 foglamps that were used until sometime in April 1968. Later cars received Lucas FT8 foglamps and, in October of that year, all Marchal-equipped cars were recalled for a Lucas swap. Obviously, not all owners chose to return to the dealers. Shelby American franchised dealers numbered 111 for the 1968 model year, with nine of those located in Canada.

Cobra Jet 428 Engine Specifications

Horsepower	335 at 5600
Torque	440 at 3400
Displacement	428ci
Bore	4.13in
Stroke	3.98in
Compression ratio	10.7:1
Cylinder heads and valves	Large intake port with 2.06in intake valve, 1.625in exhaust valve
Intake manifold	Large iron version of aluminum manifold
Exhaust manifold	New header
Carburetor	735cfm 4-V
Tappet - Cam	Hydraulic
Rocker arm	1.73:1
Oil pan	Conventional
Camshaft lift	.481in intake .490in exhaust
Camshaft duration	290deg

Source: Full-page advertisement for Shelby Automotive, Inc., *Car Life*, June 1968.

Mustang interior: its center console with the Cobra-embossed padded armrest and mini glovebox. Woodgrain appliques appeared on the inner door panels and dash area, but, fortunately, the oil-pressure and ammeter gauges remained, as well as the 8000rpm tachometer.

Beneath those luxury touches could be found the progressive-rate suspension used in 1967, a less-harsh ride for smoother road travel. Power brakes, power steering, shoulder harnesses, and the Fastback fold-down rear seat were mandatory options, and the Tilt-Away steering wheel was also available.

Exterior trim changed slightly in transition from 1967. The nose section was reshaped, and hoods received a wider split scoop closer to the nose, twist-type latches, and two rows of louvers near the cowl, which Shelby referred to as air extractor vents. The small rectangular front fender emblems were replaced by sculpted Cobra emblems. For a similar yet flashier look, the 1967 Cougar taillights of the 1967 Shelbys gave way to 1965 Thunderbird units with a more substantial chrome frame and five vertical chrome "teeth." The rear turn signals had sequential blinkers (except in California). These taillights would carry over to the 1969 and 1970 Shelbys as well.

As on the 1968 Mustangs, the front and rear fenders had safety reflectors near the bumper tips; the appearance of the rear reflector changed slightly during the model year. Once again, a steel 15x6 wheel was standard equipment, with a generic Ford wheelcover and Shelby logo center ornament. The Shelby cast-aluminum 15x7 ten-spoke wheels introduced in 1967 were optional for 1968.

New for 1968 were the rectangular rear fender reflectors, the 1965 Thunderbird taillights, a pop-open fuel filler cap with a Shelby Cobra center emblem, and a fresh look for Shelby exhaust tips.

The 428ci engines in GT-500s (and later GT-500KRs) were required to have anti-smog systems—hence, the blue plumbing. Unlike the previous year's big-block cars, the 1968 GT-500s were fitted with only one four-barrel carburetor, a 715cfm Holley. This fine restoration includes the Cobra Le Mans valve covers and all the smaller details needed for factory originality.

In addition to the Deluxe Mustang door panels, woodgrain dash, door panel, steering wheel appliqué, and Deluxe upholstery, Shelbys were fitted with a Cobra logo-embossed center console, a Shelby Cobra emblem at the center of the steering wheel, a GT-350 or GT-500 emblem on the dash panel above the glove compartment, and a rollbar MIG welded to the floor pan. This saddle color interior also features in-dash air conditioning.

The exterior styling of the Mustang Fastback had evolved modestly from 1965 to 1968 but, as this Candyapple Red GT-500 demonstrates, the Shelby touch dramatically upgraded the effect. The expanded grille, forward hood scoop openings, rear-quarter and C-pillar scoops, and up-swept deck lid were, by themselves, minor changes. The car's tasteful statement of power contributed to the sales of over 4,400 1968 Shelby Cobras.

At the beginning of the model year, Marchal 656/322 foglights were mounted in the lower outboard corners of the grille. These were highly rated French lamps that had been used on several European cars, including several versions of Ferraris. During the production year, due to fluctuations in international currency values, the Marchal lamps became markedly more expensive for Shelby.

Because of both price and their cleaner appearance, Lucas FT8 "Square Eight" foglamps were chosen to replace the Marchals. According to Paul M. Newitt's excellent *California Special Recognition Guide and Owner's Manual*, the Lucas lights, after April 26, 1968, were installed by A. O. Smith Company on all new Shelbys and Mustang California Specials. Later, in October 1968, California ruled that the Marchals were too bright to be used safely on the highway. In response, Shelby issued a recall for the retrofit of Lucas lights for early 1968 Shelbys.

White Le Mans stripes on a Gold Metallic exterior help highlight the extended nose area and aggressive hood scoops of a 1968 Shelby. Previous year's Klik pin hood fasteners were deleted in favor of Dzus fasteners on 1968 models, and the Lucas FT8, or "square eight," foglamps replaced the Marchal units in late April 1968.

The Cobra name came into expanded usage with the decision to call the 1968 cars the Shelby Cobra. In a campaign to tie the product to the AC Cobra roadsters' rocket-like reputation, Ford's specifications sheets and most of that year's advertising stressed the term "Cobra GT." This GT-500 front fender detail shows the elaborate and elegant Cobra emblem designed for 1968 GT-350s and GT-500s. Later "King of the Road" models would get a modified version of the emblem.

In mid-April of the 1968 production year, Ford introduced the new 428ci Cobra Jet engine in the 1968½ Mustang GT. With beefed-up front shock towers, staggered rear shocks, and sturdier internal engine components, the cars seemed intended for straight-line performance. At that point, the GT-500KR replaced the GT-500, and all subsequent big-block Shelbys, through the 1970 model year, were powered by the Cobra Jet engine. The initials KR stood for King of the Road, a fitting title but, as legend has it, a name swiped from a pending General Motors project. This Candyapple Red Fastback displays the new GT-500KR side stripe and the updated front fender emblem.

The powerful lines of the twin hood scoops and Shelby lettering on the nose section proclaim the presence of power.

221

Not often seen on 1968 Shelbys is the subtle but elegant Highland Green exterior color. This car also has the cast-aluminum ten-spoke wheels and Tilt-Away steering wheel. The GT-500KR also received dual-quad exhaust outlet tips and a unique Cobra Jet inset emblem for its pop-open fuel filler caps.

Next page
"Try the complete surprise. . . ." Lifestyle is for sale when a new car is photographed next to a private jet or zipping along a beach just yards away from the crashing surf. Pleasure, comfort, styling, and safety are being promoted: "a richly fitted console;" "full instrumentation;" "high-intensity fog lights and other safety items;" "deep bucket seats;" "strictly limited editions designed by Carroll Shelby. . . ." Is this what the former chicken farmer-turned road racer really had in mind?

The KR-model Shelbys' fender emblem combined the sculpted cobra, the words Cobra Jet, and the numerals 428.

Try the <u>complete</u> surprise . . .
Carroll Shelby's COBRA GT

Carroll Shelby reasons that a *true* GT needs *everything* for high performance pleasure, comfort and safety engineered right in, not just offered as afterthought options. That's why his Cobra GT is a *complete* surprise to those who see it and drive it for the first time. □ Surprise number one is style. Subtle changes in grille, hood, sides, rear deck add a fresh, exclusive look. Interior luxury follows through with deep-bucket seats, walnut-grain appliques, front seat center console-armrest, courtesy lights, full instrumentation. □ Naturally, you expect performance . . . but the GT 500's Shelby-ized 428 cubic inch V-8 rewrites the performance charts with surprising smoothness. A 302 V-8 is Shelby-prepared for the GT 350. Special wide-path tires, 16-to-1 power steering, modified suspension and adjustable super-duty shocks deliver firm control but with enough velvet to make an all-day trip a pleasure. □ Safety features are engineered-in, too. These include an overhead safety bar and inertia-reel shoulder harnesses, impact-absorbing steering wheel, dual braking system. □ By engineering his other surprises into the great-to-start-with Mustang, Carroll Shelby's biggest surprise is the small price. □ Your Shelby dealer will prove just how big *that* surprise can be.

Shelby COBRA GT 350/500   POWER BY Ford

77

Carroll Shelby's COBRA GT ...for the man who wants everything in one car

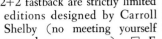

Distinctive styling, superb performance, reassuring safety—you can have all these at an attractively low price. ☐ Both the custom-styled Cobra GT convertible and the 2+2 fastback are strictly limited editions designed by Carroll Shelby (no meeting yourself around every corner). ☐ Exterior styling features are distinctive *and* functional — hood scoops for carburetor air, fastback louvers as air extractors. Even sequential tail lights. ☐ Interiors are luxurious. They gleam with unique simulated wood grain on instrument panel, steering wheel and door trim. There's a richly fitted console. ☐ These *road* car features were designed by *racing* car builders for you: new 302 Ford V-8 (GT 350) or 428 Ford V-8 (GT 500); disc front brakes; competition-based suspension; heavy-duty driveline and rear axle; custom hi-performance 130 MPH rated nylon tires; wide-rim wheels; full instrumentation with an 8,000 RPM tachometer; 4-speed transmission (a close-coupled automatic is a low-cost option). ☐ Cobra's safety features are built-in. These include front seat shoulder harnesses, high intensity fog lights and other safety items. Integral overhead bar is standard in both models. ☐ Carroll Shelby engineered all these features into the Mustang, winner of two Trans-Am road racing championships. ☐ Result: '68 Cobras that rival Europe's finest limited production cars— but sell for thousands of dollars less. ☐ Try "everything" at your Shelby Cobra dealer.

Shelby COBRA GT 350/500   POWER BY Ford

If Ford wanted the ultimate cruising GT, the 500KR convertible, with its luxury interior, air conditioning, tinted glass, AM/FM stereo, and close to 400hp, certainly filled the bill. Only 318 were produced during the period between the introduction of the Cobra Jet package and the end of the 1968 model year.

In late April 1968, due to owner complaints and state regulations, the Marchal 656/322 grille-mounted foglamps were replaced by these Lucas FT8 units, which required a custom-fabricated mounting bracket.

The two-piece folding glass rear window of this Acapulco Blue KR convertible was a $38.86 option for 1968 Mustangs. Shipping tie-down plate removal instructions for receiving dealers are on the paper affixed to the center rear valance.

The Cobra Jet engine used a Ram Air induction system, so the blue circular air cleaner and snorkel arrangement replaced the signature Cobra aluminum oval. The fiberglass chamber fitting to the underside of the hood funneled outside air directly to the air cleaner.

Overall, the 1968 Shelby represented a nod toward performance and a salute toward powerful highway cruising. Again, the public responded and, again, sales figures climbed. Still many steps above a standard Mustang, the Shelby offered a mixed message to enthusiasts. As *Motor Trend* pointed out in March 1968, "The 'establishment' has had its impact on Shelby American, and they've succumbed and resisted. Styling reflects the adoption of the 'great' philosophy, but performance and safety still are Shelby's own exclusives."

The Shelby nose consisted of the lower panel assembly, upper panel (to which the letters Shelby were affixed), and two side panels to shroud the headlights. Note the special attaching brackets that hold the Shelby grille to the forward hood bumpers and the two brackets that connect to the upper panel assembly.

With a 735cfm Holley four-barrel, low-riser heads from Ford's 427 engine, dished pistons, and strengthened connecting rods and crankshaft, the 428ci KR engine produced a nominal 335hp. Most folks knew that figure was an attempt by Ford to low-ball the power rating.

The 1969 Shelby de Mexico GT-350 was a Mexican-built Mustang hardtop with fiberglass roofline extensions and a vinyl roof. It sported 15in ten-spoke wheels and ran an upgraded 302ci engine. Courtesy Eduardo Velázquez.

Shelby de Mexico
Dust Clouds in the Neighbor's Yard.

In 1965, Mexican auto parts distributor Eduardo Velázquez bought a Hi-Po 1965 Mustang hardtop and delivered it to Hi-Performance Motors in Los Angeles for conversion to competitive status. Equipped with a race-ready 289ci engine and the complete Shelby suspension, the Mustang became a winner in Mexico. By the end of 1966, Velázquez's team had won ten of the seventeen events they had raced.

Ford Motor Company, S.A., the Mexican branch of the corporation, had begun producing Mustang hardtops. During 1966, Velázquez became a Shelby parts dealer, and the victories provided great promotion for Shelby aftermarket parts for those Mustangs. In 1967, Velázquez formed a friendship and partnership with Carroll Shelby. Their company, Shelby de Mexico, would create modified Mustangs to be marketed through Ford of Mexico dealerships.

The Shelby de Mexico models of 1967 and 1968 were powered by 289ci engines and looked nearly identical to their 1967 and 1968 stateside namesakes. Production totaled 169 units in 1967 and 203 units in 1968.

The 306 Shelbys produced in 1969 were based on 302hp-powered Mustang hardtops, but had fiberglass roofline extensions that created a Fastback look. Their front sheetmetal was near-stock Mustang, but the slightly bulged hoods were fiberglass, their deck lids had spoilers, and the taillights were the 1965 Thunderbird units used by US production 1968 and 1969 Shelbys. Several of the 1969 Shelby de Mexico GT-350s have been brought into the United States during recent years, and two have been featured in *Mustang Monthly* and other enthusiast magazines.

During those years, Shelby de Mexico campaigned Mustang race cars throughout Mexico, including two Shelby-built 1966 and 1967 Group 2 hardtops. Much advice was received from Al Dowd, Phil Remington, and Lew Spencer at Shelby American, and Carroll Shelby made a point of attending several races in Mexico. The company created two race cars in 1969 and only one in 1970. Only one of those race-specific models is known to survive.

Shelby de Mexico, during the 1971 model year, built approximately 200 Shelby Mustang GT-351s (Windsor engines) and 300 Shelby Mavericks powered by 302hp engines.

In 1967, Freddy Van Beuren won twelve races in Mexico driving one of the earliest 1967 Shelby de Mexico hardtops. Courtesy Eduardo Velázquez.

Memo Rojas drove a Shelby de Mexico race car (based on a 1969 Mustang hardtop) to a class victory at the Mexico City Race Track in 1969. Courtesy Eduardo Velázquez.

The only significant changes to the GT-500KR Deluxe interior were the additions of a wooden Cobra-logo shifter handle and a new Cobra Jet medallion on the panel above the glove compartment. This Fastback model also has optional in-dash air conditioning.

Shelby Europa
Fourteen Cars into the History Books.

Belgian road-racing veteran Claude DuBois, a Ford of Belgium employee and a Shelby dealer, campaigned 5R209, a Shelby R-Model, for Ford of Belgium throughout 1967. By 1969, he had become Shelby's direct importer for the European Common Market, and his stock had included approximately 125 Cobras and Shelbys, as well as numerous De Tomaso Mangustas and products of AC Cars.

When Ford and Shelby elected to close down the GT-350/ GT-500 program in the United States, DuBois found himself in a dilemma. He would not have the volume to remain in business. In a creative move, he proposed to Carroll Shelby that he would oversee the continuing production of Shelby Mustangs in Europe. The cars would be based on 351ci 1971 Mustang convertibles, Mach 1s, and standard SportsRoofs.

While Shelby agreed to the "Shelby Europa" plan and the cars were no-nonsense performers in the same spirit of the mid-1960 versions, only fourteen cars were built before the project was halted in 1972. No factory records were kept for these cars, but thanks to owner response to SAAC queries, a handful have been located in northern Europe and New Zealand.

In addition to the Mustang Deluxe instrument cluster, this Shelby has the optional Tilt-Away steering wheel. Note the location of the climate controls and the left-side air conditioning register.

This Cobra Jet engine also drives an original air conditioning compressor. The shock towers of CJ cars were reinforced at their bases. The inner fender detailing of this car helps make it a concours champion.

The passenger-side dash emblem indicates a
Cobra Jet, as does the Cobra logo wooden
shifter handle.

The GT-500KR side stripe and Cobra Jet 428 fender emblem appeared on only 318 convertibles and 933 fastbacks.

When Shelby production moved from California to Michigan, Shelby American split into several entities. Shelby Automotive, Inc., named on the doorsill plate, oversaw the building and selling of the automobiles.

In 1968, a Dzus twist-type hood lock, positioned adjacent to the leading edge of the hood scoop, replaced the Klik pins of previous years.

Two different designs of rear fender reflectors were used in 1968 to comply with new highway safety regulations.

Next page
Original spec sheet: 1968 Shelby Cobra GT 350/500. Dated August 1967, this general-specification flyer helped to launch the new-for-1968 convertible model with its "overhead safety bar." Presumably, it could not be called a rollbar because of implied protection and potential liability. The sheet also lists the specs for the optional "all-new Cobra hydraulic OHV 427ci V-8." Though it never actually appeared in production, the engine was rated at 400hp at 5600rpm; 460 lb-ft of torque at 3200 rpm; with a compression ratio of 11.6:1.

The Shelby lettering on the flared fiberglass deck lid, the Cobra Jet pop-open gas cap, and the striking 1965 Thunderbird taillights provide an elegantly simple, yet strong, rear view.

marketing office

shelby automotive inc.
box 7390, north end station
detroit, michigan 48202

Dear Friend:

Thanks for your request for information about my Shelby Cobra GT cars. The enclosed material should give you a pretty complete idea of what these cars are like.

Please note that my new GT 500-KR is being marketed in addition to the GT 350 and GT 500 described in the color brochure. The GT 500-KR is powered by Ford's fantastic new Cobra Jet 428 cubic inch V-8. I've Shelby-ized it a little, for just a tweak more top-end performance, although it's pretty unbelievable as it is. (The Cobra Jet replaces the 427 engine which was proposed but not produced for '68.)

You'll find a Cobra dealer not too far from you. He'll be glad to answer your questions about prices, trade-ins, terms, delivery, options and equipment...and to give you the pleasure of trying a new Cobra GT 350, GT 500 or GT 500-KR for yourself.

Thanks again for your interest in Shelby cars.

Cordially,

Carroll Shelby

Carroll Shelby

builders of fine sports cars • Cobra GT-350 / GT-500   POWER BY *Ford*

SHELBY COBRA GT 350/500
SPECIFICATIONS & FEATURES

All-new GT 350 and GT 500 convertibles feature integral overhead safety bar, many other performance, handling, safety and comfort features.

Get behind the wheel of a Shelby Cobra GT and you command a new motoring dimension. Carroll Shelby has worked a bit of racing car magic on the Ford Mustang. Result? The Shelby Cobra GT . . . a **true** road performer that rivals Europe's finest limited-production cars—but for thousands of dollars less. ☐ That's not all the news. Now you can own a Cobra GT 350 or GT 500 **convertible!** Same great features as the famed GT 350 and GT 500 fastback 2+2 coupes. ☐ If you love driving, you'll appreciate the pleasure of Cobra's thrilling GT performance and exclusive styling. It's a pleasure you can afford, as your Shelby Cobra dealer will gladly prove.

ENGINE SPECIFICATIONS

GT 350

Standard: All new OHV 302 cu. in. V-8; 250 horsepower @ 4800 rpm; 310 lbs./foot of torque @ 2800 rpm; 4.0" x 3.0" bore and stroke; compression ratio 10.5:1; hydraulic valve lifters. Cobra high velocity high volume intake manifold with 4 bbl carburetor with 600 CFM flow rate.

Optional*: Cobra centrifugal supercharger, 335 horsepower at 5200 rpm; 325 lbs./foot of torque @ 3200 rpm.†

NOTE: All Cobra GT engines include high velocity high flow intake manifolds, die-cast aluminum rocker covers, low restriction oval design diecast aluminum air cleaner, chromed filler caps, high capacity fuel pumps.

GT 500

Standard: All new Cobra OHV 428 cu. in. V-8; 360 horsepower @ 5400 rpm; 420 lbs./foot of torque @ 3200 rpm; 4.13" x 3.984" bore and stroke; compression ratio 10.5:1; hydraulic valve lifters. Cobra high velocity high volume intake manifold with advanced design, 4 bbl Holley carburetor with 600 CFM (flow rate) primaries, 715 CFM secondaries. High capacity fuel pump.

Optional*: All new Cobra hydraulic OHV 427 cu. in. V-8; 400 horsepower @ 5600 rpm; 460 lbs./foot of torque @ 3200 rpm; 4.235" x 3.788" bore and stroke; compression ratio 11.6:1; hydraulic valve lifters, advanced design cathedral float 4 bbl Holley carburetor. High capacity fuel pump.**

YOUR COBRA DEALER

Original letter responding to KR information request. This letter, mailed from Shelby Automotive, Inc., in Detroit to anyone requesting information on the 1968 Shelbys, accompanied the standard literature packet. It is interesting to note the mention that the Cobra Jet engine "replaces the 427 engine which was proposed but not produced for 1968."

Buy It . . . or watch it go by

King of the Road!

Carroll Shelby has pulled the trick of the year. He's combined Ford's new *drag champion* 428 Cobra Jet engine with his *complete* road car, the Cobra GT 500. Result? Cobra GT 500-KR . . . King of the Road.

Drag champion engine? The 428 Cobra Jet grabbed Super Stock Eliminator honors at the Pomona Winternationals. It delivers 335 hp at 5400 rpm, churns up 440 lbs/ft of torque at a usable 3400. Look for 0 to 60 times that will snap your eyeballs! "Hot Rod" Magazine calls it ". . . the fastest-running Pure Stock in the history of man."

The complete Shelby Cobra GT is ready-made for the "all-there" Cobra Jet. Power is controlled by adjustable shocks, heavy-duty suspension, four-speed transmission (with automatic a low cost option), beefy driveline and torque-sensitive locking rear. All standard—along with 16-to-1 ratio power steering, high performance tires, power disc front brakes. These essentials—plus safety features, luxury interiors and limited-edition styling—are engineered-in, not just offered as options.

The game is Follow-the-Leader. The name of the game is Cobra GT 500-KR. Or play a slightly tamer game with the Cobra GT 350. But make your play at your Shelby dealer . . . today.

 Shelby COBRA GT 350/500-KR

Original dealer brochure: 1968 Shelby Cobra GT 350/500. The first piece of dealer literature regarding the 1968 Shelby Cobra GT-350/500 had a printing date of August 15, 1967. "Just for fun," it says, "Drive the Race-Proved Road Cars." It touts the Goodyear Speedway 350 tires and only seven colors: Red, Lime Gold, White, Gold Frost, Acapulco Blue, Black, and Dark Green. One photograph has Carroll Shelby posing next to a red convertible and green fastback, with an airport in the background. The fastback sports an early-design 350 fuel filler cap insert.

Original dealer promo postcard. Standard for 1968 Shelbys was the generic 15in Ford wheel cover with Shelby center cap shown on this original promotional postcard. The ten-spoke cast-aluminum wheel was optional. The models posing with the two cars are not road-racing types; obviously, the sales pitch had moved upscale during the Shelby Mustang's midlife crisis.

'Just for fun . . .
DRIVE THE RACE-PROVED ROAD-CARS

'68 Shelby
COBRA GT 350/500

1969-1970 Shelby - The Last Big Storm

Beauty and Power.
But the Mustangs Were Catching Up

The 1969 Shelby enjoyed what many felt to be the most elegant styling of the 1969-1973 Mustang era. With the first fiberglass front fenders since the marque's inception, its unique full-width grille opening, wild NACA-scooped hood, striking rear view, and Shelby-only front bumper, the car had a significance all its own. For the third straight year, its styling made it stand apart from the standard Mustang—but maybe not far enough.

Introduced during the same model year as the successful Mach 1, the venerated Boss 429, and the rugged Boss 302, the 1969 Shelby GT-350s and GT-500s found their toughest competition close to home. Equipped with the Mustang's new Windsor block 351-4V in the GT-350s, and the 428ci Cobra Jet engines introduced to Mustang GTs and Shelby GT-500s late in the 1968 model year, the newest Shelbys had to compete with three new Mustang performance Fastback models—now called SportsRoofs—in action as well as appearance.

The Shelby was described in the February 1969 *Sports Car Graphic* as, "No longer a Mustang look-alike." But under the skin, they were more similar to Mustangs than their predecessors, and that caused consternation in the automotive media. Brock Yates, then senior editor at

Car and Driver, called it "a garter snake in Cobra skin." Oddly, three sentences later, he wrote, "I personally can't think of an automobile that makes a statement about performance in sheet metal and fiberglass any better than the current edition of the GT-350."

Once again, base vehicle production was shifted, this time from Metuchen, New Jersey, where the 1968 Shelbys had begun their existence, to Ford's Dearborn assembly plant. From there, the knockdown models went to Shelby Automotive's plant in Ionia, Michigan. The SportsRoof was based on a Mach 1 (data code 63C), which came with its own Deluxe interior, and the convertibles began as data code 76B Deluxe interior models. Dozens of unique components were added in the Shelby Automotive second stage, and the changes to the Shelby exteriors read somewhat like a map of scoops and badges.

Because the Ford stylists assigned to the 1969 Shelby project were able to replace the Mustang front fenders with custom fiberglass pieces, they enjoyed more latitude in redesigning the final Shelby. Even the front bumper was unique to the GT-350/500 models. This Grabber Blue convertible gives a clear view of the trademark Shelby rear-quarter scoops that fed cool air to the inner fenderwell and rear brakes.

The 1969 and 1970 Shelbys were identical except for the chin spoiler, twin black hood stripes, VIN codes, and additional emissions equipment on the later models. The Grabber Orange on this 1970 GT-350 convertible was also available on Mustangs in 1970. Styled wheels, chromed steel rims with cast-aluminum centers, were standard on all 1969 and 1970 models, and Shelby Automotive offered no optional wheel.

The annual SAAC conventions provide members the opportunities to drive their vintage performance vehicles on racetracks, coast to coast. This unmodified 1969 GT-350 SportsRoof is doing what comes naturally at the 1989 Pocono SAAC event.

This Grabber Green 1970 GT-500 convertible displays the updated 428 Cobra Jet emblem on its upper rear front fender. The roll bars for the 1969-1970 Shelbys were not as substantial as the 1967-1968 versions, nor were they MIG-welded to the floor pan as they had been. Only the SportsRoof models used inertia reel front seat safety harnesses. The reflective full-length mid-bodyside tape stripes, in blue, gold, white, and black, keyed off the exterior colors.

One is first drawn to the grille, with its inset chromed rectangle and offset Cobra insignia. The extended, sculptured hood boasts three air inlet scoops, two relief vents just forward of the firewall, and chromed twist-type latches. The fiberglass front fenders have scoops just aft of the grille and ahead of the wheel openings. They may or may not be effective in cooling the front disc brakes, but the quarter-panel scoops ahead of the rear wheel openings are specifically ducted to route air to the

rear drums. The convertible quarter-panel scoops are more oblong and are positioned lower than the SportsRoof versions so their ducting can clear the convertible top mechanism. There was no roof-mounted air scoop for 1969.

The trademark Shelby lower body panel stripe, in a change mirrored by the new Mach 1, was moved upward to draw the eye from the headlight rearward, ending at the rear bumper. The reflective tape stripes came in white, gold, blue, and black to complement the cars' exterior colors. There was only one style of 1969-1970 wheel: a hefty-looking five-spoke aluminum center in a chrome steel rim with a Cobra logo center cap.

At the rear of the car, 1965 Thunderbird taillight reflector housings, lenses, and chrome bezels filled a fiberglass taillight panel. The gas filler inlet was hidden behind the hinged license frame, so no special cap was needed. Just below the

license frame, a custom aluminum exhaust outlet handled the dual exhausts. This location led to a problem several months into production: The GT-500 models, after decelerating from highway speed, could backfire and ignite fuel vapors collected in a "dead air" spot above the filler cap. This almost always occurred to cars that had had the distributor timing advanced and either the fuel mixture or carburetor jets changed. The fires would damage the fiberglass tailpanel and deck lid.

A proper recall was put in motion, and owners of record were notified of the fire hazard by a September 18, 1969, letter from Ford's National Service Office. A September 16 letter to Shelby dealers provided detailed instructions on carrying out the recall, replacing the vent-type gas filler cap and installing a vent tube to direct fumes under the car to a framerail area.

Finally, the fiberglass deck lid again matched custom fender extensions, and a

The Factory Had It Rough

The 1969 Shelbys were built under District Special Order (DSO) codes allocated to Ford's Home Office Reserve. Therefore, every 1969 Shelby door data plate DSO code begins with 84. It is known that, at times, several vehicles would be ordered under a single six-digit DSO number. These knockdown models, or Base Vehicle Shells, could be delivered for conversion and sale only to dealer 84-999, the Shelby Automotive Company. The final six digits of their VIN codes would begin with 48 (with one or two exceptions on the earliest prototypes).

Creating the 1969 Mustangs to be shipped to Shelby Automotive's Ionia, Michigan, plant was directed by a Special Competitive Vehicle Product Letter dated July 19, 1968, and issued August 15, 1968. The vehicle release and special equipment parts list indicated that four separate situations be recognized:

Parts List 9393-400 provided guidelines for modifying a Mach 1 to Shelby specifications. Everything from omitting the production steps of drilling sheet metal holes for Mach 1 trim to installing a Cougar console (C9WB-65045A06-N1A) was included.

Parts List 9393-450 upgraded a base Mustang convertible to Shelby specs. From the addition of the GT Equipment Group and Mach 1 Sound Package to the deletion of interior rear-quarter trim (where the rollbar would be installed), the steps were detailed. Preparing the front ends for Shelby's unique fiberglass pieces and custom grille/bumper assembly required the systematic deletion from the Mustang process of eighty-four separate components. At

least sixty-four additional deletions were needed to complete the task.

Parts list 9393-350 directed the creation of the factory input to the GT-350 package. Because the fastbacks began as Mach 1s and the convertibles as base (no option) convertibles, certain items such as the Heavy Duty (or GT) suspension and Deluxe Interior were already standard for a Mach 1. Only the Shelby convertibles received specific instructions to add those two items. The Mustang shocks were replaced with Gabriel Adjustables (C9ZX-18045-B, front; C9ZX-18080-C, rear), the exhaust system was readied for the Shelby rear exhaust outlets, and 0.95in stabilizer bars replaced 0.85in units. Even details such as the inclusion of Cougar-type gearshift knobs (C8WA-7213-C) for four-speed cars and the addition of a C4DB-16A238-A radiator support-to-hood rubber seal were listed.

Parts list 9393-500 directed the factory input to the GT-500 package. Here, the convertibles got high-back bucket seats with knitted vinyl trim, the Deluxe Interior Decor Group, the tachometer and trip odometer for automatic transmission cars, and power tops with glass backlights. The Cougar-style 428-4V air cleaner for Ram Air (C9ZF-9600-D) was slated to replace the C9ZF-9600-E Mustang unit; likewise, a C7ZF-9601-A air cleaner element and C7ZF-9661-A cover assembly were noted. Part number C9ZX-5556-A two-stage rear springs replaced those slated for Mach 1s (C9ZA-5556-G) and convertibles (C9ZA-5556-E). Dozens of other changes were made before the Base Vehicle Shells left Ford's Dearborn Assembly Plant.

chrome-trimmed black expanded aluminum section was inset vertically into both the deck lid and extensions. Similar aluminum pieces also were inset into the two most forward hood scoops and the rear quarter-panel scoops.

The End of the Road

This is not a mystery book, so the reader knows that the 1969 model was, for all intent, the final Shelby Mustang. Carroll Shelby had seen his small manufacturing operation outgrow two facilities, generate volumes of dominating race cars, and bring unending attention to Ford and to the teams and work force of Shelby American. He also had seen it moved away from California and closer to Ford, and had seen the initial, highly successful "Cobra-Mustang" program become twisted by the demands of the corporation and the marketplace. He had seen the muscle cars of the era begin to receive increased scrutiny from the powers of government and insur-

---

Road Test Specifications, 1969 Shelby GT-500

Options

as Tested:	Traction-Lok, fold-down rear seat, Tilt-Away steering wheel, automatic transmission, AM radio

Engine

Type	V-8, iron block, water-cooled
Head	Cast-iron, removable
Valves	Pushrod/rocker-actuated ohv
Maximum bhp	335 at 5200rpm
Maximum torque	440lb-ft at 3400rpm
Bore	4.13in
Stroke	3.98in
Displacement	428ci; 7019cc
Compression ratio	10.7:1
Induction system	Ram Air, single Holley four-barrel carburetor
Exhaust system	Standard, dual
Electrical system	12 volt, distributor ignition

Transmission

Type	Three-speed automatic with manual override

Ratios

First	2.46:1
Second	1.46:1
Third	1.00:1

Differential

Ratio	Hypoid, 3.50:1
Drive axles (type)	Enclosed, semi-floating

Steering

Type	Recirculating ball-and-nut-type gear, power-assisted
Turns, lock to lock	3.5
Turning circle	37ft

Brakes

Type	Ventilated front discs; heavy-duty drum rear, dual system, power-assisted
Disc diameter	11.3in
Drum diameter	10.0in

Chassis

Frame	Unit steel, welded
Body	Steel and fiberglass
Front suspension	Unequal A-arms, independent coil springs, anti-sway bar, heavy-duty adjustable tube shocks
Rear suspension	Hotchkiss-type, unsymmetrical, variable-rate semi-elliptical leaf springs, heavy-duty adjustable tube shocks
Tire type and size	Goodyear Super Wide-Oval F60x15

Weights and Measures

Wheelbase	108.0in
Front track	58.5in
Rear track	58.5in
Overall height	50.6in
Overall width	71.9in
Overall length	190.62in
Ground clearance	6in
Curb weight	3,850lb
Test weight	4,230lb
Crankcase	6qt
Cooling system	20qt
Gas tank	18gal

Acceleration

0-30mph	2.4sec
0-40mph	3.5sec
0-50mph	4.7sec
0-60mph	6.0sec
0-70mph	7.3sec
0-80mph	9.0sec
0-90mph	11.6sec
0-100mph	13.9sec
Standing quarter-mile	102mph in 14sec
Top speed, observed	115mph

Fuel consumption

Test	9.4mpg
Average	11-12mpg

Braking Test

Deceleration average	.73g
Fade	Encountered on seventh stop

Source: *Sports Car Graphic*, February 1969.

Ford officially renamed the Mustang Fastback the SportsRoof, and the Shelby GT-350s (like this Black Jade model) and GT-500s were based directly on the new-for-1969 Mustang Mach 1. SportsRoof Shelbys had their rear-quarter-brake cooling scoops mounted higher for 1969 and 1970, just aft of the doorhandles. Note the eye-catching Mach 1 red inserts on the front seat backs.

Next page
Inlaid into the deck spoiler and fender end caps of 1969-1970 Shelbys were sections of expanded aluminum. This Grabber Blue SportsRoof also has optional rear window slats.

The Shelby interior for 1969 and 1970, adapted from the Mustang Mach 1 interior, included the Mach 1 woodgrain dash treatment with a Shelby emblem.

1969 Shelby Color Chart

Like the 1968 Shelby and its 1969 Mustang counterpart, the 1969 Shelby had a Ford warranty/data plate riveted adjacent to the driver's door latch. Colors were noted by a letter code. Interior color codes also were noted on the data plate; 1969 Shelbys offered 3A for black vinyl, 3W for white vinyl, and 3D for red vinyl.

Color Code	Color Name	DuPont Number	Ditzler Number
B	Royal Maroon	4864	50746
C	Black Jade	88	9300
D	Acapulco Blue	4857	13357
F	Gulfstream Aqua	4868	13329
M	Wimbledon White	4480	8378
T	Candyapple Red	4737	71528
J	Grabber Blue	5205	2230
U	Grabber Orange	5208	2232
Z	Grabber Green	5206	2231
4	Silver Jade	4975	2048
6	Pastel Gray	5053	2038
None	Grabber Yellow	5194	2214

1969 Shelby Prices

GT-350 SportsRoof	$4,434.00
GT-350 Convertible	4,753.00
GT-500 SportsRoof	4,709.00
GT-500 Convertible	5,027.00

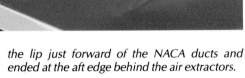

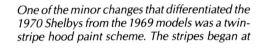

One of the minor changes that differentiated the 1970 Shelbys from the 1969 models was a twin-stripe hood paint scheme. The stripes began at the lip just forward of the NACA ducts and ended at the aft edge behind the air extractors.

In 1969, the Lucas foglamps were no longer installed in the grille, making room for the left-side Cobra logo emblem (that the company parts list referred to as a "two-inch snake-over-Shelby"). The newly designed hood featured outboard forward NACA scoops that fed air to the engine compartment.

ance. He had seen what happens when a pet project outgrows its purpose. None of it looked good to a stubborn, independent, promo-minded, throttle-jumping, race-winning competitor.

Shelby had created race cars in 1965; only several years later, the automobiles were, to his mind, boulevard cruisers headed in a direction he did not comprehend or enjoy. He asked Ford Motor Company to bring the pact to an end.

Almost 800 1969 Shelbys remained unsold as Ford's 1970 sales season began. To prevent their instant devaluation and to ease their sale through Ford dealerships, the remaining 1969 stock was converted into 1970 models through minor changes and the major change of updating their windshield VIN plates. To remain within the law, Shelby Automotive asked the FBI to oversee the renumbering process. To update the cars, black stripes were added to the hoods, door data decals were changed, and emissions controls were brought up to 1970 standards. Lower front spoilers, similar to those on Boss 302 Mustangs, were shipped with the 1970 Shelbys to be added by dealers after the hazardous rides on the transport trucks.

Oddly, there are conflicts in the old paperwork regarding the total number of 1969-1970 Shelbys produced. The official Ford tally, based on a document from 1969, is 3,153 units. But the Shelby American Automobile Club, based on serial numbers observed, holds that as many as 3,294 were made. Either way, looking back, the numbers indicate a reasonably successful swan song sales record.

Finally, the production operation ceased. Fortunately, in intent and image, the Shelby maintained its reputation and mystique through the waning days of the era. Wonderfully, today, it all survives.

The familiar Cobra logo/Shelby emblem was positioned on the SportsRoof C-pillars.

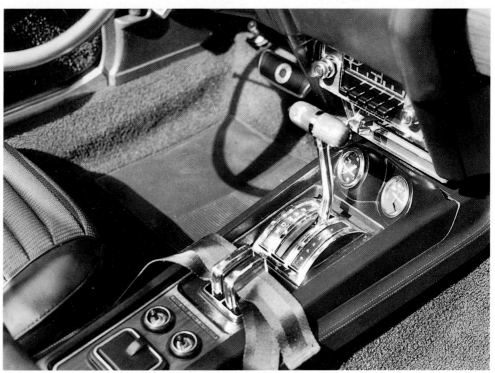

Consoles in the 1969 and 1970 Shelbys were adapted from Mercury Cougar units.

A Cobra Jet GT-500 emblem replaces this Shelby's Mustang Mach 1 emblem on the wood-grain passenger dash area. Note the wood shifter handle, stock in-dash Mustang air conditioning vents, and Shelby gauges mounted in the console.

Taillights from the 1965 Thunderbird were used on all Shelby Mustangs after 1967. Note the expanded aluminum insert in the flared sections of the rear-fender extensions and deck lid.

Shelby Automotive installed a Cobra logo steering wheel center insert, a wood shift handle (CJ cars had cobras on the handle), and consoles from the Mercury Cougar line.

The 1969-1970 fuel filler cap is located behind the flip-down license plate bracket. The first caps were vented, and the proximity of fumes to the aluminum exhaust outlet caused fires that damaged the adjacent fiberglass panels. After eleven fires were reported between early May and mid-July, Ford issued a Special Service Letter dated July 14, 1969, instructing dealers to modify GT-500s in stock so that their gas tanks would vent into a frame rail. On July 22, an internal Product Development Letter recommended a recall of the 567 cars in the hands of individuals and the 784 cars held by dealers (1,351 total) as of July 11. In September, Ford issued a formal recall to all GT-500 owners.

All 1969 and 1970 Shelbys used Ram Air induction. This 428ci Cobra Jet engine compartment incorporates not only the complete anti-smog system, but the correct factory quality control markings and properly dated hoses. Its 735cfm Holley carburetor and aluminum intake manifold are flanked by finned aluminum valve covers.

Previous page
This underside detail of the Ram Air hood used on all 1969 and 1970 Shelbys, regardless of engine size, shows that the outboard forward NACA scoops fed air to the engine compartment, while the center scoop led directly to the Ram Air assembly. The two rear-facing extractors near the cowl allowed heated air to escape the engine compartment.

Afterword

One of Carroll Shelby's earliest performance claims was that a Cobra roadster could go from a standstill to 100mph and back to a standstill in 12sec flat. That, of course, was almost unbelievable for any car. But books should not screech to a halt.

Let's jump away from the year-by-year production, sales, and competition of the 1960s, and close out this history with an overview of what we now observe.

These days, we seem to be witnessing a cross between a benevolent personality cult and a de-centralized marketing empire. Just as Florida tourist concessionaires know that any ashtray, T-shirt, lamp, or housing development will sell faster if a palm tree is attached to it, the auto paraphernalia vendors of the world know the effect of the name Shelby. Of course, the various Shelby trademarks and the use of the name are vigorously policed by an experienced staff. But the fact cannot be disputed: The name carries a cachet of power, class, adventure, and money.

Carroll Shelby tours the SAAC-16 popular vote car show at Charlotte Motor Speedway with Lee Morse of Ford Special Vehicle Operations (a Cobra roadster owner) and Howard Pardee, an R-Model owner and member of the SAAC.

Recent years have seen an escalation in values for the cars and comparisons to the great European builders. Legends grow under their own steam. All individuals can do is witness and contribute, recognize and perpetuate. The history of the Shelby evolves: More production details will be discovered, more people will become fascinated by the marque, and attention and respect will grow with time. It all stems from the personality, instinct, gumption, inventions, and wisdom of one man.

Carroll Shelby went to work for Chrysler in the early 1980s. When pressed by an earnest fan for reasons behind his apparent defection, Shelby explained his move succinctly: Lee Iacocca was the main individual at Ford who got behind the 289 Cobra concept. Iacocca, then the Ford Division Sales Manager, went out on a professional limb to front money and support so that Shelby American could become a reality.

There came a time when both Chrysler and Iacocca were in trouble. Carroll Shelby offered his assistance. And that's all there was to it. The man would not forget the origins of the phenomenon. He would not let a brand loyalty displace a personal loyalty.

The man believed in what could be done, stuck by his guns, built cars of character, proved what could be done,

and, when the project sidetracked from its original concept, stopped while all four tires were still on the pavement. The cars continue to go fast, and their beauty will endure.

Let's let that thought bring our book to a close.

Performance comes to the kitchen. Carroll Shelby's Original Texas Brand Chili is a national favorite, and older-style packages are considered collectors' items.

Not only did one Shelby owner arrange for a special license tag, but got Carroll Shelby to personalize it.

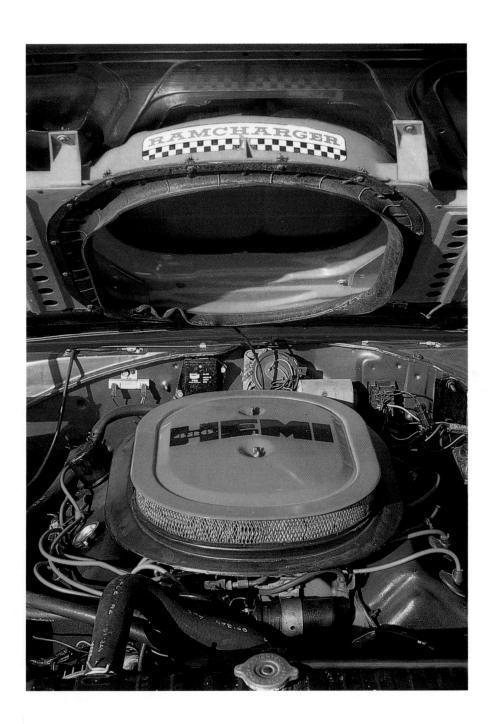

HEMI

Acknowledgments

Thanks to the willingness and cooperation of all I spoke with at Chrysler Corporation, the Chrysler Hemi story has finally been told.

I want to thank John Wehrly for arranging the interviews, and Rose Mueller for her deft handling of appointments. Bruce Raymond produced a great deal of printed matter for me on the 426 Hemi, and got the ball rolling for the all-important photographs.

Special thanks go to Bill Weertman. He not only gave me a great deal of heretofore unknown information on the 426 Hemi's initial development, he also told me where I could reach other engineers who contributed to both the first- and second-generation Hemi V–8s. I obtained the majority of black-and-white photos in the book through him. I also received from him copies of SAE papers, memos and other documents, giving me valuable information. His

This 1970 Dodge Coronet R/T with the optional 426 Hemi is one of only a few examples in existence today. Fewer than fifteen were originally built. This kind of rarity ensures its collector value. This car is owned by Ken Funk of Los Angeles, California. David Gooley

careful editing of each chapter and comments helped to make this history accurate and more than just a story.

Contributing their recollections for chapter one were Bill Drinkard, Everett Moeller, Harold Welch, Fred Shrimpton, Robert Cahill, Bert Bouwkamp, Tom Hoover and Troy Simonsen.

Tom Hoover also offered a wealth of information for chapter two, as did Bill Weertman. Bob Rarey, Dick Maxwell, Brian Schram, Steve Baker, Ted Flack, Troy Simonsen, John Wehrly, Bob Tarrozi and Dan Mancini all contributed to the chapter also. Dick Landy loaned me some rare photos of the 426 Hemi cars he raced, and some great background on his winning A/FX car.

For chapter three on the street 426 Hemi, I must again thank Bill Weertman for all the documents he offered me from his files that helped me trace the creation of these mightiest of Mopars. Ted Flack, Oscar Willard, Bert Bouwkamp and Tom Hoover gave their input to the chapter also.

Kathy Donovan was most helpful in supplying me information on her husband's work on the first aluminum-block Hemi, the Donovan 417, recalled in chapter four. Keith Black was generous with his time in telling me how he

got into the engine-building business, and how the Keith Black aluminum 426 Hemi block came to be. His secretary Judy Rodriguez made sure I received the KB literature and photos. Larry Shepard at Chrysler's Mopar Performance division not only contributed to chapter four, but also offered constructive criticism on the other chapters in the book, as he did with my first book, *Mighty Mopars.*

The assistance of Barbara Fronczak and her staff at the Chrysler Information Resources Center was also appreciated.

I would like to thank the editors of *Automobile Quarterly* in granting me permission to use material from my 1984 article, "HEMI—Four Letters for Performance," that appeared in Volume 22, Number 2.

The idea for this book must really go to my editor at Motorbooks International, Michael Dregni. It was he who called me at work one day and asked if I would be interested in writing a book on the Chrysler Hemi V–8 engines. Silly question, Mike.

Finally, I want to thank my wife Annie for her encouragement while writing this book. The dream is coming true.

Dodge "426" Hemi-charger V-8

DODGE DIVISION CHRYSLER MOTORS CORPORATION

Introduction

A New Era of Performance

The first-generation Hemi V-8 of the 1950s and the 426 Hemi of the 1960s built by Chrysler Corporation are among the most significant automotive engine designs of the twentieth century. They broke new ground in terms of performance for their day.

The performance era might have taken longer to arrive had not the Chrysler FirePower, Dodge Red Ram and DeSoto FireDome V-8s made their appearance. It has been said that these Hemi-head engines launched the horsepower wars by forcing General Motors and Ford to match their performance. While output was initially modest compared to what came later, the real proof of the first-generation Chrysler Hemi's performance potential was achieved with its tire test car.

This car, a Kurtis Kraft rear-engine design with a modified 331 ci FirePower V-8, put out roughly 400 hp and developed a top speed of over 180 mph. Its performance surpassed that of the Indy cars themselves. It was so fast, the rulebook was rewritten before Chrysler could enter one in the Indianapolis 500.

Enthusiasts could still experience that feeling of power with the advent of the Chrysler 300 in 1955. During the 1930s, the mighty Duesenberg J and SJ cars were the fastest on the road; lesser

Hemi graphics went from mild to wild, above. By 1971, huge, billboard-size graphics covered the rear quarter panels on the Hemi 'Cuda. Left, this display engine of the 426 drag Hemi with its cutaway parts drew crowds at SAE conventions and car shows. Dodge called its version the 426 Hemi-Charger V-8. David Gooley; Chrysler

cars had no choice but to get out of the way. The Depression was the death knell of the Duesenberg and other performance marques, and it wasn't until the Chrysler 300 appeared that auto enthusiasts once again witnessed a similar

quantum leap in automobile engine performance.

With its 300 hp 331 ci FirePower Hemi-head V-8, nothing could touch a Chrysler 300 in terms of acceleration or top speed. More than a few men thought of the ways to scrape together the money—somehow—to buy that gleaming red Chrysler 300 they stared longingly at through the showroom window. Whenever one was parked on the street, it always drew a crowd.

Suddenly, Chrysler was a name to be reckoned with in stock-car racing. Chrysler 300s were the cars to beat, and they truly were stock cars in those days. The racing success only lent more prestige to the 300s on the Chrysler showroom floors across America.

The recession of 1957 had a stunning effect on car sales. Compared to 1956, sales of DeSotos plunged fifty-four percent and Dodge sales were off forty-seven percent; the story was pretty much the same for every manufacturer. Chrysler had been working on a new, more economical Wedge-head engine family to replace its Hemi V-8s and the recession added impetus. Quietly, the Hemis disappeared from the Dodge, DeSoto and Chrysler line of cars.

The engines, however, were discovered by hot rodders. The 392 Chrysler

FirePower was the Hemi of choice, and the intercorporate Dodge Ramchargers were the first to capitalize on the Hemi's power on the quarter-mile strip. These engines found their way into boats as well. Keith Black made a name for himself modifying these engines for racing boats off the coast of California before moving on to Hemi-powered cars.

In the early sixties, Chrysler had shown it could truly build high-performance engines for the quarter-mile strip with its Max Wedge 413 and 426 V-8s. Stock-car racing was another matter, as the Wedge-head engines had a more difficult time. A corporate decision was made to design and build a new racing engine that would reign supreme on both the track and the strip. That engine would become the 426 Hemi V-8.

This new Hemi V-8 borrowed the lessons learned from the first-generation Hemi and with incredible speed, Chrysler unveiled its new engine at the 1964 Daytona 500 with spectacular results. During the sixties, Ford and GM waged war with Hemi-powered Dodges and Plymouths.

It can honestly be said the 426 Hemi drag engine experienced even greater success than its circle-track counterpart. Regardless of class, the 426 Hemi was king—from Super Stock to Top Fuel Eliminator. The inherent strength and extraordinary breathing ability of the 426 Hemi enabled the horsepower levels to be dialed in. How fast you wanted to go was limited only by money, and only the 426 Hemi was capable of delivering the horsepower levels to drop elapsed times from ten seconds to nine, then eight, seven, finally into the sixes, and even lower. As ETs (elapsed times) went down, horsepower shot up, with the most powerful Hemis now generating close to 4000 hp!

While the circle-track Hemis raced for less than a decade, the Chrysler Hemi has continued to prosper on the quarter-mile ever since its inception. The drag-racing Hemis found their way into wild factory cars like the altered-wheelbase AF/X cars of 1965 and the Super Stock Darts and Barracudas of 1968. Once Chrysler ceased production of the drag Hemi, drag racers continued to use the 426 Hemi with such enthusiasm, engine builders came forward to fill the void.

The 426 street Hemi, of course, was one of the most respected engines of the muscle-car era. Having only the most

rudimentary changes necessary to make it streetable, the 426 street Hemi carried with it a level of prestige no other engine could match. Many of these Hemi-powered cars spent much of their time at the strip, and that was the idea!

The collectibility of these 426 Hemi-powered Dodges and Plymouths was dormant for more than a decade after the street Hemi ceased production with the 1971 model year. For performance enthusiasts, the latter seventies were depressing. It was obvious that high-output engines from the car manufacturers were gone forever. These enthusiasts began looking around for used muscle cars, and the most desirable among them had the 426 Hemi. In the early eighties, it was still possible to pick up a 426 street Hemi Mopar for $10,000 or so. Prices began rising rapidly in the late eighties. These Hemi-powered Mopars were destined to become the most collectible—and expensive—cars from the supercar era. Some of the rarer examples are offered for sale in excess of $100,000.

With the continuing popularity of the 426 Hemi at the drag strip, many of the old iron-block Hemis were finally wearing out with replacements hard to find. In 1990, Mopar Performance—the performance parts division of Chrysler Corporation formerly known as Direct Connection—announced plans to retool a new 426 Hemi iron block and cylinder heads to fill the needs of aftermarket enthusiasts.

In this book you will read about these engines—how they were conceived, designed, built, tested and raced. To give a truly comprehensive racing history of Chrysler's Hemi V-8s, however, is really beyond the scope of this book. Many of the key designers, engineers and technicians of both the first-generation Hemi and the 426 Hemi were interviewed, and their comments are used extensively.

To all the Chrysler Hemi enthusiasts around the world, this book is for you.

Hemi 'Cudas were rare, and rarer still were the 1970 Hemi 'Cuda convertibles. This was the first year the Barracuda was available with the 426 street Hemi. Stuffing a 426 Hemi into a 'Cuda convertible resulted in what is today the most collectible combination. Musclecar Review

FirePower, FireDome & Red Ram

First-Generation Hemi Engines 1951–1958

K. T. Keller said, "Bill, I think maybe you've got the
right plan." That was the thing that turned the
whole thing around.

—William E. Drinkard

World War II had a pervasive effect on the corporations of America. Practically every type of company manufacturing consumer goods halted production to take on military contracts. The automobile companies were no different; the automotive assembly lines were shut down to make way for what came to be known as the arsenal of democracy.

In January 1942, Chrysler Corporation shut down its Dodge, Plymouth, Chrysler, DeSoto and Imperial assembly plants and began the massive conversion to manufacturing war materiel. With amazing speed, Chrysler tooled up and began building wings for bombers, tanks, anti-aircraft guns, parts for ships and aircraft, as well as jeeps and trucks. From the crucible of this effort came the genesis of the idea for what would become the Chrysler hemispherical-combustion-chamber V–8 engine.

With the end of the war, Chrysler slowly resumed passenger car production in the closing months of 1945. Like the other auto makers, it looked to the postwar economy with promise. Work was begun on new engine designs as a means of getting more power and smoother performance. In a real sense, the engine that finally emerged represented the forthcoming power, prestige

On the DeSoto, above, the Hemi V–8 under
the hood was announced with a medallion
mounted to the fuel-filler door on the right
side, as well as the left rear fender. Left, the
Chrysler 300 of 1955 instantly became the
most powerful American production car on
the road. Musclecar Review; David Gooley

and prosperity of postwar America.

Two areas were felt to hold the most promise in improving engine performance: compression ratio and volumetric efficiency. Boosting compression was an old horsepower trick, but the ability to do so was dependent on the octane rating of available pump-grade fuel. Efforts to increase octane rating of gasoline after World War II were slow, and this limited engineering in the area of higher compression ratios for cars.

Volumetric efficiency was a product of combustion-chamber design specifically and engine breathing in general. Chrysler decided on a concurrent design and engineering program to evaluate compression ratios and combustion-chamber designs as a means of boosting power.

Hemi Research and Development

Chrysler used a unique single-cylinder engine to evaluate cylinder head designs with a compression ratio of 7.0:1. The familiar L-head and F-head were tested, as well as a conventional valve-in-head design and a hemispherical cylinder head. Chrysler had practical reasons for wanting an improved cylinder-head design. Combustion-chamber deposits could significantly reduce power over a given period. These depos-

The first application of the Chrysler hemispherical-combustion-chamber cylinder head in a passenger car was on this straight-six prototype engine. Chrysler

The straight-six Hemi-head prototype engine allowed Chrysler engineers to confirm the cylinder head's performance before tooling up for the prototype V–8. These photos show the juxtaposition of the intake and exhaust valves and double rocker shafts. Chrysler

its affected thermal and volumetric efficiencies, resulting in power losses of as much as ten percent after only 5,000 to 10,000 miles. A combustion chamber with a low surface-to-volume ratio minimized these losses. All indicators were pointing to a hemispherical combustion chamber, which inherently had a high thermal and volumetric efficiency as well as low surface-to-volume ratio.

Hemispherical combustion chambers were really nothing new. One of the first, if not *the* first, uses of the Hemi head was on the 1904 four-cylinder Welch passenger-car engine. The Hemi head was the design of choice for such famous racing marques as Duesenberg, Stutz, Miller and Offenhauser.

The fledgling aircraft engine industry seized upon the hemispherical cylinder head as the best power-producing design for air-cooled engines. In fact, during World War II, Chrysler engineers were engaged in developing a V–16 aircraft engine and a V–12 tank engine, both of which had hemispherical combustion chambers. Although neither of these engines reached production status due to the war's end, their performance and efficiency were excellent, impressing the engineers involved.

With some known advantages of a hemispherical combustion chamber, why hadn't it achieved more widespread use in automobiles? There were two basic reasons, Chrysler found. The Hemi head had a reputation for roughness and proclivity for high-octane fuels. Also, the inherent complexity and cost didn't lend itself to mass production. However, Chrysler Corporation had years of experience building relatively high-compression engines. In 1924, Chrysler introduced high compression in its namesake line of cars. Four years later, it turned the automotive world on its ear with the 1928 Red Head engine with an unheard-of 6.2:1 compression ratio.

The Chrysler engineering team was up to the task of developing a truly revolutionary passenger-car engine. James C. Zeder was director of Engineering and Research. He was the younger brother of Fred Zeder, who, along with Carl Breer and O. R. Skelton, left Studebaker in 1920 at the behest of Walter P. Chrysler to establish the Chrysler Corporation. Working under James Zeder was Ray White, in charge of experimental design; William E. Drinkard, head of laboratory research and development;

and Mel Carpentier, in charge of production engine design. These men relished the challenge of working the bugs—real or imagined—out of the Hemi head and making it viable for mass-produced automobiles.

Chrysler began testing a great many passenger-car engines from both domestic and foreign auto makers. Ev Moeller witnessed these engines being tested. He started with Chrysler in 1939 and graduated from the Chrysler Institute in 1941. He was assigned to the aircraft engine program during the war, and in 1947, he was moved to the Engine Development Laboratory.

"We tested every engine in site," Moeller says. "One of the engines that we worked on was the Healey, which was an English small passenger-car engine that had a pushrod-operated overhead valvetrain. It had two camshafts, one on each side of the block. The pushrods came up to operate the overhead valves. It was a long-stroke, Hemi configuration and the thing that was surprising was it was the highest powered and most efficient engine we had ever tested."

Lab testing of the single-cylinder engine with the four different head designs was supervised by John Platner, who had joined Chrysler in 1931 as a member of the first class of the Chrysler Institute of Engineering Graduate School. Platner worked in Engine Development his entire career with the company, and made his presence felt over the years.

What they found was contrary to what had been doctrine concerning the Hemi head: this cylinder head actually displayed knock-limiting characteristics. To achieve the thermal efficiency of the Hemi head at 7.0:1, the L-head required a compression ratio of 10.0:1 at 1200 rpm, 9.4:1 at 2000 rpm, 8.9:1 at 2800 rpm and 8.5:1 at 3600 rpm. The F-head performed much like the L-head. The overhead-valve head was somewhat better than these two, but it suffered losses of volumetric efficiency and valve durability.

The Hemi head was a superior performer in all respects. With the intake valve closest to the intake manifold and the exhaust valve directly across from it on the other side of the hemispherical chamber with an included valve angle of 58½ deg., the fuel-air mixture entered, burned and exited efficiently. The Hemi-

This V–8 Hemi-head prototype engine shows how the spark-plug wires were originally grouped on the valve covers. The left-hand exhaust pipe passed underneath the oil pan to join the right-hand exhaust pipe for a single exhaust system. Chrysler

The Chrysler FirePower 331 ci V–8 was introduced in 1951. The engine shown on this display stand featured chrome-plated parts for show. The spark-plug wires were hidden by the small cover on top of the valve cover. Chrysler

267

The Chrysler FirePower V–8 was standard equipment in such cars as the Chrysler New Yorker. Chrysler

head design also extended valve life and promoted sealing by aiding effective uniform cooling of the valve seats. The engineers found the stability of the valve seats in the Hemi head to be excellent.

With these encouraging results, Zeder's team decided it was time to test the Hemi head on one of its engines. A standard Chrysler straight-six engine was selected and a special double-overhead-camshaft head with hemispherical combustion chambers was designed and built. Bench tests showed a significant performance gain over the standard six-cylinder engine. The engine, with the designation A161, was installed in a Chrysler to test real-world conditions by Wallace E. Zierer, who was in charge of automobile testing. The car

ran effortlessly on the then-standard eighty-octane regular gas. Roughness, which had been a theoretical concern, was absent, thus affirming the use of a Hemi head in a passenger car. It was a research and development milestone for Chrysler.

From a production standpoint, however, the chain-driven double-over-head-valve design was complex and expensive, and serviceability would be a problem. A simpler, less costly valvetrain design had to be worked out. What the team developed was a pushrod-actuated Hemi-head straight-six with a greatly simplified valvetrain at less expense.

Birth of the FirePower

Despite the successful test results, a Chrysler Hemi engine, or even a Hemi

V–8 for that matter, was by no means certain. Convincing Chrysler upper management was a formidable task, because there were detractors within management, as well as the engineering staff itself, of both the Hemi head and the proposed V–8 configuration.

Drinkard, who joined Chrysler in 1934 and became manager of the Engine Development Laboratory in 1943, remembers the battles in the boardrooms of Chrysler over this new engine. "There were just two guys, as far as I'm concerned, that believed in the idea of the Hemi V–8 engine and tried to sell it," Drinkard recalls vividly. "Those two guys were John Platner and myself. There wasn't anybody else. Anytime you work in a big corporation, if you've got some

268

idea and try to sell it, look out for all those guys who are going to sell something else and belittle you. That is exactly what happened. Fred Zeder said, 'Look fellas, I'm not going to have any part of a V–8 engine. We've made our money on a straight eight and that's all we're going to have.' We had all these research guys in there trying to confuse the waters. Finally, K. T. Keller, the chief operating officer, said, 'Bill, I think maybe you've got the right plan.' That was the thing that turned the whole thing around." Drinkard later co-authored a paper with Mel Carpentier published by the Society of Automotive Engineers (SAE) in July 1951 detailing the laboratory findings.

Prior to and just after the war, Chrysler had tested a number of engine configurations with a multiplicity of intake manifold designs, intake and exhaust valve juxtaposition, and other mechanical variations. These included one inline five-cylinder engine, several inline six-cylinder engines, one 90 deg. V–6, and several 60 deg. V–6s and 90 deg. V–8s. One experimental V–6, the A93, had both overhead and underhead valves. The overhead intake valves were pushrod actuated while the underhead exhaust valves were directly actuated by the camshaft tappets. No concept was beyond consideration in Chrysler's search for increased engine performance. The 90 deg. V–6 was found to be unsatisfactory for smoothness, and the length and weight of a straight-eight were no longer thought to be acceptable. The compact V–8 engine appeared to be the standard for the future. Cadillac and Oldsmobile were working on V–8 engine designs for introduction in 1949, so it was this configuration Zeder and his fellow engineers selected for use with the Hemi head.

By 1948, Chrysler had a 330 ci Hemi-head V–8 undergoing testing, the A182 designed by Ray White's department. The A182 prototype Hemi V–8 was run extensively on the dynamometer to evaluate its performance after optimizing variables like camshaft timing, fuel mixture and ignition timing. It was then evaluated in a road-test Chrysler car with satisfactory results. Chrysler management was sufficiently impressed with the results of all of the A182 engines tested that approval was given for an engine of this type and size to be designed for production.

Mel Carpentier's department then designed the A239 engine, which became the first production Hemi V–8, later christened the Chrysler FirePower. It had a slightly larger displacement of 331 ci. The resulting design was shorter and lighter than the A182, and was designed with manufacturing considerations in mind.

Robert Cahill joined Chrysler in 1936. He started working in the engine development lab in 1938 and stayed there until 1953. He witnessed the first-generation Hemi's development firsthand within the tough parameters established by Drinkard. Cahill recalls, "Drinkard laid down the spec that he wanted us to be able to pass a thousand hour test on a certain schedule we had. He wanted the engine to be able to run 100,000 miles without having to replace major parts. He wanted the bearings, valves, pistons and rings to last 100,000 miles. There was a lot of effort made to do that."

One of the most worrisome problems was in the area of camshaft wear. Bert Bouwkamp knew firsthand the difficulties encountered in making this key engine component last the requisite number of miles. He entered the Chrysler Institute in February 1949, graduating in June 1951. Starting work in the Engine Laboratory, he coordinated development of the 241 ci Dodge Red Ram Hemi. He remained in the lab for one year, then moved on to the DeSoto engine plant to supervise production of the DeSoto FireDome V–8, where he was assistant motor engineer.

"This was our first overhead valve engine," Bouwkamp says, "and the biggest problem with the Hemi was camshaft wear. We didn't have experience with valvetrain loads, and we ran into severe wear between the camshaft and the face of the tappet. Some engines failed in a few thousand miles. We had some failures right within the engine plant and after tearing them down, [it was clear] they wouldn't have gone 100 miles."

Bob Rodger was head of the group assigned to solve this accelerated wear problem. It became apparent the problem had to be attacked on a number of different levels.

"To solve this," Bouwkamp continues, "it took a change in the material of the tappet to chilled cast iron, a change to the spherical radius of the tappet to try to reduce the unit loading, a graphite-based anti-scuff coating, and an additive in the oil to finally solve the problem."

Fred Shrimpton was truly unique among all the designers, engineers and drafters who have worked at Chrysler. His career there spans more than six decades and he has been able to observe virtually every major engine design in that time. He recalls the first day he applied for work at Chrysler in 1929 as if it were yesterday. The current six-story building at Oakland Avenue in Highland Park was only three stories then. He started work as a tracer and had risen to chief layout man when interest in the Hemi V–8 and the prospect of its production finally crystallized.

"Mel Carpentier came up to me one day," Shrimpton remembers, "and said, 'I want you to lay out a Hemi head.' I laid out all three engines—the Chrysler, the Dodge and the DeSoto. That was a lot of fun. I really liked it. It was something different. Then we had a strike, so I rolled all the stuff up. We were gone for 104 days; it was a long strike. When I came back, those drawings were gone, but we had already started on detailing drawings. In fact, we knew so little about them, we made details right off the layout drawings. The big problem was getting spark plugs down through the center and how to seal them."

Because the spark plug was located between the intake and exhaust valves and slightly offset from the cylinder's centerline, some means had to be developed to permit changing the plugs without having to remove the large valve covers. A steel tube was designed with a flange at the lower end that acted as a gasket as the spark plug was screwed into the cylinder head. Snapping the spark-plug wire onto the spark plug was facilitated by a long ceramic boot. To prevent oil from leaking between the tube and the valve cover, an ignition wire cover, or channel, compressed a neoprene O-ring with a steel washer, creating a seal around each tube as the ignition wire cover was screwed into place. The ignition wires were hidden by the ignition wire cover until they exited the back of the valve cover near the distributor, giving this first-generation Hemi engine a clean look.

Chrysler's new engine featured other improvements. The crankshaft employed shot-peened and machined undercut fillets to eliminate tool marks

For the 1951 model year, Chrysler introduced the Chrysler FirePower V-8. The engine had a displacement of 331.1 ci and produced 180 hp at 4000 rpm and 312 lb-ft of torque at 2000 rpm. This represented a more than forty percent boost in horsepower and a sixteen percent increase in torque over the straight-eight engine of 1950. And it was 9½ in. shorter than the inline engine.

The Chrysler FirePower V-8 was introduced in the long-running (since 1939) Chrysler Saratoga and New Yorker, as well as the Chrysler Imperial and Crown Imperial. The Imperial was the flagship of Chrysler; the Chrysler Imperial 80 had been introduced in 1926. The engine was a marketer's and advertiser's delight. While not a high-performance engine per se, it was Chrysler's first V-8 passenger-car engine and it bristled with features that made great advertising copy. It developed more power than either the Cadillac or Oldsmobile V-8s, and didn't require premium-grade fuel like its competitors.

Harold Welch began working at Chrysler in 1935. As did all graduate engineers, he entered the Chrysler Institute, a two-year work-study program. In 1937 he was assigned to the mechanical laboratory. In 1940, he moved to the engine development laboratory and became assistant manager, under William Drinkard. He recalls the impact the new Chrysler FirePower had on the automotive industry.

"It was jokingly said," he says today, "it made the lights on the top floor of the General Motors building burn extra hours at night. It's sometimes blamed for kicking off what was generally referred to as the horsepower race."

As planned, Chrysler expanded availability of the Hemi-head design to other makes. In 1952, the DeSoto Fire-Dome V-8 made its debut with a displacement of 276 ci with 160 hp at 4400 rpm. Dodge received its Red Ram Hemi V-8 in 1953. It was the smallest of all the Chrysler Hemi V-8s, with a displacement of 241.3 ci; it generated 140 hp at 4400 rpm and 220 lb-ft of torque at 2000 rpm. The engine was offered in the 114 and 119 in. wheelbase versions of the V-8-equipped Coronet that year.

High-Performance Development

The Chrysler Hemi-head V-8 had untapped reserves of power, and the engineers knew it. The research, design

Chrysler Division president Ed Quinn, left, and James C. Zeder, vice-president of engineering, pose with the A311 Indianapolis 500 racing engine. Chrysler

was forced to reduce displacement from stock to meet the rules, cutting the engine's power. Chrysler

and surface roughness and greatly improve fatigue strength. The use of hydraulic tappets was to achieve quiet valve operation and to enhance the life through constant control of opening and closing ramps.

Chrysler worked with Carter to design a water-jacketed carburetor throttle-valve body with integral automatic choke to prevent engine stalling due to carburetor icing. A dual-breaker

distributor provided a reserve of ignition voltage at high speeds.

The durability of this new Chrysler engine—given the name FirePower—was as important as all the engineering that went into it. More than 8,000 hours of dynamometer testing and more than 500,000 miles on test cars were involved in ensuring long-term durability. The engine was finally ready and released for production.

and development of the engine had been slow and deliberate. Increasing performance was, indeed, the engineers' goal, but high performance was not—at first.

In a paper presented to the SAE at the National Passenger Car, Body and Materials Meeting in Detroit in March 1952, Zeder recalled how further development—high-performance development—came about.

Zeder wrote: "Then we met the 'hotrod' boys—or rather they adopted us with all the gusto attending induction into any other tribe of wild Indians. We, who live within the industry, have learned to accept without too much resistance the utilitarian place which our product holds in the scheme of things; but it was a pleasure and, in many ways, an inspiration to meet a group of men in whom are rekindled the enthusiams [sic] of an earlier era; men to who owning and driving a car are sport and adventure, and not merely a chore inherited by default from the streetcar motorman."

Zeder and his team were just as intrigued as the "hotrod boys" in learning what the maximum performance potential of the engine was, even if there wasn't a real-world application for it. Once again, two key areas were explored: compression ratio and volumetric efficiency. A production Chrysler FirePower was fitted with pistons, giving compression ratios of 7.5:1, 10.0:1 and 12.5:1. The rest of the engine remained stock. The engineers achieved a fifteen percent boost in power with 12.5:1 pistons over the 7.5:1 pistons. However, the engine required the equivalent octane rating of 130 performance number. Running double-digit compression ratios would have to wait for the advent of superior-grade gasoline.

The most dramatic gains in power would come from attacking the engine's volumetric efficiency. To establish a realistic baseline from which to work, it was decided to discard the stock exhaust manifolds for the streamlined, steel-tube exhaust type. This alone produced an 18 lb-ft increase in torque and a further 13 hp. The other three areas affecting volumetric efficiency were valve ports, intake manifolding and carburetion, and camshafts.

While the Hemi head permitted larger intake and exhaust valves, there was room to make them even larger. The

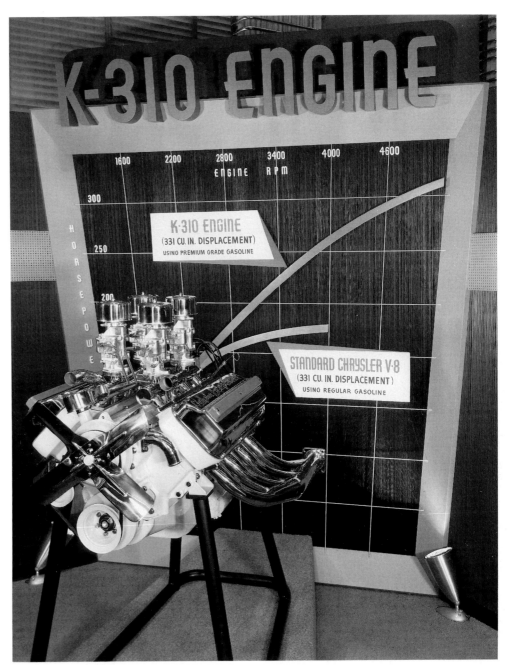

One of the high-performance Chrysler FirePower derivatives Zeder and his team developed was the K–310. It featured four carburetors, log-type intake manifold and streamlined exhaust manifold. Chrysler

intake valve was increased 0.125 in. and the exhaust valve by 0.25 in. The ports were increased to match the increase in flow.

Chrysler engineers decided on two approaches regarding intake manifolding and carburetion. For mid-range, or high torque, they designed a manifold to accept four inline single-barrel carburetors, each one feeding two cylinders. For high speed, or high power, the

four carburetors sat atop a simple runner manifold, similar to racing designs of the day.

The standard FirePower engine used a camshaft giving 252 deg. intake duration, 244 deg. exhaust duration, with 30 deg. of overlap. Three special camshafts were developed for the test engine. The first was a 260/260 deg. design with 40 deg. of overlap. The second was 270/260 deg. with 50 deg. of

Introduced in 1952, the DeSoto FireDome V–8 had a displacement of 276 ci and was rated at 160 hp. Chrysler

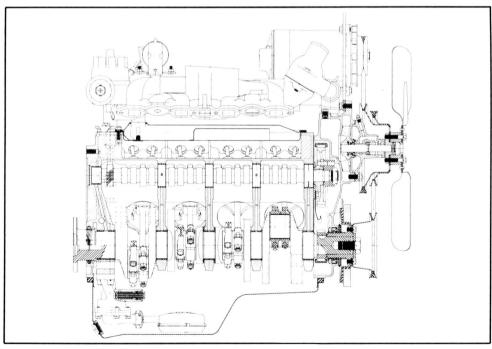

This assembly layout drawing of the DeSoto FireDome V–8 displayed the draftman's art, now lost in the age of computer-aided design. Chrysler

overlap, and the most radical design was 280/270 deg. with 60 deg. of overlap. Lift was increased with all three camshafts. "This is one of the earliest places the electronic computer was used to design the camshaft," Welch states. "The computer came along just in time to develop a new mathematical formula that permitted better cam design with minimum stress and maximum performance."

Test results surprised no one. The Hemi responded exceedingly well to these modifications. With the high-flow heads and high-torque intake manifold, the engine gained 42 hp with a 30 lb-ft boost in torque. The three camshafts were tested in this engine with the 270/260/50 cam giving the best all-around performance increase. The total increase in the Hemi's output over the new baseline engine was 60 lb-ft of torque and 95 hp.

The high-torque induction was replaced by the high-speed carburetor-manifold setup, and the tests were run again with all three camshafts. The 280/270/60 camshaft produced the best results throughout the rpm range. Corrected brake horsepower was 308.6 with 341.7 lb-ft of torque—with stock pistons! To see what a boost in compression ratio could do, the 12.6:1 pistons were installed. All previous runs were made using premium-grade gasoline; for this run they ran the equivalent of iso-octane plus 1.0 cc of lead to prevent knock. Torque increased to 385 lb-ft with 353 hp—all this from a 331 ci engine.

In typical engineering understatement, James Zeder wrote, "the basic FirePower cylinder gives performance comparable with Indianapolis engines, which have been developed for power without regard to any other purpose." In his concluding remarks, Zeder was more enthusiastic, stating, "we remain unalterably convinced that, in the battle of the combustion chambers, the spherical segment chamber has demonstrated unquestionable supremacy."

Production Performance Increases

In 1954, the first wave of increased power appeared. The Chrysler Fire-Power now developed 195 hp at 4400 rpm, still at a 7.5:1 compression ratio, but a new four-barrel-carburetor version developed 235 hp. The Dodge Red Ram was offered in a 7.1:1 compression ratio developing 140 hp at 4400 rpm, and a 7.5:1 version with 150 hp. The DeSoto

FireDome now produced 170 hp at 4400 rpm.

Chrysler Corporation was poised to throw off its conservative image. The high-performance development work that showed the Hemi's potential was about to bear fruit that would attract the attention of the entire automotive world, and it was decided that this new car would be introduced for 1955. The car was the Chrysler 300.

Bob Rodger joined Chrysler in 1939 and entered the Chrysler Institute. After graduating, he was assigned to the Engine Development Lab in 1941. He was a key man on Drinkard's team in the development of outstanding durability for the A239 FirePower engine. By 1954, he was resident chief engineer of the Chrysler car division. He knew well the performance potential of the FirePower engine and proposed the concept of a high-powered model with good handling and unique styling. This early product planning proposal resulted in the 1955 Chrysler 300.

From the time it began rolling off the assembly line in January 1955, it became *the* car to road test by automotive journalists. The 300's performance left them agog, establishing a high-water mark in acceleration, handling and top speed. The 331 ci FirePower now had a compression ratio of 8.5:1, a 280/270/60 mechanical camshaft, and two Carter four-barrel carburetors. It developed 300 hp—hence the car's designation—at 5200 rpm and 345 lb-ft of torque at 3200 rpm. The only other car that even came close was the Cadillac Eldorado with 270 hp, but it weighed nearly half a ton more than the 4,000 lb. Chrysler 300.

A less-potent 331 FirePower was offered in the Chrysler New Yorker Deluxe and the Imperial, having 250 hp at 4600 rpm and 340 lb-ft of torque at 2800 rpm. To round out the Chrysler FirePower line-up, a new smaller-displacement V–8 with 301 ci was offered in the Chrysler Windsor Deluxe with an 8.0:1 compression ratio, developing 188 hp at 4400 rpm and 275 lb-ft of torque at 2400 rpm.

Over at Dodge, the Red Ram Hemi received an increase in displacement to 270 ci, boosting output to 175 hp. This new, larger mill was standard in the Coronet and Royal. The Custom Royal had slightly more power—8 hp to be exact. An optional engine was available in all three models. The Custom Royal

Dodge introduced its Hemi, the Red Ram V–8, in 1953. Its displacement was just over 241 ci and was rated at 140 hp. Plymouth was the only division not to offer a Hemi V–8 of its own. Chrysler

engine could be ordered with a Special Equipment Power Package that used a four-barrel carburetor. This produced 193 hp at 4400 rpm with 245 lb-ft of torque at 2800 rpm.

For 1955, the DeSoto FireDome also was increased in displacement, to 291 ci. With a two-barrel carburetor, it was rated at 185 hp. A four-barrel version, called the Fireflight, was offered which developed 200 hp.

Racing Success

Until the advent of the Chrysler 300 in 1955, Chryslers were not the car of choice for circle-track and endurance races. During the early fifties, however, Briggs Cunningham was the most visible privateer who believed in the Chrysler Hemi V–8 and campaigned his cars, most

visibly at LeMans. Cunningham had raced various automotive concoctions during the forties. In 1950, his team won tenth and eleventh places overall at Le Mans in mildly modified Cadillacs.

Cunningham's first attempt with the Hemi at Le Mans was in 1951, after founding the B. S. Cunningham Company with partners Bill Frick and Phil Walters in West Palm Beach, Florida. Chrysler was willing to help as much as it could, and the high-performance development work on the FirePower found its way into his C Series race cars. The cars were uniquely Cunningham, using an American V–8 engine in a chassis of his company's own design, as was the body. The striking blue-and-white C-2s that hit Le Mans were heavy but they were fast—152 mph down the long

The Chrysler 300 quickly became a legend on the racetracks around the country, lending credence to the words "stock car." It was one of the most desirable cars of the fifties to own and drive—a true gentleman's express. The combination of two four-barrel carburetors, a stiff mechanical camshaft and the hemispherical-combustion-chamber cylinder heads produced 300 hp from the 331 ci FirePower V-8. No other American-made car at the time could match its performance. David Gooley

Mulsanne straight. The following year the sanctioning body of Le Mans issued a new requirement, stating a manufacturer had to build a minimum of twenty-five cars in order to race as a production car. Cunningham built exactly twenty-five C3 and C4 roadsters and coupes combined to qualify.

In the 1952 Le Mans race, Cunningham drove twenty of the twenty-four hours and finished in fourth place, all the more remarkable since he was in

his forties. Team Cunningham also raced the cars in America over the next several years as well, before closing his company in 1955.

On the NASCAR circuit, Oldsmobile and Hudson seesawed for dominance during the early fifties. That all changed in 1955. The Bob Rodger-conceived Chrysler 300 won twenty-seven of the forty-five races that year, winning the Grand National title.

Back in the fifties, there was room for a full-size spare tire—wire wheels, huge whitewalls and all. The small fins on the car would grow to amazing proportions in a few years. David Gooley

Factory racing of the Hemi might have taken other forms if the A311 engine program had reached fruition. Harold Welch remembers how Chrysler almost went racing at Indianapolis. "This engine," he says, "was first used to test tires for Firestone, then Goodyear. The A311 was made with large ports and roller tappets. John Platner and Don Moore were deeply involved with the project. They used a Hilborn fuel-injection system, which was common at Indianapolis at that time. That car was used

for many miles of high-speed testing and it was able to easily run at regular Indianapolis speeds.

"As part of the dedication of the Chrysler Proving Grounds in June of 1954," Welch continues, "the first four finishing drivers of that year's Indianapolis 500 mile race were invited to bring their winning cars to try them on the new highly banked 4.7 mile oval track. All of the drivers held their cars wide open through the turns, which was the first time any of them had had an opportunity to do so. Jack McGrath was the fastest, with an amazing 179 miles per hour. Even more amazing was that the Chrysler-powered Kurtis Kraft tire-test car then ran 182 miles per hour!

"It showed this Hemi with its push-rod valvegear could definitely compete very nicely with the Offys. The rules at

Indianapolis permitted stock-block engines to have that much displacement, but then they changed the rules to 272 cubic inches. We shortened the stroke to get 272 cubic inches, and that's how they entered the race the next year, but didn't quite make it. It's interesting that at 331 cubic inches, it was so successful they changed the rules."

It wouldn't be the last time a sanctioning body would change the rules again because of the Chrysler Hemi's inherent performance superiority.

Production-Car Improvements

There were changes in the Hemi-engine line-up for 1956. At Chrysler, the 301 ci Hemi was dropped and a new 354 ci Hemi was introduced. The displacement increase was achieved by increasing the bore from 3.81 to 3.92 in. while

275

The Chrysler 300 had its own distinctive escutcheon mounted between the grille openings. And it had the horsepower to match the numbers. The car blazed a trail of wins on the NASCAR circuit that lent status to the version in Chrysler showrooms. David Gooley

Previous page
The Chrysler 300 of 1955 was a traffic-stopper. There were more expensive cars on the road, but none was faster. It ushered in a new era of large fast cars, soon to be known as muscle cars. David Gooley

keeping the 3.63 in. stroke. The 354 Hemi had a 9.0:1 compression ratio and produced 280 hp at 4600 rpm, with 380 lb-ft of torque at 2800 rpm. This engine

was standard in the New Yorker, New Yorker Newport and New Yorker St. Regis. This was the last year for the Chrysler 331 ci Hemi in the Windsor line, which was now offered in a 225 hp version, or the optional 250 hp powerplant. Chrysler's performance flagship, the 300, now took on its famous letter designation sequence. The 300 B was powered by a 340 hp 354 Hemi, churning out 385 lb-ft of torque at 3400 rpm. The optional 10.0:1 compression engine developed 355 hp at 5200 rpm, and 405 lb-ft of torque at 3400 rpm.

The Chrysler 300 really did have a mystique about it. With its now-legendary racing victories and awesome horsepower, the 300 B turned heads whenever one drove by. The legend grew in 1956, with Chrysler again taking

the NASCAR title. The colorful Carl Kiekhaefer-sponsored team won sixteen races in a row. Chrysler capitalized on the success of its 300 in its advertising. In an ad picturing a 300 B getting the checkered flag under the bright lights of a nighttime race, the copy read, "Let's get one thing straight . . . Chrysler has won every major competition in 1956! And don't confuse Chrysler's Grand Slam wins in all the big events with those 'in their class' wins that you may have read about. When Chrysler competes it competes against all comers!"

Almost lost in the hoopla over the 300 B were improvements in the Dodge and DeSoto Hemis for 1956. Dodge introduced a raised-block (RB or raised-B) Hemi with 315 ci, having a bore and stroke of 3.63x3.60 in. It developed 218 hp in standard trim for use in the Custom

278

Under the hood, the Chrysler 300 had an air cleaner in the shape of a flying wing to span the two inline carburetors with two air cleaners, one on each side. This powerplant was the one to beat on the NASCAR circuit in the mid-fifties. David Gooley

and Custom Royal. There were two optional 315 ci Hemis, one developing 230 hp and the other 260 hp. The small 270 ci Hemi was still standard in the Coronet, now rated at 189 hp. The 354 ci Hemi was optional in the Coronet; with a 10.0:1 compression ratio, it pumped out 340 hp at 5200 rpm and 380 lb-ft of torque at 3800 rpm.

DeSoto also received a raised-block Hemi in 1956. This new two-barrel, 330 ci FireDome V-8 developed 230 hp, but

the four-barrel Fireflight version offered 255 hp. DeSoto buyers demanding maximum power ordered the dual four-barrel 341.1 ci Adventurer with 320 hp. The DeSoto received a boost in its lagging image when it was selected as pace car for the 1956 Indy 500.

All of Chrysler Corporation's car divisions received all-new sheet metal for 1957, and the Fin Era was now in full swing. Chrysler reduced its offerings from seven distinct models to four: Windsor, Saratoga (absent since 1953), New Yorker and the 300 C. Horsepower kept climbing, as did compression ratios. The venerable 331 Hemi was dropped. The Windsor was now powered by a 285 hp 354 ci Hemi, running a 9.25:1 compression ratio. The Saratoga had 10 hp more. Now, there was a new Hemi: the

392 V-8. This was a raised-block design with a bore and stroke of 4.00x3.90 in. With the new increase in displacement came larger valves: intake valves were 2.0 in. and exhaust valves 1.75 in. This increased displacement and breathing, of course, brought increased power: 325 hp at 4600 rpm with 430 lb-ft of torque at 2800 rpm. The New Yorker came standard with this engine.

The most powerful Chrysler 392 Hemi that year was reserved for the 300 C. The dual four-barrel, radically cammed 392 Hemi with 9.25:1 compression developed 375 hp at 5200 rpm, with 420 lb-ft of torque at 4000 rpm. The optional 10.0:1 compression 392 was rated at 390 hp, with 10 lb-ft more torque at slightly higher rpm. Some wondered just where this horsepower would end,

Briggs Cunningham was one of the first American road racers, and as the jewel in his crown, he strove to win the French Le Mans race with an all-American team. He developed his own sports cars for the purpose, the most successful being the C4 Series. The C4R shown here was powered by a Chrysler Hemi, producing 325 hp in race tune. This vintage racer won Sebring in 1953 and finished third at Le Mans in 1954. George D. Lepp

but in truth it had already begun to level off.

The Chrysler Imperial also received its annual horsepower boost. The 280 hp 354 Hemi of the previous year was replaced by a 325 hp 392 for 1957. There was no optional engine for the three Imperial models, and really, in a luxury car like this, one didn't need it.

The Dodge line of models was expanded and now included the six- and eight-cylinder Coronet, Coronet Custom, Royal, Custom Royal, Suburban, Sierra and Custom Sierra. The standard V–8 in the Coronet, Royal, Custom Royal and Suburban was the 315 bored out to 325 ci. Power was now 245 hp with 320 lb-ft of torque. There were three optional V–8 engines for the Coronet: the 285 or 310 hp 325 with 9.25:1 compression, or the top-of-the-line 340 hp 354 from the previous year. Optional in the Royal and Custom Royal were the 285 and 310 hp 325s. If you ordered the optional 285 hp 325 for your Suburban, it became the Sierra; if you opted for the 310 hp version, it became the Custom Sierra.

Some automotive pundits felt the late 1950s were the era of excess. This was evident in model names as well as aesthetics. DeSoto was a prime example. For 1957, you could choose from the Firesweep, FireDome, Fireflight and Adventurer. For less fanciful types, there was also the Explorer and Shopper station wagons. This was to be the last year for the Hemi engine in DeSotos. There was the two-barrel FireDome 341 ci engine with 270 hp, the four-barrel 341 ci Fireflight with 295 hp, and the dual four-barrel 345 ci engine offered in the Adventurer with 345 hp. The Hemi would be replaced the following year by the Turboflash V–8. All this fire and flash was to no avail, however, as DeSoto ceased car production with its 1961 line.

The days for the Chrysler Corporation Hemi were indeed numbered. The company had been working on a less-expensive Wedge-head design, and engines with the new cylinder head made

280

The Hemi V–8 version used in the DeSoto was called the FireDome. Note the absence of spark-plug wires; they were hidden under the DeSoto FireDome Eight wire cover on the valve cover. Musclecar Review

their debut in 1958. At Dodge, the lone Hemi offering was the 325, which was at a distinct disadvantage when stacked up against the new 350 and 361 ci Wedge engines that developed more horsepower.

The situation was somewhat better at Chrysler, where the Hemi still dominated the engine line-up. The Windsor

came equipped with the 290 hp 354, the Saratoga with the 310 hp 354 and the New Yorker with the 345 hp 392. The new 300 D came with a 380 hp 392; the optional 392 with fuel injection was rated at 390 hp. All Chrysler Hemi engines this year packed a 10.0:1 compression ratio. The Imperial models came with the same engine as the New

Yorker. According to Chrysler Corporation literature, this was the last year of production for the first-generation Hemi engine in Chrysler, Dodge and Imperial.

Why was such a thoroughly proven engine scrapped? Drinkard will be the first to state the Hemi was replaced for purely economic reasons. Welch agrees, but says there were other reasons involved as well.

"To our chagrin," he says, "our management thought we were spending more producing our engine than Ford and General Motors were with their wedge-shaped combustion chambers, and manufacturing was interested in building a new, central engine plant to build engines [for all divisions]. So, for primarily economic reasons, the B and raised-B engines built at Trention eventually replaced the Hemi. They were somewhat lighter than the Hemi and more economical as far as material is concerned, and then, of course, the cars began to get heavier, so that the V–8 for the Dodge and DeSoto ended up being too small. That combination of things replaced the first generation family of Hemis with the B and raised-B."

The Ramchargers

The Hemi was gone but not forgotten by some at Chrysler. Around 1958, a small group of Chrysler engineers formed a club to share their interest in cars in general and high-performance cars in particular. Tom Hoover was one of the men in this group. Having received his masters degree in physics in 1955, he entered Chrysler through the Chrysler Institute and in 1957, went to work in the area of fuel injection. He got to know like-minded engineers over the next year, and what first started out as casual gatherings eventually evolved into one of the most aggressive drag-racing teams in the United States.

"In the cafeteria in Engineering at lunchtime," Hoover recalls, "a number of us who had performance vehicles, which was rather rare in those days among the Chrysler cars, would get together. There were six or eight [of us] initially. Wayne Erikson and myself were the two primary instigators. The idea was to have just a group so that we could go to the drag races together, cooperate and help one another out."

This group called themselves the Ramchargers. At night, they would demoralize other drag racers on North Woodward Avenue in Detroit and on weekends, set records at Detroit Dragway. These engineers had access to the research and development work that had been done on the Hemi and they applied it to their personal cars. Then they concocted a plan to build an altered vehicle for the B/Altered class in sanctioned drag racing, and the *High and Mighty* started to take shape. The car they used was a 1949 Plymouth Business Coupe, and it was extensively modified in the home garage of Jack Mc-Phearson, one of the Ramchargers.

"Dan Mancini and I built the engine," Hoover says. "Gale Porter over at Dodge got for us a 354 Hemi truck engine that had dropped an exhaust valve. It became the engine for the *High and Mighty*. It was a joke with us at the time because we had roughly $200 invested in it. We bought a new set of Jahns pistons. Jim Hider had a place over near the Detroit Airport. We came up with a camshaft profile and ol' Jim would do it for a reasonable price. Jeff Baker at Chrysler designed the plenum-ram manifold, and we used reinforced radiator hose for the trumpets. The *High and Mighty* was the grandaddy of the tunnel-ram manifold."

Getting all this new-found horsepower to the ground was a problem due to the limitations of tires in the late fifties. Troy Simonsen joined Chrysler in 1958 and the Ramchargers shortly thereafter. He relates how they solved the problem of traction.

"With the *High and Mighty,* we sat down and thought about the vehicle dynamics of drag racing. The problem was getting all the traction you can. We wanted the car high, to get weight shift. We had a unique suspension that was intended to transfer the weight equally to both the rear wheels so that the torque of the driveshaft and the tendency to lift the right wheel was offset.

That car," Simonsen remembers, "was tall enough that you could crawl under it on your hands and knees, almost."

This impromptu club grew from its rather inauspicious beginnings over the years to race the Max Wedge and 426 Hemi engines, and the Ramchargers became one of the biggest draws in sanctioned drag racing. More importantly, the Ramchargers had a dramatic impact on Chrysler Corporation's racing engine development. The company's racing success and attendant public image were a direct result of the enthusiastic efforts of these engineers. Some of the others who joined the Ramchargers included Dick Maxwell, Dan Knapp, Tom Coddington, Jerry Donley, Herm Moser, Jim Thornton, Mike Buckle and Gary Congdon.

"I doubt that there would have been a drag-racing program without the Ramchargers," Hoover says. "I really believe if the company had made an attempt to do drag racing as they did, I doubt they would have been successful at all if the Ramchargers cornerstone had not been available."

The ability of the hemispherical-combustion-chamber cylinder head to make power would prove itself again when the new Wedge-head engines showed their limitations on the high-banked ovals of NASCAR racing around the country. The Hemi was momentarily eclipsed by the Wedge head until it became clear that something more—much more—was needed.

426 Race Hemi

In the Winner's Circle 1964–1970

Larry Adams, who was in charge of race-engine development, came into my office, just sat down in the chair and said, "Bill, that engine isn't going to last. We aren't going to finish the race."

Willem L. Weertman

As the first-generation Hemi faded from the scene, the Wedge-head engines took over the dynamometer labs and engine bays. In 1957, the 318 ci Wedge was introduced in the Plymouth Fury. The 350 and 361 ci Wedge engines were released in the Dodge line in 1958; Plymouth got the 350 ci Wedge the same year. The 383 and 413 Wedges in Chryslers came out the following year. The Imperial was now powered by a 413 Wedge, not the Hemi.

Interestingly, the 1959 Chrysler 300 E, now powered by the Golden Lion 413 Wedge, produced no more power than the 392 Hemi of the previous year. Some automotive writers thought this a moot point. Horsepower was horsepower, after all. One test pegged the 380 hp 300 E at 17.2 sec. for the quarter mile doing 92 mph through the lights.

The Wedge V–8 continued its evolution into the new decade. In truth, the new Wedge engines were more than adequate in the street cars that Chrysler built. The Max Wedge 413 and 426 high-performance racing engines proved their capabilities on drag strips around the country, whether they were campaigned by the Ramchargers (and Plymouth's rival Golden Commandos) or the big and small names in drag racing. Circle-track racing—NASCAR—was another matter.

In 1964, Mopar and its new Hemi swept the Daytona 500, and in 1969, Dodge built its Daytona and named it in honor of the race, above. Left, the drag-race Hemi engine on this Dick Landy Dodge 330 was fitted with chrome valve covers. The block and intake manifold were painted Hemi Orange.
Michael Dregni; David Gooley

Chrysler cars, specifically Dodge and Plymouth, were not frequently in the stock-car winner's circle. A resolution passed by the Automobile Manufacturers Association (AMA) on June 6, 1957, banned car manufacturers from openly supporting racing wins as a reflection of their street car's performance. The AMA felt such practices encouraged reckless driving. The manufacturers went along with the resolution, fearing that failure to do so would result in unfavorable legislation from Washington. The car makers were forced to sell the racing cars and parts, usually to those teams they sponsored, and back off. The AMA did not clamp down on the production of high-performance street cars, however. NASCAR did not view the AMA ban as a threat, because it once again permitted the little guy to have a fighting chance for the winner's circle.

What the resolution succeeded in doing was force the handful of car makers active before the ban to become creative in their means of researching, developing and distributing racing hardware. This was achieved in part by the NASCAR rules that took shape stating that if a given make, model and engine was to be raced, it had to be a production vehicle or option. This had more or

The Chrysler 426 Hemi was conceived, designed, built and tested with unprecedented speed. It swept the 1964

Daytona 500 race and has endured as one of the finest V–8 automotive engines ever built. Chrysler

less been the case for some years, but it was made explicitly clear when rather exotic engines or induction systems made their way into cars that had no production-line counterpart that could be verified, and NASCAR would immediately disqualify the entry.

The manufacturers shifted the research and development to street cars with racing parts available over the parts counter at the dealer. There was some under-the-counter activity between the factory and now-independent racing teams to be sure, but the major objectives by the AMA had been achieved. Thus, the late fifties and the early sixties stock-car racing was pretty much a team effort as opposed to a factory effort.

February 22, 1959, was the biggest day in NASCAR history—the first running of the 500 mile race of the newly opened Daytona International Speedway. The Daytona 500 race would play a pivotal role in the decision to implement a crash program for a new Chrysler racing engine.

The Wedge Rules

In the early sixties, the 413 Wedge was Chrysler's performance engine of note. In 1962, the company introduced the Max Wedge 413. The release of this engine was directly tied to Chrysler Corporation's new president, Lynn Townsend, who stepped up to the presidency in the middle of 1961. The company gained a new advocate of performance and racing, and the change, Hoover remembers, was almost immediate.

"When Lynn Townsend came in as president of Chrysler, the good fortune was he had two teenage boys. They were known to travel North Woodward Avenue late at night. They made it known straightaway to Dad that this stuff [Chrysler Corporation cars] was nowhere. He was highly sensitive to the fact that the product line was nowhere out there with the young people. The rationale was, you can sell an old man a young man's car but you can't sell a young man an old man's car.

"There were," Hoover continues, "encouragements from Bob McCurry over at Dodge, certainly Gale Porter, Frank Wylie from Dodge public relations, and Jack Shirapar. Jack was our champion. He was the guy who could carry the message from the trenches—from North Woodward and Detroit Dragway—right upstairs. Jack knew what had to happen out on North Woodward.

"When Mr. Townsend, by whatever mechanism, let it be known that it was time to change the image of our product, it was just like having the clouds separating and the sun shining through. Engineering division was given the directive to get some cars out there that would do the job. I was made engineering coordinator for the whole engineering division for the race program. That was in October 1961.

"A program began in October 1961 to release in the standard-size cars performance packages based on the RB [raised-block] engine, which at the time was 413 cubic inches. I'll never forget that because Mr. Townsend himself had signed the project request to initiate it, so that was like walking into engine design with a blank check.

"The first of the cross-ram, eight-barrel 413 Wedge cars we got running was a white Plymouth two-door. Mr. Townsend himself, the chairman of the board, came out to the proving grounds one day and I took the car out there. He stood out there at the east-west straightaway and had me make a pass with the car so he could listen to the car and watch it. He had the ability to understand what it meant, and I'll go to my grave believing it was his two teenage boys who put that sparkle there.

"Those [Max Wedge] cars," Hoover explains, "hit the drag race scene like an H-bomb. They just blew everything else away by eight to ten miles an hour. I think that there's no question that the experience that all the Ramchargers had gained the preceding three or four years at the drag strip and North Woodward was fundamental to making those cars successful.

"The 413 Wedge was less successful as a Grand National stock-car engine," Hoover reveals. "If the Wedges had been more successful in Grand National racing, the need for the 426 Hemi wouldn't have existed, because the Wedges were doing a good job in drag racing, and that success was related to modifying the TorqueFlight automatic transmission for drag-racing purposes. Pontiac was the job to beat at the time, if I recall correctly. It became evident that in order to really make a big splash at Daytona Beach in the Grand National cars, we needed a better level of power."

The 413 Max Wedge and later the 426 Max Wedge were Chrysler's first true high-performance racing-engine programs. The managers of these successful programs were under the direction of Bob Rarey. He had joined Chrysler in 1942 and became assistant chief engineer of engine design in 1955 when Mel Carpentier died. By the early 1960s, Rarey had become chief engineer in charge of engine, transmission and engine electrical. When asked by Bob Anderson to take over all racing-engine work at Chrysler, Rarey balked. However, he did agree to set up a separate group, apart from production-engine design, to handle this activity. The success of the Max Wedge 413 and 426 was a tribute to his foresight and support. The engines, however, could not realistically double for circle-track racing.

The reason for this was not just the Wedge-shaped combustion chamber of the 413 and 426, but the size of the intake and exhaust valves and the design of the intake and exhaust ports. While the engines performed well on the short, quarter-mile strip, the high rpm, high horsepower requirements of stock-car racing exposed the Wedge's limitation in producing the level of horsepower necessary to win.

Willem L. Weertman would become closely involved with the new racing engine that evolved. A 1947 graduate of Yale, Weertman joined Chrysler that year and entered the Chrysler Institute. After graduating from the two-year work-study program, he began work at the Plymouth Road assembly plant. When the Mound Road engine plant was built for the production of V-8 engines, he was selected as the first resident engineer of the plant. In 1955, Bob Rarey, as the new assistant chief engineer of engine design, selected Weertman to be manager of engine design.

"We had a fairly strong factory effort with the Wedge V-8 in 1962 and '63," Weertman says, "but it was obvious to those managing the program we were not competitive with it. About that time,

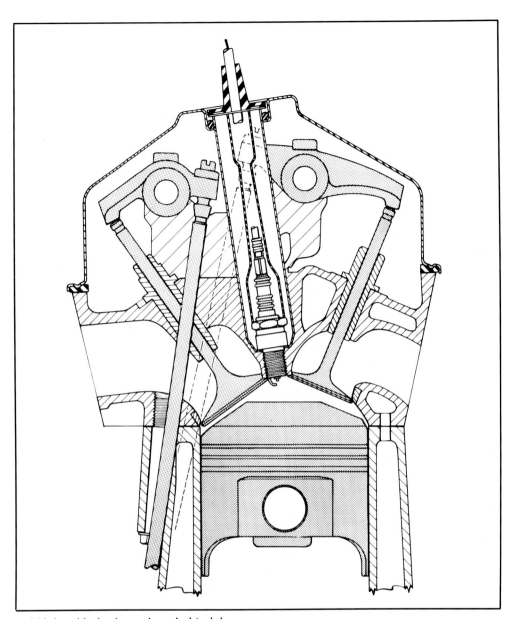

A fifth head bolt, shown here behind the intake valve pushrod, was a key feature of the 426 Hemi. Chrysler

in late '62, early '63, it was a collective decision by our race policy people, which included Bob Rodger, who said in effect, 'Either we do something big or we should get out. What we are doing is not meaningful to the company, to our dealers or to car sales.' So [Rodger], Tom Hoover and Bob Rarey had to think about what might be possible and immediately the thought came to their minds, 'Can we have a Hemi version of our B and raised-B engines?'"

Engine Code: A864

"I remember exactly where I was on the second floor of the main building in

Highland Park," Hoover says. "Don Moore was there, I was there and a couple of other people. It was the winter of '62-'63, and the big Wedges had not done well in NASCAR. A couple of us offered up the argument, I suppose it was Don Moore and myself, 'If we're going to make a new head for the engine, let's go with what we know is right. We know the Hemi will do the job, and we have all the A311 and Cunningham background upon which we can rely to proceed forward.' Jack Shirapar picked up the ball and he's the one who carried it right up to the executive

The cylinder-head design of the 426 Hemi was similar to Chrysler's first-generation Hemi of the fifties.

group was Frank Bialk. We were racing the 426 Wedge-head engine at the time. We had the displacement set up, now we had the challenge of trying to put the Hemi head on that engine. A critical decision was made by that group to stay with the included valve angle from the old Hemi engine, because we had a background that describes the chamber, valve sizes and the performance of the engine."

With a maximum vertical separating load of 18,800 lb. at 7200 rpm along the crankshaft centerline, durability of the bottom-end was of paramount concern. To ensure durability and rigidity, the main-bearing cap design of the 426 Wedge was abandoned.

"Steel bearing caps appeared in the early Hemi for testing Firestone tires at Indianapolis," Hoover explains. "Also, Briggs Cunningham used early Hemi engines for some road racing in Europe and the need for good structural support for the crankshaft bearings became evident during that program."

Bialk designed a new set of number two, three and four main-bearing caps that took advantage of the current deep-skirt walls of the raised-block by adding cross-bolts that went through the block walls into the bearing caps. This enabled the engine-block skirt structure to aid the bearing caps to resist the horizontal loads pushing the cap across the engine. This cross-bolt main-bearing cap design used $\frac{1}{2}$–13 bolts vertically through the bearing cap to the block and $\frac{3}{8}$–16 bolts horizontally through the block skirt to the main-bearing caps. Later in the 426 Hemi's development, these were increased to $\frac{9}{16}$–12 and $\frac{7}{16}$–14 bolts, respectively.

The cylinder head was a unique design challenge for a number of reasons.

"One thing that we had on the new engine that was better than the old engine was the headbolt pattern," Weertman says. "Our B and raised-B engines had a five-bolt headbolt pattern as compared to four on the prior engines. The ability to clamp the head is crucial to how much you are ever going to get out of the engine. The problem that we faced in doing the Hemi became the solution that made a real engine out of it: how to handle the fifth headbolt. The fifth headbolt was literally in the way of the pushrods and intake port. This area would be so restricted it wouldn't

committee. I got to carry the drawings up there for Jack. He made the pitch and Townsend didn't hesitate a bit. [He said] 'Do it.'"

The decision to put a Hemi head on the raised-block 426 was borne of necessity. Lynn Townsend wanted the new racing engine in time for the Daytona 500 race in February 1964. The Hemi design team was faced with an almost impossible deadline. Thus, the decision was made to use the same basic machin-

ing dimensions as the 426 Wedge in order to use existing tooling. Cylinder bore centers were 4.80 in. Height along the bore axis was 10.725 in. Vertical height from the crankshaft center was 10.875 in., and overall length was 23.46 in. Bore was 4.25 in. and stroke was 3.75 in.

"In March 1963," Weertman continues, "we gave that assignment to our advanced engine group under Bob Dent, and the lead designer of that have much more power than the Wedge-head engine. What Frank Bialk came up with was to bring the bolt up from underneath. It took him awhile to be sure that, indeed, we could bring a bolt up from underneath."

The juxtaposition of the intake and exhaust valve within the combustion chamber was also crucial. If the two valves were equidistant from the bore centerline in the transverse view, the resulting engine would be so wide it couldn't fit into the cars it was designed for. It also resulted in an exhaust-valve rocker arm of alarming proportions. The solution was achieved by rotating the included valve angle of 58 deg. across the hemisphere toward the intake manifold.

"We looked at that rocker arm and that thing kept looking like a huge pump handle," Weertman laughs. "We reduced its length until we thought, 'That's going to work.' That set where the valve was going to be. We had daily meetings on the board to see what Frank had, then we'd let him work for several days to come up with his best thinking. He was really an amazing guy. He would say whenever he would get into a corner, 'Sometimes I just go home and I'll have a vision. I'll come back to work and [it will be] just fine.'

"That was part of the challenge of getting the chamber design in place," Weertman continues, "to come up with just the right compromises on the top-end. The use of the rocker shafts was sort of ordained because of their use on the prior-generation engine. It was a sturdy arrangement, with forged-steel rocker arms."

Once the design for the cylinder block and heads was finalized, these two long-lead items were procured for manufacture. Chrysler's American Foundry Division in Indianapolis, Indiana, was chosen for casting the cylinder block. Campbell, Wyant and Cannon Foundry Company in Muskegon, Michigan, was selected to cast the cylinder heads. Weertman explained how Chrysler was able to get these new engine parts into production so quickly: "We took the production [426 Wedge] parts, making just the changes we needed to. Where we could, we would take an existing box, or pattern, and change it. We were able to go from our prototype design to the first casting quickly. However, many

The 426 race Hemi used these steel-tube and cast-iron flange headers. The tube pattern on the right header was distinctly different from that on the left. Chrysler

The connecting rod was designed to withstand a separating load of 18,000 lb. at 7000 rpm. Chrysler

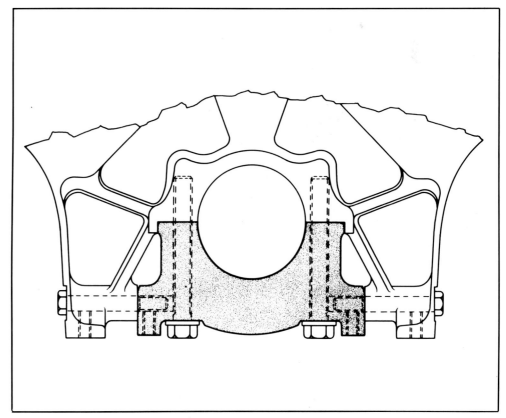

Another key to the 426 Hemi's durability was the use of cross-bolted and recessed main bearing caps.

291

The 426 Hemi for NASCAR events in 1964 and 1965 used a single Holley four-barrel carburetor on a dual-plane high-riser intake manifold. Chrysler

The intake manifold designed for sanctioned drag racing was a plenum-ram design with staggered dual four-barrel carburetors. Chrysler

parts, like the cylinder heads, did require all-new equipment."

When the 426 Hemi engine was given the go-ahead for development, the decision was made to have a parallel design program for a drag-racing Hemi. Thus, two distinct intake manifolds were designed by Forbes Bunting at Chrysler. The circle-track single-four-barrel intake manifold was a dual-plane design for use with a Holley carburetor. The drag intake manifold was a plenum design with two staggered four-barrel carburetors. Each carburetor sat atop a plenum chamber that fed the four cylinders on the bank opposite the carburetors. The Carter carbs on the drag manifold used $1\frac{11}{16}$ in. primary and secondary bores with a rating of 770 cfm (cubic feet per minute). The track-engine Holley carburetors used the same primary and secondary bore diameters. Both intake manifolds were cast aluminum.

Reciprocating Parts

As originally designed, the pistons would be impact extruded from an aluminum slug. To achieve the 12.5:1 compression ratio required for the track and drag engine, the top of the piston was contoured to protrude 0.755 in. into the combustion chamber. Valve timing at top dead center—the end of the exhaust stroke and beginning of the intake stroke—resulted in both valves being partially open. This required circular depressions in the top of the piston to permit 0.070 in. clearance between the valve and the pistons.

The connecting rod would go through two redesigns at the crankshaft end, but initially it used two $\frac{7}{16}$ in. bolts loaded to 16,300 lb. each—close to their yield point. The rods were forged. The distance between the piston pin and crankshaft bores was 6.871 in., with a minimum I-section of 0.35 sq-in.

The crankshafts for both the track and drag engine were identical in dimensions but made of different materials. Main journal diameter was 2.75 in. Crankpin journal diameter was 2.375 in., and the stroke was 3.750 in. Undercut journal fillets were incorporated, as in the previous Hemi. Initially, all journals were finished to 0.015 in. but later were reduced to 0.015 in. to prevent oil film breakthrough under high rpm. The circle-track crankshaft was forged from SAE 4340 high-strength alloy steel; the drag-racing crankshaft was forged from SAE 1046 carbon steel. Both cranks then underwent the same finishing procedure. They were first heat treated, then machined, with the exception of the finish grind on the journal surfaces. After being entirely shot-peened, the journals were ground. The entire crankshaft was then surface hardened by a nitride-immersion process call Tufftride. Finally, the journals were lapped.

The mechanical camshafts for circle-track and drag racing differed also. The 1964–1965 track camshaft had an intake and exhaust duration of 312 deg. with 88 deg. of overlap and 0.54 in. of valve lift. The 1964 drag camshaft had 300 deg. of intake and exhaust duration with 76 deg. of overlap and 0.52 in. of lift.

The valvetrain was designed to withstand the punishment of flat-out racing. The valve angle from bore centerline was 35 deg. for the intake valve and 23 deg. for the exhaust valve. Intake valve diameter was 2.25 in., with a hefty 0.309 in. diameter stem. The 1.94 in. diameter exhaust valve had a stem diameter of 0.308 in. Dual valve springs were needed on each valve, requiring 384 lb. to fully open. A spiral spring damper was placed between the inner and outer spring.

Forged rocker arms featured full-length steel-backed bronze bushings. The rocker-arm valve tip was hardened and ground to 0.030 in. These rocker arms were adjustable, using a ⅜–24 UNF thread with a locknut.

The rocker-arm shafts had an outside diameter of 0.872 in. and an inside diameter of 0.60 in. The rocker shaft was hardened at the location of each rocker arm. Light helical springs were necessary on the shaft to keep the rocker arms in place against the adjacent brackets.

Malleable-iron rocker-shaft brackets were attached to the cylinder heads using five of the cylinder head bolts. A solid dowel accurately located each bracket. Holes were drilled in the brackets to permit oil to flow from the bracket mounting surface to each rocker shaft.

Valve tappets were mechanical, made from extruded steel and having a brazed-on iron face. The pushrods were made of steel tubing, 0.375 in. in diameter with a heft 0.083 in. wall thickness. Hardened-steel inserts that contacted the tappet and rocker arm were pressed in and then welded to the ends.

A 426 Hemi undergoing assembly. Test engines were assembled in Chrysler's Highland Park, Michigan, engine lab. Production racing engines were assembled at Chrysler's Marine and Industrial division in Marysville, Michigan. Chrysler

View of the assembled 426 Hemi cylinder head. Note the CWC foundry mark of Campbell, Wyant and Cannon Foundry Company. Chrysler

A drag-racing intake manifold after machining. This intake manifold was also used on Chrysler's famous 1968 Super Stock Barracudas and Darts, which are still campaigned today. Chrysler

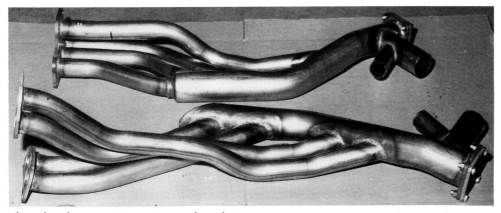

These header extensions were used on the 426 race Hemi and incorporated the use of cutouts where rules permitted. Chrysler

Chrysler also designed new exhaust headers for the 426 Hemi. The headers were made from 2 in. diameter steel tubing, welded to cast-steel flanges which bolted to the cylinder head. Initial dynamometer testing resulted in 45 in. tube length before discharging into a 4 in. collector. Subsequent testing showed an improvement in high-end power when the tubes were shortened to 30 in. and mated to a flange plate, to which undercar header extensions were

294

bolted. The configuration of the four exhaust-header tube centers differed for the left and right. In addition, the tubes on the left exhaust header were grouped to one flange, while the ones on the right of the engine had two separate two-tube flanges.

Machining and Assembly

The raw cylinder blocks and heads were shipped from their respective foundries to the Trenton, Michigan,

engine plant for machining. Changes were made to the 426 Wedge-block line to allow for the Hemi's requirements.

"Trenton could put the blocks down their main machining line," Weertman says, "and then they had offline operations for the block, for example, to put in [the main-bearing cap] side bolt holes. Trenton was giving us virtually hour-by-hour service on the blocks. I was in touch with the factory manager, and he understood our desire. Of course, he had his own production schedules to meet. We challenged them to do this whole job quickly because the corporation had almost no time to get the job done."

Although the production 426 street and race Hemis were to be assembled at Chrysler's Marysville, Michigan, engine plant, the test and early racing engines were assembled at the engine labs in Highland Park. The Hemi parts shipped there from the Trenton plant underwent minute inspection and checking before being approved for final assembly.

"Prior to building each engine," Troy Simonsen relates, "we did a lot of dimensional checks. We Zyglowed the pistons to look for cracks, and we Magnaglowed the blocks, the cranks, the rods and the heads. Steve Baker and I had the responsibility of the day-to-day, nuts and bolts—was the engine holding together?—and analyzing and testing anything that required mechanical development. We supervised and wrote the orders for building up all of the engines, which included all of the ones that went to the Daytona race."

Steve Baker joined Chrysler in 1960 and entered the Chrysler Institute. He had the good fortune to be assigned to the engine lab that would eventually oversee assembly and testing of the 426 race Hemi. With so much riding on the success of the Hemi, it was essential each engine was assembled with great care.

"Our only secret here," Baker says, "was that we took extreme care in cleanliness and making sure the parts were good. It took about eighty man-hours to assemble a race Hemi, not counting the machining time. Most of that time was in inspection, checking all the parts to make sure they were within tolerance. Things like taking a white cloth through each cylinder bore, not just to make sure they were clean, but to make sure the assembly guys understood this was the way it was done."

Chrysler had no previous experience testing an engine designed purely for circle-track racing. Weertman called in Larry Adams, in charge of the race Hemi engine testing program.

"I said to Larry, 'How do we find out if our engine's going to be durable enough for Daytona?' We had durability schedules for testing passenger-car production engines—long 800 hour tests. We didn't have any durability schedules for our racing engines."

Weertman and Adams came up with the idea of running the engine testing in the lab identical to the demands made on the engine during an actual 500 mile race, including straightaways, banked turns and pit stops.

The first 426 race Hemi build-up started the last week in November 1963 and was ready for lab testing the first week in December. The Daytona race was only two months away. Before putting the new engine through its race-profile testing, the engineers thought it prudent to bring it up to speed slowly to establish power readings in the dyno room.

"At the time," Baker remembers, "that room had a 400 horsepower Amplidyne dynamometer. Well, we knew we had a hell of a lot more horsepower. There were several of us there—the operator, myself, and the department manager, Ev Moeller. So we slide-ruled the observed power. We got 400 horsepower around 4800 rpm. There was a possibility we were going to break the dyno. Moeller was in charge and said to go ahead. He would take responsibility so the operator wouldn't get into trouble for damaging equipment. As I remember, we got up to more than 425 horsepower the very first run we made with the engine—and the dyno didn't break. Everyone was pretty pleased with that."

Preparation for Daytona

This engine, and others, then began their rigorous race-profile testing, and the dyno rooms in Highland Park reverberated with the unmuffled roar of 426 Hemis running at full power. With the Daytona 500 qualifying races just a few weeks away, the pace at Chrysler reached a fever pitch. The prestige of Chrysler Corporation was riding on the 426 Hemi and it was a make or break situation. Yet, for many of the engineers and technicians, these months of frantic

A fully assembled 426 drag Hemi, minus only the air cleaner, with manual four-speed transmission. This configuration was offered in Chrysler's 1964, 1965 and 1968 factory drag cars. Chrysler

effort are the most memorable of their careers.

"Some of my fondest memories," Simonsen recollects, "would be coming to work in Highland Park very early in the morning before daybreak in the winter. We were running three shifts of operators with the dynamometer crew. The engines ran headers with an exhaust system that dumped into a six or twelve inch stack that then went up and exhausted out over the roof on the third story of the building. As you came across the parking lot at 5:30 in the morning, it just echoed all over Highland Park."

Problems arose quickly, however. Weertman co-authored a 1966 SAE paper with Bob Lechner chronicling the saga of the 426 Hemi's development, and the first problem encountered would prove the most nerve-racking.

"Shortly after the first engines were run at full power," Weertman and Lechner wrote, "several engine failures occurred due to vertical cracks in the thrust side of the right hand bank bore walls. A quick analysis showed that these block cracks were occurring in the bore wall opposite the piston pin pier.

"A reduction of this load concentration could have been obtained by increasing the piston cam so that the bore wall would be loaded more uniformly by adding load to the center of the bore while reducing it at the crack location area. The piston, however, had just undergone an intense development program of its own and further changes to it were ruled out."

"We were bringing the engine up to as much power as we could get out of it with this deadline of the Daytona race in February in front of us," Weertman says. "It was in fairly quick succession that they found cracked cylinder bores in the lab engines. I was in my office when Larry Adams, who was in charge of race engine development, came into my office, just sat down in the chair and said, 'Bill, that engine isn't going to last. We

In 1966 Chrysler offered a new intake manifold for NASCAR competition. Chrysler engineers nicknamed it the Bathtub intake manifold. Chrysler

aren't going to finish the race.'

"I told him, 'Well, Larry, what's it going to take?'

" 'We have to thicken up the bores. There's really no other way.'

"I said, 'OK, we'll see what we can do.' The date was January 28, 1964.

"What we did on the board," Weertman reveals, "was we made a template that could be used to take an existing water jacket core at the foundry, scrape it away and as we scraped the sand away, we would add metal to the block. So we made up these templates to give the thickness in the areas we thought would do the job. We handed them off to our foundry liaison who worked in engine design by the name of Louie Taylor. He flew down to the Indianapolis foundry where the blocks were being cast. He took with him another man—Earl Pinches.

"Louie took the templates we had

set up and he attempted to scrape some cores and get the cores ready to make castings, but the cores cracked apart. We took away so much sand, that he couldn't get a good core. He called from Indianapolis and said, 'Bill, we can't get any good cores with these templates. You're going to have to come here and help me.' So, at that point, I flew down to Indianapolis and I saw that we had added too much metal to the bore walls to solve the cracking problem, but now we couldn't get a block casting. We then proceeded to file a number of cores in batches of twelve cylinder blocks which required both the right- and left-hand cores. We did these by hand with modified templates so the foundry could reproduce this, because at some time Louie, I and Earl Pinches were going to leave that foundry, but we would want them to continue to make good blocks for us.

"We put the cores through their normal process, which requires a core wash, then the core is dried out before it's put into the mold and the casting made. We had worked late on a whole bunch of castings and we went back to

the motel to get some sleep, and the people called us from the foundry and said, 'All the blocks are scrapped that came out.' We went back to the foundry and the blocks were missing large segments of the metal. We had a giant mess on our hands.

"The foundry people were really cooperative. They were doing whatever we wanted them to do. We looked at it and we got our heads together. They said, 'What we think happened is that those cores were not baked out enough and that there was still water retention in the cores.' When those cores went in the mold and when the iron went into the mold and hit the moisture, it blew the metal away, and we were seeing voids in the metal.

"We went through the process again, and I think we went through that about three times. The whole process took about three hours, from scraping the cores, processing them, putting them in the mold, pour the iron, and let the iron cool down before going through shakeout before we got a casting at the other end. We were so anxious to know if we had a good block, we just kept at it. We indeed worked twenty-four hours straight. We were totally exhausted, but we finally came out with a block that looked like a sound casting. We had several blocks and we said, 'Ship it!' "

The date was February 3, 1964. Three blocks from this group would be in the final race. These blocks, however, were not shipped directly to the engine plant for machining. They were shipped first to a stress-relieving furnace for a reheat and slow cool-down. This was done because, along with the bore-wall cracking, bulkhead cracking was also found during engine testing. Considering the substantial design of the Hemi block, the consensus at Chrysler pointed to this being a problem of residual stress in the block casting and not to a design problem. The stress lab and the metallurgists went to work on it. Oscar Willard began work in Chrysler's stress lab in 1956, and remembers well the problem with the 426 Hemi block.

"We worked as a service group almost exclusively in the stress lab," Willard says. "Anytime a problem arose in the corporation from a strength standpoint with failures involved, they usually came to our area to get help to determine what the cause of failure was and what had to be done to remedy it. I worked with some pretty brilliant people and I was at the working level. The problem was presented to them, and the engineers and technicians would stress analyze the blocks.

"We were heavily into residual stress back in an era where it was an art more than a science. There was so much that was unknown about metallurgy: how it reacts when it is poured, where does the residual stress come from? The time after pouring the metal until it is taken out of the mold and cleared of sand is very crucial.

"We were working around the clock in the stress lab along with the people who were running the dynos," Willard says about the 426 Hemi's pre-Daytona 500 race development. "We had prepared an engine block, heads—anything that was having problems. We had completely strain-gauged the block, and that meant bringing the wires out of the crankcase so that we could get to them and hook them up to the electronics. We worked in shifts around the clock for the whole weekend when we were having this crisis. We would come in for our eight-hour shift, compile the data and give it to the next shift, and by Monday morning we had all the answers. We got in the think tank and the decisions of what had to be done were based on that. This was within two weeks of the Daytona race."

With the data and recommendations from the stress-lab engineers in hand, the foundry received new instructions to eliminate the 426 Hemi's residual stress. All previous core preparations and casting procedures were followed. After cool-down and shake-out of the sand core, with care to ensure all sand was removed so as not to allow a temperature concentration, these blocks were placed in a large furnace and reheated to 1,200 deg. Fahrenheit to relieve the blocks' internal stresses. Then the furnace temperature was slowly lowered before the blocks were removed and shipped to Trenton for machining, then to Highland Park for assembly into engines.

Car testing had already been started with the original-design Hemi well before the dyno testing was completed. Steve Baker remembers the first vehicle test with the 426 Hemi.

"The first track test we did with a Hemi in the car," Baker says, "was at the

Straight-on view of Bobby Isaac's Charger Daytona shows off the car's sleek aerodynamics. The car was slick enough that Isaac had earlier set a closed-course record, running a similar car up to 201.104 mph. Isaac allowed how the car was so stable, any driver could turn 180 mph laps straight off the showroom floor. Dr. John Craft

Goodyear track at San Angelo, Texas, with Ray Nichols and his crew. Paul Goldsmith was the driver, and he complained the track was kind of rough. We went out and you could see where the car had become airborne and then came down, leaving tire marks. We had timed him at 180 miles per hour. This was the very first time the 426 Hemi was installed in a stock car."

The date for check and pre-race inspection for the Daytona 500 race was February 4, 1964. Engines had been built and shipped to the teams ahead of this date to give the teams time to make the car installations and to start their own preparation and testing. These engines, of course, were the original design. The gamble had to be taken that these engines would hold up long enough to get through practice, the qualifying laps and the qualifying races. Then the miracle had to happen: beginning with the new, heavy-wall castings that American Foundry started making on February 3, the blocks had to be machined, built into engines and delivered to Daytona in time for all the teams to change their engines before race day on Sunday, February 23, 1964.

As the first engines were built and shipped to the racing teams for installation in their Dodges and Plymouths, there was a secret among all of them that was never revealed to anyone else. The Hemi could develop power that would put the other cars to shame, but Chrysler didn't want to tip its hand. Troy Simonsen explains what that secret was.

"When we went to Daytona in '64, Ford had been dominating the race and Chevy had had the 'Mystery Chevy' engine the year prior and had done very well with that engine; it was the quickest engine on the track at that point. Chrysler had been getting beat regularly. We weren't much of a contender. Of course, NASCAR wants to have a good show, and they wanted three participants.

"We were coming out with the Hemi, and the NASCAR rules were essentially that it was to be a production engine in a production car. We intended that this was going to be a production engine in a production car, but at the time we went to NASCAR we didn't have any production cars out there. We were able to convince NASCAR—who wanted to be convinced because they wanted another participant—that it was going to be a production car in the spring, two months later, which we did make. We knew Ford was going to object if we were really wild and tough, and they would lean on NASCAR not to say it was a recognized production car, so we were careful when we went to Daytona.

"During the weeks of qualifying and getting the cars ready," Simonsen reveals, "we never, during that time, did a wide-open lap. Never. Junior Johnson was one of our drivers. He had driven the Mystery Chevy engine the year before and he said it was just unbelievable the amount of difference in the power between the Mystery Chevy engine and this [Hemi] engine. Going down the back stretches, they would lay their foot in it and feel what it did, and they would feel what it did in the corners, but they never, ever made a complete lap wide open, because they didn't want somebody in the stands timing them and finding out they were eight or ten miles an hour faster than Ford. We were turning 170 mile an hour lap times just like the Ford guys were doing. It looked like it was going to be a good race. NASCAR was happy and everybody was getting comfortable with the fact that we were there. That was the whole plan."

Plan or not, the drivers couldn't resist using enough of the Hemi power to set new course records. On Friday, February 7, 1964, Paul Goldsmith qualified with a two-lap average of 174.91 mph. Richard Petty qualified at 174.418. The next day two fifty-mile pole position races were held with half of the qualifiers in the first race and half in the second race. Goldsmith won his race at an average of 170.94 mph. Petty won his at an average of 171.99 mph. With his original qualifying speed, Goldsmith won the pole position, with Petty on his right, for the Daytona 500.

The rest of the starting positions were determined in two 100 mile qualifying races held on Friday, February 21, 1964. Junior Johnson won the first race with a speed of 170.777 mph. Bobby Isaac won the second race at 169.811 mph. Every one of these speeds broke prior records.

Not everything went according to plan, however. The qualifying races served to put the Hemi through actual racing conditions, even if the engine was not being run flat out. Yet another weakness had surfaced during the qualifying races.

"In the car that Junior Johnson drove," Simonsen says, "the engine finished the race with twenty pounds of oil pressure. We knew what we were going to find without tearing the engine down. The block cracked right down the oil line between the cam and the main-bearing bulkhead."

The fears about the durability of the first cylinder blocks had been underscored.

Two days after the fifty-mile pole position races, a ladle of molten iron at 2,600 deg. Fahrenheit was poured in a mold at American Foundry. This casting would become the cylinder block of the engine that was destined to win the final race.

As each heavy-wall, stress-relieved block arrived at the engine labs, assembly of the Daytona 500 426 Hemi engines began with all the other, pre-inspected

The Dodge Charger Daytona dominated NASCAR's superspeedways throughout the 1969 and 1970 seasons, and Bobby Isaac drove the K&K Insurance car to victory at many of the venues. His sponsorship was irony at its peak; while K&K sponsored this NASCAR racer, the whole muscle-car era would soon be doomed due to the insurance companies' excessive rates on similar performance cars. Dr. John Craft

The 426 race Hemi of the Isaac NASCAR Daytona. The large airbox plenum fed the single carburetor through the air slots at the base of the windshield. Dr. John Craft

Previous page
Rear spoiler of the Isaac Daytona, photographed along pit row on the Talladega, Alabama, superspeedway. The Daytona inherited the flush-mounted rear window from its predecessor, the limited-production-run Charger 500. The giant spoiler was all its own. Dr. John Craft

parts to expedite assembly. The assembled engines were painted, then sent to the dyno labs for performance confirmation. Each engine was then bolted to an engine stand for transportation to the waiting racing teams at Daytona.

Millions of dollars had been spent to develop the 426 Hemi, and there were fears about sending the engines by plane. Oscar Willard remembers with bemusement this crucial next step to the hoped-for Daytona 500 win.

"I remember we had a bunch of skeptics here," he laughs. "I asked a question once and they said, 'They're building an engine over there in the motor room right now, and they're going to be sending it down to Daytona tonight, so make sure if there's anything you have to add that it's included.'

"'They're shipping it down tonight?' I asked.

"'Oh yeah. They've got a truck waiting for it.'

"'Truck? Why don't they put it on a plane and fly it down? Why don't they take two at a time?'

"'What if they have a plane crash?'

"The thinking was, at the time, they did not trust the plane. The mechanic from, say, Petty's crew, would come up here, pick up the completed engine, drive it down there, throw it in the car and they'd be testing it the next day. They couldn't stand the thought of shipping two in an airplane at one time because there was such a scarcity of the parts."

Bob Lechner was assigned the task of taking additional 426 Hemis to Daytona, with the added bonus of watching the race.

"I took three or four Hemi engines down to Daytona in a pickup truck with another fellow," Lechner says. "Most of the major racers already had theirs; these were strictly spares. I had tickets in the grandstands area. It was the first time I had ever seen a Grand National race."

The 1964 Daytona 500

February 23, 1964, dawned cool but sunny. As the stock-car fans filled the stands, there were countless discussions and bets as to who would win the race and what make would take the checkered flag. The qualifying races gave the best indication and determined the starting line-up. Out of a starting field of forty-six cars, the first seven positions were Dodges or Plymouths.

Paul Goldsmith held pole position in his Plymouth Belvedere. Next to Goldsmith was Richard Petty in his number 43 Plymouth. Junior Johnson was in third position, driving a Dodge Coronet. Bobby Isaac was in fourth, also driving a Dodge Coronet. In fifth position was Buck Baker behind the wheel of a Belvedere, as was Jim Pardue in sixth position. David Pearson was in seventh, driving a Dodge Coronet. Jim Paschal was in tenth position driving a Coronet. The race program stated these cars were

Hemi Engines at 1964 Daytona 500

Cylinder block	Casting date	Car number	Crew	Driver	Final position
0726	2–10–64	43	Petty	Petty	1
0688	2–7–64	54	Burton and Robinson	Pardue	2
0704	2–10–64	25	Nichols	Goldsmith	3
0583	2–3–64	5	Owens	Paschal	5
0641	2–5–64	3	Fox	Johnson	9
0589	2–3–64	41	Petty	Baker	12
0586	2–3–64	26	Nichols	Isaac	15
0647	2–6–64	6	Owens	Pearson	DNF

powered by "Chrysler Corporation's Hemispherical Combustion Chamber Maximum Performance Engine."

The miracle had happened. Every one of these cars was powered by a new, heavy-wall Hemi engine. The race teams had done their part in making the engine changes the day before the start. Chrysler, and the teams, were ready to race.

Ronnie Householder, Chrysler's director of stock-car racing, was in the pits, making sure the pit crews had the needed fuel, tires, parts—and spare 426 Hemi engines. As the official 12:30 pm start of the race approached, the field of cars began their pace laps.

"Ev Moeller and I were in the stands across from the pits," Bill Weertman smiles. "They started off and I don't know how many laps it was, maybe twenty-five or fifty laps, [when] the cars came into the pits and the hoods went up! We just about died. That was a sign that you've got trouble. What happened was there was so much paper and debris on the track, that it was being sucked up and plastered on the front of the radiators, and the engines were overheating. What they had to do, of course, was get all this stuff cleared off the radiators. Down went the hoods, off they went onto the track, and they really dominated the race."

That day racing history was made and a legendary engine was born. Three hours and fifteen minutes later, Richard Petty was first across the finish line followed by Jim Pardue and Paul Goldsmith—a one-two-three sweep by Plymouth. Jim Paschal was fifth, seconds behind the leaders. Junior Johnson was ninth. Hemi cars set a new average speed record of 154.334 mph.

"Ford had had a major ad campaign with the slogan, 'Total Performance,'" Troy Simonsen remembers fondly. "Within days after taking first, second, third and fifth at Daytona and having dominated that race, everybody here, on the teams, in the lab and in public relations was wearing a little button that said, 'Total What?'"

Chrysler president Lynn Townsend was jubilant. Chrysler had not only won the most prestigious stock-car racing event in NASCAR, it dominated the top finishers. Townsend immediately looked for other fish to fry, and looked to

The interior of the Bobby Isaac Daytona is all business. The essential gauges are mounted in a simple, lightweight, fabricated dash. Dr. John Craft

Indianapolis. He called Bob Rarey into his office.

"'We've wiped those guys out of Daytona, now let's wipe them out of Indianapolis. Build an engine that will take care of them at Indianapolis,'" Rarey remembers Townsend telling him. "So we designed a small-displacement Hemi engine. Townsend came to me and said, 'I've just gotten the cost figures on this thing. We're going to go racing with those guys, but it's going to cost $7 million. You've got to tell me what our chances are to win.' I said, 'I don't know what kind of a racer you are or how many races you've been to, but if you've

ever seen an Indianapolis race, there are thirty-three cars in the race and some of them don't make it through the first turn. I would say since there are thirty-three cars in the race and we have two of them in there, we'll have about a one in sixteen chance.' And he said, 'For seven million dollars, we're cancelling the program.' So, we never built that one."

The Woodward Avenue Race Shop

Chrysler's fledgling race group was faced with a corporate structure that was not experienced in building the race cars needed to get the job done. The development of the 426 Hemi for NASCAR and sanctioned drag racing made that clear. There was no convenient place to do prototype development cars at Highland Park. In order to do the job professionally and avoid corporate red tape that would slow pro-

Dick Landy established a colorful and enduring reputation for himself racing Hemi-powered Dodges during the sixties. With cigar clenched firmly in cheek, he comes off the line in one of the first factory Maximum Performance Package 426 Hemi Charger Dodges, racing in Super Stock/Automatic. Dick Landy

gress, a separate facility had to be found.

Dick Maxwell joined Chrysler in February of 1959 and graduated from the Chrysler Institute two years later. He joined the Ramchargers and immediately began working in the race group on Chrysler's drag-racing efforts. It was clear to Maxwell, as well as others in the race group, that they needed a place to build their test cars.

"There was really no place inside engineering where we could do the sort of things we wanted to do," Maxwell says. "We needed a specialized facility where we could do prototype race cars, or whatever."

After some searching, Hoover felt he had found the ideal building: an old Pontiac dealership on Woodward Avenue that had gone out of business. Its location was appropriate, too. Woodward Avenue had become the street to cruise—and race. It had developed a mystique and was known to enthusiasts all over the country.

Dan Mancini was put in charge of running Chrysler's new race-car shop. Mancini had joined Chrysler in 1953 as a driver and mechanic, and quickly moved on to the dynamometer lab. Later, he was responsible for engine build-up for the engines that were tested in the lab. This was followed by work in the carburetor lab. It was while working there he learned of the Ramchargers and became involved. Hoover chose him to supervise the running of the garage.

Mancini gathered a crew of five mechanics from within Chrysler with a keen interest in racing and skill in engine building and car fabrication. They were Roger Lindamood, Larry

304

The Little Red Wagon *was one of the wildest applications of 426 Hemi power seen during the sixties. With its built-in wheel-standing capability, it routinely set elapsed times in the low tens at speeds over 125 mph.* Chrysler

Knowlton, Fred Schrandt, Dan Knapp and Ted Macadaul.

"This was where we built the racing mules for testing," Mancini says, "whether they were for drag racing or NASCAR. Tom Hoover and Jim Thornton supervised the drag cars and Larry Rathgeb handled the stock cars."

The 426 Hemi Drag Cars

It was the production of the 426 Hemi-powered drag cars that ostensibly made the Hemi a production engine. How many engines constituted a production engine? Curiously, this was a nebulous point with NASCAR, and no engineers at Chrysler today can remember any definitive minimum production run specifically requested by

NASCAR for homologation. Bill Weertman and Bob Lechner, however, did state in their SAE paper roughly how many 426 drag-race Hemis Chrysler built.

"Immediately following the initial introduction of the engine," they wrote, "a production run of several hundred drag racing engines and cars were planned to be built. The production of the several hundred drag engines was completed by the end of the 1964 model year. Another production run of several hundred drag engines was made for the 1965 model year automobiles, with a considerable weight decrease for the engines obtained by use of aluminum and magnesium components."

The Dodge and Plymouth factory drag cars truly were set up for the strip. The 12.5:1 compression ratio 426 Hemi was factory rated at 425 hp at 6000 rpm, but to racers who knew better, this rating was obviously conservative. The standard rear-axle ratio was a Sure-Grip 4.56; optional ratios available ranged from 2.93 to 5.38. Dual Carter AFB four-

barrel carburetors sat atop the short-ram aluminum intake manifold. The cars came standard with the TorqueFlight three-speed automatic transmission. The A–833 four-speed manual transmission was optional.

Dodge called its Hemi the Dodge 426 Hemi-Charger. In its booklet Dodge added this disclaimer in bold type to discourage any would-be racers from taking the car to the public streets:

"The Hemi-Charger 426 engine is designed for use in supervised acceleration trials and other racing and performance competition. It is not recommended for general every day driving because of the compromise of all around characteristics which must be made for this type of vehicle. In view of its intended use this vehicle is sold "As Is" and the provisions of Chrysler Corporation's manufacturers passenger car warranty or any other warranty expressed or implied does not apply."

In the booklet section describing features, it stated a lightweight aluminum front-end package was available as optional equipment for better weight distribution. This included aluminum fenders, hood, dust shields, front bumper, bumper-support brackets and doors. Door glass and front quarter window winders were replaced with plexiglass and the window winders were eliminated. The rear window was replaced with 0.08 in. tempered glass. The hood was fitted with a large air scoop to feed colder, denser air to the angled, oval air filter spanning both carburetors.

"The Super Stock drag-race cars were intended only for drag-strip use," states Troy Simonsen, "but were production-built cars and we built a lot of them, both manual and automatic. They had a minimum amount of equipment in them. You could take one out the door, put a set of M&H tires on it, uncork the headers and go turn 11.50."

Naturally, this was *the* vehicle of choice for the Ramchargers and they did extremely well with it. At the American Hot Rod Association (AHRA) Summer Nationals, the Ramchargers achieved an 11.06 sec. elapsed time in the quarter-mile at 132.62 mph, seizing the Top Stock Eliminator title. At the National Hot Rod Association (NHRA) Nationals in Indianapolis, where the Hemi blocks had been cast, the Ramchargers set an NHRA record of 11.23 sec. at 130 mph in the Super Stock class.

Racing Parts Procurement

A key facet in the 426 race Hemi story is the procurement of parts. It's one thing to design and manufacture the parts, but once made, how did they get to the engine lab for assembly and testing and to the racers themselves? The product lines of Dodge, Plymouth and Chrysler had their own system for procuring parts, but the race group had no such system; one had to be created. The man responsible for setting up the racing parts procurement system was Brian Schram.

Schram joined Chrysler in 1949 as a clerk at the Dodge plant. In 1955, he had the opportunity to join the product engineering office at Dodge, building new-car prototypes and procuring the parts. By 1960, he was working for Gale Porter and Frank Wylie, ensuring parts supply to Carl Kiekhaefer and Lee Petty. Through Porter, Schram began to help Robert Cahill in Dodge's drag-racing program, procuring parts first for the Max Wedge 413 and 426 and then for the 426 Hemi. The Ramchargers also turned to him to meet their racing parts needs.

Schram established a parts depot at Dodge's Product Planning Lynch Road garage. He operated the depot by himself at first, systematizing everything from the air cleaner to the oil pan and every part in between. As the 426 Hemi stock-car and drag-racing programs mushroomed, Schram was assisted by Gene Carr, Dave Johnson and Mo David.

Notification of a parts requirement would come to Schram via a memo, usually from an engineer affiliated with the race group. "For example," says Schram, "Dick Maxwell would send me a Speedi-memo stating, 'Send Sox and Martin two Hemi cylinder heads,' or something like that. I'd crate the parts and take them to Detroit Airport for shipment to the racers."

Schram says the stock-car racing parts program was structured differently. Race-car builder Ray Nichols, under contract to Ronnie Householder in charge of Chrysler's stock-car racing program, would receive the parts from Schram; the parts were not sent directly to the racing teams themselves.

Twin-Cam and Aluminum Hemis

Chrysler did not sit still with the 426 Hemi's development. The corporation rightly surmised GM and Ford would

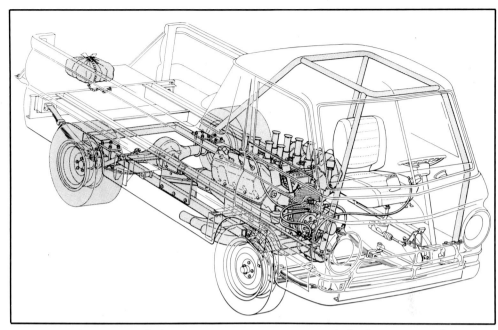

The Little Red Wagon took shape in Chrysler's Woodward Avenue garage. Based on the Dodge A–100 compact pickup, the 426 Hemi with Hilborn fuel injection was bolted into a rugged new frame to add strength to the pickup's unibody. Bill "Maverick" Golden campaigns the Little Red Wagon to this day.

Dick Landy got one of the six 1965 Dodge altered-wheelbase factory drag cars designed to compete in A/FX class drag racing. Dick Landy

307

Stock-car driver Bobby Isaac piloted his 426 Hemi-powered Dodge Daytona to twenty-eight national and world records on the Bonneville Salt Flats, Utah. Chrysler

redouble their efforts to beat the Hemi.

"After the first several races [in 1964]," Simonsen recalls, "Ford made a major drive and improved their performance of both the engines and the cars, and from then on out, the races were pretty much competitive."

One of the designs intended to improve the 426 Hemi was the A925 engine program. This was a double-overhead-camshaft design with four valves per cylinder. A prototype was built, and although it never ran in Chrysler's dyno labs, this prototype served an important purpose.

"Ford went down to Daytona for 1965 with their racing engine," Rarey says, "which wasn't a Hemi exactly but was darned near, I guess. They said they wanted to race *that* against us. Ronnie Householder went into Bill France and said, 'Hey, look fellows. If you run that Ford engine, we're running this engine.' He takes the cover off it and shows the

four-valve Hemi. This engine had a sixteen-branch intake manifold. It was unbelievable. France just said, 'As of now, the Ford engine isn't running and neither is *that*.' We eliminated the Ford competition with that one engine."

Unfortunately, the NASCAR ban on the Ford single-overhead-cam 427 and Chrysler double-overhead-cam 426 Hemi also extended to the 426 Hemi they were currently racing. Although Ford and Chrysler filed protests, Bill France did not waiver. Chrysler withdrew its factory support for the 1965 season. Ford, however, took advantage of the void left by Chrysler and opted to race its mass-produced 427 ci Wedge-head engine. Many Dodge and Plymouth stock-car drivers, faced with the NASCAR Hemi ban, shifted their efforts to NHRA, AHRA and USAC (United States Auto Club) sanctioned events in 1965. Richard Petty, for example, raced a Hemi-powered Barracuda in B/Altered.

One of the Hemi engine programs that did see the light of day was the A990 program, originally an offshoot of the A864 Hemi program. Ways of reducing the weight of the 426 Hemi for drag racing were studied. Bill Weertman made

his first entry regarding the program in his monthly progress report dated June 2, 1964: "A reduction in power plant weight has been effected by use of aluminum and magnesium parts." In his progress report of July 29, 1964, he wrote: "The first aluminum cylinder head was cast on July 24. The cast was almost perfect with only one small area of porosity. Changes to eliminate this porosity are being made. Additional castings will be made on July 28 and July 29, 1964."

In August 1964 the lightweight 426 Hemi engine program officially received the A990 designation. The new parts included aluminum cylinder heads, oil-pump body, oil-pump cover, water-pump housing, water-outlet elbow and alternator bracket. The intake manifold was cast in magnesium. The aluminum heads were first cast by Alcoa and later by various small foundries around the country, one of which was Ross Foundry in Ohio. The magnesium intake manifold was cast in California and the machining was performed by Keith Black.

Other changes for the A990 Hemi included increasing the exhaust branch manifold outside diameter from 1.88 to

Miss Chrysler Crew *was an unlimited hydroplane powered not by the usual Rolls-Royce or Allison aircraft engine but by two supercharged 426 Hemis. The boat was campaigned by Bill Sterett in the late sixties.* Chrysler

2.00 in., and the switch from Carter to Holley carburetors.

In his progress report dated August 25, 1964, Weertman announced the production schedule: "The production volume of this engine will be 210. The production build schedule is: First Car—11-16-64; Last Car—1-8-65."

After the first A990 was run by the dyno lab, only four minor changes were necessary for production to begin. These were use of copper head gaskets instead of steel, thicker head bolt washer, longer head bolts to accommodate the thicker washers and increased length of the chrome plating on the valve stems.

The A990 Hemi was installed in some of the wildest factory-built drag cars ever offered by a major car manufacturer. The most radical Chrysler offer-

ing to date was built for the Altered/Factory Experimental and Ultra/Stock classes. Dodge shortened the wheelbase of its Coronet by moving the front wheels and rear axle forward for vastly improved weight transfer. The hood, doors and trunk lid were made of fiberglass. Dick Landy was among many of the drag-racing greats who bought and raced these cars.

"Those cars," Mancini recalls of the A/FX drag cars, "turned out to be a little bit too light. We had taken a lot of strength out of the car when it was acid-dipped and as a result, on a very hard acceleration you could actually bend the car. So we had to go through another program to strengthen the car with a rollcage and a couple of bars underneath."

With Chrysler absent from the high-banked ovals for the first half of 1965, Bill France was once again faced with a dominant factory presence—in this case, Ford. He contacted Henry Banks, director of competition for USAC. The outcome of their discussions was a NASCAR bulletin released to the press on June 15. The joint agreement covered rule changes affecting both sanctioning

bodies for the remainder of 1965 and 1966. The rule changes pertaining to NASCAR were: "(1) A minimum weight limit of 9.36 lbs. per cubic inch of displacement for a car ready to run with a full load of fuel, oil, and water. For example: a car with a 427 cubic inch engine must weigh 4000 lbs. (2) The Hemi engine will be permitted on NASCAR tracks of over one mile in the 1965 Dodge 880, and 1965 Dodge Polara. All 1964 Dodges competing on these tracks must use the wedge-type engine. (3) The Hemi engine will be permitted in the Plymouth Belvedere and the Dodge Coronet on all USAC and NASCAR tracks of one mile and less and road courses."

France and Banks also announced that in 1966 a joint committee composed of USAC and NASCAR officials would categorize all American production cars. The four categories were standard, intermediate, compact and sports. For 1966, intermediate-size cars, such as the Plymouth Belvedere and Dodge Coronet, would be permitted to race on oval circuits of more than one mile with a 405 ci limit. In a statement that seemed directed at the Chrysler 426 Hemi and

Ford sohc 427, Banks said, "One of the objectives of the committee will be to eliminate the high cost/low volume engine from competition."

This was a moot point. Chrysler had already decided to make the 426 Hemi available in Dodge and Plymouth passenger cars for 1966. Consequently, the Hemi wasn't eliminated from competition, but it did have to conform to the displacement-reduction rule.

To meet these new rules, Chrysler started the A117 program. This Hemi had a shorter 3.558 in. stroke requiring a new crankshaft and longer connecting rods with 7.174 in. center to center. Displacement was 404 ci. To offset the inevitable loss of power, the two key areas studied were the intake manifold and camshaft timing.

Hemi Variants

John Wehrly joined Chrysler in 1962 and the Ramchargers shortly thereafter. After working in the area of engine cooling, he moved on to the engine development lab. In 1971, he became race engine development supervisor. The intake manifold for the 1966 404 ci circle-track Hemi was a new approach involving extensive development.

"We developed a single four-barrel manifold we called the Bathtub manifold because it dipped down in the center," Wehrly says. "The purpose was to get the hood clearance down and still have the length of the runners we needed. The longer runners in that type of intake manifold were a real challenge—to have a manifold that had good driveability because of all the sharp angles and the fact that the air had to twist through the manifold. We did a great deal of work on that design, looking at dozens and dozens of manifolds."

The camshaft was even more radical than the one used in the A864. Intake and exhaust duration was now 328 deg., with 112 deg. of overlap and 0.565 in. of lift.

A number of variations of the 426 Hemi were pursued by Chrysler which never saw production. One of the first was a spin-off of the A990 program called the 300 Hemi. This was a serious consideration to provide the Chrysler 300 Letter Series luxury sport sedan with Hemi engine power in addition to its Wedge engine. Since the engine would be somewhat detuned for street use, the block and bearing cap structure would

be made more like the production 440 Wedge engine. This would make it easier to produce at the Trenton Engine Plant.

In a November 2, 1964, program memo, Weertman described the proposed 300 Hemi alongside the A990 Hemi. This engine had a larger 4.32 in. bore with the same 3.75 in. stroke, resulting in 440 ci. The block was to forgo the lengthy and expensive heat treatment and would not have the cross-bolt main-bearing caps, opting for the less-expensive standard two-bolt main-bearing caps. Other concessions for the street included a 268 deg. hydraulic camshaft, single instead of double valve springs and new, less costly exhaust headers. The hot induction setup included three two-barrel Carter carbs on an aluminum intake manifold—a precursor to the Six-Pak that would appear in 1969. Effort was made to install an air-conditioning compressor on the engine. Sadly, the 300 Hemi remained a proposal and nothing more.

Another race Hemi design was the A148. On December 2, 1965, a Performance Planning Letter initially requested a variant of the A864 with a larger 4.363 in. bore and shorter 3.558 in. stroke to allow for the use of larger valves. Intake valves were 2.44 in. in diameter and the exhaust valves were 2.06 in. Longer valve springs were used to permit greater valve lift. Flow testing of the prototype cylinder head early in 1966 proved this design flowed better than the A864 but not as well as the double-overhead-cam A925. Both iron and aluminum cylinder heads were procured for this 426 Hemi. Engines were built and tested, but says Wehrly, "What we really found was that so much development was required to get the same reliability that we didn't pursue it any further."

Dyno Testing: "Good Luck Guys"

The pace of Hemi design development and testing throughout the sixties never slackened, as Chrysler worked to keep up with the ever-changing NASCAR rulebook and performance gains by its competition. Ted Flack joined Chrysler in 1967 and landed a job that 426 Hemi enthusiasts dreamed about.

"I was 20 years old and wanted to go racing. I figured if I could get into a car company, I could learn more—the se-

crets of this engine stuff," he remembers. "So I walked into personnel and asked, 'Have you got any openings for mechanics?' And they said, 'Yes. We have one here in the dynamometer section.' They brought me around and walked up and down the dyno buildings. They were running a couple of Hemis—racing engines. I felt like a kid in a candy store.

"When I was working there, there were six guys in the motor room just building Hemi engines. Many times we'd put an engine on a dyno stand while the paint was still wet. Then, after a power run, we'd have to back off to deliver it to somebody for a race and the engine would still be hot when we loaded it onto a truck. When they would ship engines for a race, they would write notes on top of the manifold like, 'Good Luck Guys.' When it came time for the race, the guys down there would send up reference charts, so we knew which engine was in which car and the guys here who built it would know which car actually had his engine."

The dyno labs literally performed destructive testing on the 426 Hemi to learn its limits as well as confirm performance. Explosions were unpredictable because of the test cycle and the number of hours on an engine. When a Hemi finally came apart under the most grueling test conditions, the results were spectacular.

"We had them blow up," Flack recalls, "where there was nothing on the stand—the crankshaft would be on the floor, the heads blown off into the corner. One fellow here had a picture where one engine actually sawed itself in half. The back half was gone and the front half was hanging there by the radiator hose. There are holes in the ceiling down there still to this day.

"The back side of the dyno cell used to be all windows. When we'd run the engines, the headers would glow red. A lot of guys would stand and look in the windows to see what we were doing, sometimes with their face pressed against the glass. It wasn't really safe because you never knew what was going to happen. One day, we shut down the engine, went outside and told the guy, 'We don't want you standing right by the window.' He left, we brought the engine back up to speed—about 7000 rpm. Thirty seconds later the engine blew up. Complete connecting rods went through the window right where he had been standing. One landed out in the driveway, still sizzling, and burned a hole down into the asphalt."

When NASCAR tightened the screws again requiring a restrictor plate using 1⅛ in. bores, the dyno lab was crucial in surmounting this supposed problem.

"We came up with a venturi-effect spacer about two inches high," Flack says, "and actually made more power with it than we did without it—about fifteen more horsepower."

Power gains came from new camshafts with ever-increasing valve lifts that were possible with the higher valve springs that had been started with the A148 program. It was also decided to change from a chain-driven camshaft to a gear-driven camshaft to eliminate any camshaft rotational fluctuations caused by chain flexing.

A flat crankshaft was tried. The theory was to improve power by always alternating exhaust pulses from one bank to the other rather than having adjacent cylinders fire, as is the case with a conventional V–8 crankshaft. The problem was that the engine was no longer in balance and the secondary forces shook the engine. There was so much trouble with bolts loosening and parts breaking that it was finally decided that the power gains, if any, weren't worth it.

The 1968 Super Stock Cars

The most awesome application of the 426 drag Hemi came with the introduction of the 1968 Hemi Dart and Hemi Barracuda. The Woodward Avenue garage had seen some wild Hemi-powered prototypes built there, and conversations often drifted around the garage of stuffing the 426 Hemi into Chrysler's two smallest cars—the A Body Dodge Dart and Plymouth Barracuda—for use in Super Stock class drag racing.

"Dick Maxwell was a fundamental champion of the Hemi A Body," Hoover says. "I can remember at the time I argued that we should keep the Hemi in the B body because that's where we sold to people, but I'm glad that Dick prevailed because by many standards, they are the world's nastiest, meanest production cars that people could go out and buy."

The 1968 Super Stock program was the most ambitious Chrysler had under-

Dick Landy tests his new 1968 factory Super Stock Hemi Dart at Irwindale Raceway. Chrysler contracted with Hurst Performance to build seventy-five Dodge Darts and seventy-five Plymouth Barracudas powered by the 426 Hemi drag engine. Many of the surviving cars are still raced today. Dick Landy

The engine bay of Dick Landy's 1968 Super Stock Dodge Dart. The power-to-weight ratio of these cars permitted them to dominate their class for years. Dick Landy

311

As this photo shows, the mold for the twin-plug cylinder head was not modified to accept the second spark plug. Several machinings converted the single-plug head to the twin-plug design. Chrysler

taken up to that time, but the procedure for getting corporate approval and funding was the same as previous race-car programs.

"We usually had to get sales division approval to do something like this," Maxwell says. "The race group at that time was in product planning. The first thing we would do was go to the product planners and sign them up in supporting the program. Then, we'd go to our leader, Bob Rodger, and get him behind it, and then the sales divisions and sell them on it, which wasn't hard because there was so much enthusiasm for racing in those days and drag racing in particular because of the muscle-car boom. We were doing so well in that market. Once we had that done, it was a matter of scraping up money—which was sales division money—to pay for the program."

Since the Dodge Dart and Plymouth Barracuda had similar chassis and body dimensions and clearances, it was felt only one prototype needed to be built. A Barracuda was selected as the mule and shipped to the Woodward Avenue garage. Bob Tarrozi was the mechanic and engineer who first worked out all the calculations on paper, then went about extensively modifying the car to drastically reduce its weight while strengthening the car to deal with horsepower and torque levels the A-body was never designed to handle.

"That car," says Maxwell, "was the mule—the test car. Everything was worked out in that car, and the purchase order contract was let to Hurst Performance, which opened up a facility up in Hazel Park and built the cars for us."

Stock Barracudas and Darts were shipped to the Hurst facility where the cars were modified and the 426 drag Hemi installed according to Tarrozi's manual that had been compiled from the prototype. The cars were left in grey primer so the racers could add their own color scheme. Dodge and Plymouth cranked up the public relations mill, getting the word out about Chrysler's new drag cars.

"We had no trouble selling those cars," Maxwell remembers. "We originally scheduled fifty of each, and we had so many orders we went back and built twenty-five more. We built seventy-five of each. I don't remember what the prices were but they were pretty reasonable, and they could be ordered through the dealers."

The D Cylinder Head Program

During 1969 and 1970 Chrysler undertook a cylinder head refinement program to experiment with various aspects of design that affected intake and exhaust flow. All these heads retained the hemispherical combustion chamber, but the engineers experimented with a great many ideas; the most feasible, from a manufacturing standpoint, were designated for prototype or limited production for use on the racing engines. Hemi enthusiasts know these as the D heads.

The D1 cylinder head used the same diameter intake and exhaust valves but had larger ports. Each intake port had 3.00 sq-in and the exhaust port had 2.10 sq-in. Intake valve angle from cylinder bore centerline was 35 deg.; exhaust valve angle was 23 deg. This head was tested for the 426 race Hemi.

The D2 cylinder head was essentially the same as the D1 but used on the 429 ci displacement Hemi as permitted by NASCAR rules, using a 0.02 in. overbore. The lab engine with this setup was run in April of 1969, but the D2 program was canceled the following month because performance gains were not sufficient.

In his program report on the D3, Bill Weertman wrote, "The A864 D3 is the first of several cylinder heads designed to provide larger valves and increase flow, intake and exhaust ports." The valve angles had to be changed due to the new intake valve diameter of 2.38 in. with a 3.65 sq-in intake port, and an exhaust valve diameter of 2.00 in. with a 2.53 sq-in exhaust port. In addition, the cylinder bores had to be notched for intake valve clearance. Displacement remained at 426 ci. Two cylinder heads were prepared in March 1969, and the intake manifold modified to match the heads the following month. The first power run was made on May 9, 1969, but ironically, power was less than the D1 Hemi.

Between the D3 and the D4 cylinder head design was the D3.5. It used the large intake port of the D3 head and the exhaust port of the D4. The castings for this head were ordered in May 1969 and they were machined in the engine lab that September. No records of the flow results are available.

The original write-up for the D4 head was made May 12, 1969. In his program report for this cylinder-head design, Weertman wrote, "The A864 D4 design was made to investigate improvements for making the exhaust port higher with less curvature and with larger area." The head was ordered March 12, 1969, but the first power runs weren't made until May 1970. The 426 Hemi with D4 heads generated 641 hp on May 1, 1970.

The race group wanted to see what the D4 heads with a gear-drive camshaft would do on the Daytona Speedway, so the engine was put in the engineering test car and shipped to Daytona. The track had already been rented for May 12, 1970, just to test the car. Paul Bruns,

The 426 race Hemi was first offered in factory-built race cars in 1964. Dick Landy was among the first to get his hands on one of these cars, this one being a Dodge 330. This fully documented example is now owned by National Hemi Owners Association member Pete Haldiman. David Gooley

manager of the engineering race-car program, and Bill Weertman were there. The car ran a lap at 191.172 mph, which was a boost of almost 3 mph over runs with a prior engine.

The D5 cylinder head was probably

Dick Landy spared no expense to make this car as light as possible. Body panels were acid-dipped and frame members were drilled to reduce weight further. These steps, combined with the best production drag-racing engine ever designed and Landy's driving skill, made him one of the most successful racers in the sixties. David Gooley

the most famous of all. This was a cast-aluminum twin-spark-plug design that incorporated all the improvements in the D4 design. The twin-plug feature aided flame propagation. This cylinder head actually saw limited production for use by 426 Hemi drag-racing enthusiasts.

There were other cylinder head variations on the 426 Hemi. One of the last investigated was the D20 Magna

design. In his progress report on this design, Weertman wrote, "The D20 'Magna' was a design study to provide extra large ports and valves. In order to avoid a long, high inertia rocker arm, a two-piece pushrod was devised connecting with a small tappet in the cylinder head." The D20 had a 4.00 sq-in intake port with a 2.50 in. diameter intake valve, positioned 31 deg., 45 min. from cylinder bore center. The exhaust port had a 2.60 sq-in cross section with a 2.20 in. diameter exhaust valve set at 36 deg. from the cylinder bore center. With this valve geometry, the head was wider, requiring larger cylinder-head covers. The aluminum version of this design was the D21. Work progressed from its first write-up in November 1968 until May 1969, when the program was canceled

The interior of the 1964 Dick Landy drag car has been beautifully restored. The red and black interior contrasts handsomely with the car's silver paint. David Gooley

Next page
The 1964 factory drag-race cars were originally equipped with magnesium wheels. Today, those wheels have been replaced by aftermarket pieces. Bigger, fatter tires have required altering the rear suspension for proper clearance. David Gooley

There was no column shift in the big Chryslers in 1964 because the corporation was exploring the wonderful world of push-button transmissions! It was a moot point in a car like this, since Landy let the TorqueFlight do the job all by itself. David Gooley

316

Even more fearsome than the 1964–1965
factory drag cars were the Super Stock
Plymouth Barracudas and Dodge Darts built
in 1968. These cars were conceived by
Ramcharger member Dick Maxwell. The
prototype was executed by the able men at
Chrysler's Woodward Avenue garage and
the cars were built by Hurst Performance.
The Barracudas, like this one, are more
frequently seen today than the Darts. David
Gooley

Two generations of factory race Hemi drag cars: Dick Landy's original 1964 car and the 1968 Super Stock Barracuda. These truly are historic quarter-mile machines. David Gooley

due to yet another sudden rule change by NASCAR.

That rule change ended further 426 Hemi development and production for racing. The rule change was a result of the exotic, aerodynamic body designs that hit the high-banked ovals in 1969 and 1970. For Chrysler, greater performance gains were achieved through aerodynamics than by further horse-power development. The first Mopar to reflect this thinking was the Charger 500, followed by the Dodge Daytona and then the Plymouth Superbird. Once again, Bill France put the brakes on these and other aero stock cars by requiring a maximum displacement of 305 ci powering them. This rule was to take effect for the 1971 season. This was too drastic a change to make altering the Hemi worthwhile.

"Actually, the manufacturing of the [race] Hemi stopped before the racing," Wehrly says. "The last batch of iron heads were cast around 1970. The last aluminum heads were cast in the early seventies."

Although production had ceased, Chrysler continued to offer technical support to the thousands of devoted 426 Hemi racers. Keith Black, Milodon and others took up the 426 Hemi and offered it in aluminum. A new generation of Hemi enthusiasts was guaranteed to continue the 426 Hemi's long, record-setting history.

Next page
Factory Super Stock cars were finished in a primer grey and owners painted their cars after taking delivery. This Super Stock Barracuda has been painted a pale yellow. When first raced, it was covered by sponsor decals. David Gooley

Previous page
The incredible speed with which the 426 race Hemi was conceived, designed, tested and built makes the enduring success of the Super Stock Barracuda and Dart even more amazing. After a quarter of a century of competition, these cars are still virtually unbeatable in their class. David Gooley

James Hylton, number 42, charges through turn 9 at Riverside, California, in his 426 Hemi-powered Superbird. The aerodynamic Plymouth Superbird and Dodge Daytona signaled the twilight of the 426 Hemi in NASCAR events. Chan Bush

Ed Miller of Rochester, New York, traveled across America to compete in the NHRA Winternationals at Pomona, California, with his Hemi Plymouth Super Stock. Chan Bush

The Ramchargers pioneered the use of
superchargers on the 426 Hemi, and every
other drag racer soon followed suit. Chan
Bush

The 426 Hemi was campaigned by the
Ramchargers into the seventies. Here,
Leroy Goldstein pilots his 1971 Challenger
funny car. Chan Bush

Sox & Martin were among the most familiar names in drag racing in the sixties and seventies with their red-and-white 426 Hemi Plymouths. Here, Ronnie Sox is behind the wheel of their 1971 Hemi 'Cuda, racing in Pro Stock at Pomona, California. Chan Bush

Judy Lilly raced Miss Mighty Mopar in SS/AA. The Plymouth 426 Hemi Super Stock factory drag car remains the high-water mark in a long line of Chrysler race cars for the quarter-mile. Chan Bush

426 Street Hemi

Ruling the Road 1966–1971

The factory rating for the street Hemi of 425
horsepower was right on. When we did a scuff test,
we'd fire up a green engine—no hours on it—and
run it at max horsepower for two hours. Those
things made 425 horsepower like clockwork.

—Ted Flack

For years, automotive enthusiast magazines have stated the 426 street Hemi was offered for sale to meet minimum production requirements by NASCAR and other sanctioned racing organizations. This is partly true, but other factors were involved in turning the 426 Hemi loose on American streets.

Early on, Chrysler looked into offering the 426 Hemi in passenger cars during the 300 Hemi program. To make the 426 street Hemi affordable, expensive steps in the engine's manufacture were to be deleted and modifications made to civilize the Hemi for street use. But the proposal went no further.

The idea of putting the 426 Hemi in street cars was not as outrageous an idea at the time as one might first believe. It was, after all, the performance era, and every car manufacturer was offering high-performance, large-displacement engines—some with multiple carburetion—in their passenger cars. Chrysler had offered Hemi-head engines in their cars before, and they were touted for their greater performance compared to Ford and General Motors. For 1964, Chrysler offered a new 365 hp 426 Wedge in its Dodge and Plymouth models, and the 426 race Hemi was offered in

When a dark paint scheme was ordered on a 1970 Hemi 'Cuda, the graphic identification was white, above. Left, in 1970, only 72 Plymouth GTXs with the optional 426 Hemi were built. David Gooley

those Dodges and Plymouths for sanctioned drag racing.

In light of all this, it is easier to understand Chrysler's decision to detune the 426 race Hemi and make it an option in select models. What Chrysler perhaps did not know is that the 426 street Hemi was destined to become the most desirable high-performance engine ever bolted into a passenger car.

During the latter months of 1964, product planning meetings were held by Chrysler management to discuss the feasibility of offering the 426 Hemi in their cars. On January 6, 1965, Bob Rodger, special car manager and chief engineer, and Robert Cahill issued a Product Planning Letter with the title: "Hemi Performance Option Super Stock and 'A' Stock Competition." It was specifically addressed to J. C. Guenther, manager of Styling Administration and H. R. Steding, executive engineer of Engineering Administration. The models affected were 1966 model-year Plymouth and Dodge B Series cars with B and C Bodies. This letter was actually a change to an earlier performance engine proposal and gave the following description of change:

"Because of continued requirements for an ultimate performance drag

5. Pistons—Forged acceptable and thermally controlled preferred.

6. Manifolding and camshaft to be designed to give best high speed power possible while still maintaining a reasonably drivable vehicle for summer and winter.

7. Automatic and four-speed [manual] transmissions required (4–speed to have development priority).

8. No air conditioning required for 'B' Series.

9. Limited warranty is acceptable for 'B' Series usage."

Projected production volume stated in the letter was 5,000 to 7,500 cars, to take effect for the 1966 model year. The letter closed with this statement: "This engine to replace eight barrel wedge requested in Product Planning Letter . . . dated 8/5/64."

With the release of the January 6, 1965, Product Planning Letter, events moved quickly to make the 426 street Hemi a reality. On January 12, 1965, W. J. Bradley issued a product description of the street Hemi, now having the designation A102. It listed all the preliminary findings of additional changes that had to be made to the 426 race Hemi for use in street cars.

Race Hemi in Street Clothing

The only changes to the cylinder block anticipated were mounting lugs on the side of the block for engine mounts in C-bodies, and some machining of the mounting areas.

The crankshaft was identical to the drag-race Hemi, made of SAE 1046 carbon steel and Tufftrided. It would be fitted with a heavy inertial vibration damper.

While the connecting rods were the same as those in the A990 Hemi, the pistons were new forgings designed to produce 10.25:1 compression ratio, so that the engine could run on extra-premium fuel available at many service stations. This piston was a floating-pin design that incorporated a bushing in the small end of the connecting rod.

The camshaft, of necessity, had to be designed to develop the power expected, yet make the car drivable for street use. Intake and exhaust valve duration was 276 deg. with 52 deg. of overlap. Lift for both valves, according to the SAE paper published by Weertman and Lechner in April 1966, was 0.46 in. The camshaft drive used the same

Willem L. Weertman posing with the 426 street Hemi in April 1966 when he presented the SAE paper co-authored with Bob Lechner. Chrysler

strip, and street type engine with expanded usage, the following change in the engine lineup has been agreed upon after discussion with the affected areas.

Please release a hemispherical combustion chamber engine for 'B' Series with the following general characteristics:

1. Intake manifold to have two four-barrel carburetors.

2. Cylinder block to maintain cross tie bolt main bearing caps.

3. Cast iron exhaust manifold.

4. Solid lifters are acceptable but not preferred.

This was the stuff of which mighty Mopars were made. The Plymouth GTX was among the mightiest, and with the 426 Hemi it was as comfortable on the quarter-mile strip as it was on the street. This car is owned by Ken Funk of Los Angeles, California. David Gooley

Identification on the 1970 GTX extended to the sides of the car over the bogus scoops. There was no 426 Hemi identification on the sides of the car when that engine option was ordered. David Gooley

The performance styling of the 1970 GTX was subdued, with no clear visible markings revealing the fact that a 426 Hemi was under the hood. When the accelerator was floored, the Air Grabber hood scoop would pop up out of the hood. David Gooley

With the hood of the 1970 GTX raised and the air cleaner removed, the inline dual four-barrel carburetors commanded attention. The Plymouth fresh-air induction system was called the Air Grabber. The operating components of the Air Grabber system can be seen under the hood. David Gooley

Next page
From a distance, there was no indication to the unwary that a 426 Hemi lurked under the hood of this Dodge Coronet R/T. Chrysler Corporation had a way of turning its standard passenger cars into muscle cars with the use of striking exterior and interior colors and scoops to drive home the performance message. When the light turned green, the Hemi took over. David Gooley

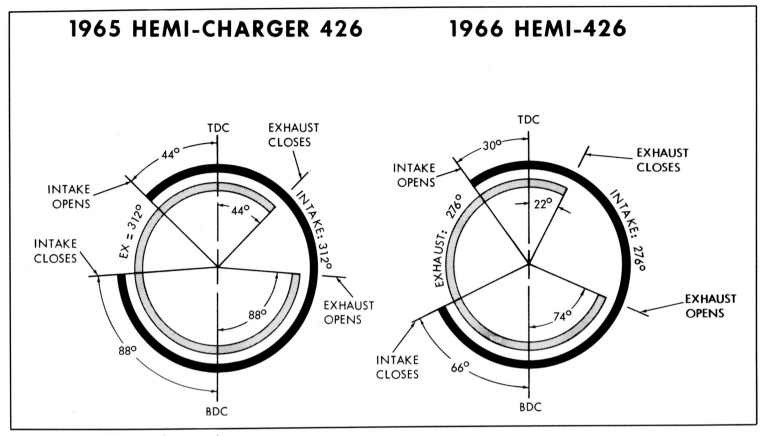

1965 HEMI-CHARGER 426

TDC

INTAKE OPENS

44°

EXHAUST CLOSES

EX = 312°

44°

INTAKE: 312°

INTAKE CLOSES

88°

EXHAUST OPENS

88°

BDC

1966 HEMI-426

TDC

INTAKE OPENS

30°

EXHAUST CLOSES

EXHAUST: 276°

22°

INTAKE: 276°

INTAKE CLOSES

74°

EXHAUST OPENS

66°

BDC

Camshaft timing differences between the 1965 racing Hemi and the 1966 street Hemi.
Chrysler

double-roller timing chain as the race Hemi. The 1964–1965 racing engines originally used a single $\frac{7}{16}$–14 screw to bolt the camshaft sprocket to the camshaft, but this was changed to three $\frac{3}{8}$–16 screws for both racing Hemis and the new street Hemi.

The valves, rocker arms, mechanical lifters and pushrods were from the A864 race Hemi, but the valve spring rates were lowered to avoid premature wear and limit engine rpm to keep rated output to the desired 425 hp.

The cast-aluminum intake manifold was a dual-plane design to use two Carter AFB four-barrel carburetors mounted inline. The front carburetor was model

A pre-production 426 street Hemi was fitted to a partial chassis in Chrysler engineering to check for clearances and possible interference problems. The valve covers on this engine do not yet have the black crackle-paint finish that would appear on production street Hemis.
Chrysler

The magnificent 1971 Hemi 'Cuda. The Hemi went out with a bang, with huge billboard graphics announcing to those with bad eyesight that ol' King Kong was under the hood. Chrysler

A TorqueFlight automatic transmission is shown bolted to a pre-production 426 street Hemi in a full chassis. Note the front suspension torsion bars. Chrysler

number 4139S. The rear carburetor was model number 4140S and, unlike the front carb, was provided with exhaust manifold heat to facilitate engine warm-up. The right-hand exhaust manifold was fitted with two aluminized steel tubes to divert hot exhaust gases to a chamber in the floor of the intake manifold at the base of the rear carburetor to achieve quicker and smoother engine warm-up. A heat control valve on the exhaust manifold would shut off the exhaust gases to the intake manifold when the engine was sufficiently warm. A special heat shield was bolted to the underside of the intake manifold to keep engine oil from contacting the heated chamber.

The only changes to the cylinder heads were those necessary to accept the new, streamlined cast-iron exhaust manifolds; these manifolds were designed to have a long service life, as the racing exhaust manifolds, made of steel tubes and cast-iron flanges, were noisier and not as durable.

To keep the 426 street Hemi properly lubricated under all street conditions, there was a new, deep oil pan with baffles. An 8 in. wide hat-section member was welded onto the chassis cross-member; this acted as a skid to protect the oil pan from damage by road obstructions. The oil pump had a larger, ⅝ in. diameter suction hole and tube.

Unlike the chrome valve covers on the racing Hemis, the street Hemi would get valve covers finished in black crackle paint. The covers had to be modified with new depressions for body drop and running clearance.

The street Hemi would have a new air cleaner and cover. It used a huge 18 in. diameter, 2 in. high paper element. As originally specified in the W. J. Bradley letter, the air cleaner was to have a black crackle-paint finish to match the valve covers, but by the time the 1966 street Hemi made its appearance, the air cleaner cover was chrome plated.

To ensure the Hemi remained cool-running, it was fitted with a high-speed water pump having a small impeller, and used a special drive belt having greater stretch resistance at high engine speeds.

It was fully anticipated that street Hemis would see a lot of competition at

the drag strip, so special front and rear engine mounts having higher rates would be fitted in Hemi-equipped cars.

The street Hemi was to be offered with either four-speed manual or three-speed automatic transmission. The competition four-speed manual transmission was modified in a number of ways for street/strip use. A new cast-iron clutch housing was made for use with new 11 in. discs. The pressure plate was made from pearlitic malleable iron. The clutch cover and release lever were made from thicker, 0.14 in. stock steel, and wear strips were placed behind the centrifugal rollers. A new flywheel-and-ring-gear assembly was bolted to the crankshaft using eight bolts. This four-speed manual transmission designation was A833.

The automatic transmission was a heavy-duty A727 version TorqueFlight. It would use a 10¾ in. high-stall-speed converter, with a governor moving the shift points up to 5500 rpm under maximum acceleration. This transmission used five discs, instead of the four used in the standard TorqueFlight. The second gear band was increased from 2.00 to 2.50 in.

Vehicle Modifications to Accept the 426 Hemi

Due to the size of the 426 Hemi, the right front shock absorber tower in the B Bodies required modifications. The power brake-cylinder booster had to be moved to clear the valve cover. However, according to Bradley's letter, the booster would have to be removed entirely for removal of the number-seven spark plug or the valve cover for valve adjustment. The left valve cover was modified to clear the battery and battery tray. Also, on C-bodies, a dash panel depression was required to clear the right valve cover.

Due to the air cleaner's size, the hood hinge torsion bar position and support bracket had to be modified. On B Bodies, the dash panel in the area of the heater motor depression required a change for proper valve cover clearance, and the heater hose routing and fittings had to be changed, also for valve cover clearance.

Electrical wiring needed to be changed too. It was thought that shielding of the starter wiring harness might be needed. Manual transmission cars required a remote-mounted starter sole-

noid necessitating special wiring.

Finally, underneath the car would be a new dual exhaust system designed for the 426 Hemi. It used 2½ in. exhaust pipes running to canister mufflers, with 2¼ in. outlets.

On January 29, 1965, a powerplant memo was released. It consolidated previous letters and memos regarding the street Hemi and authorized appropriate design and drafting to begin. Titled "Chassis–Powerplant Design Release Memo," it affected all bodystyles except station wagons. Under "Action To Be Taken" the memo read:

"Approval has been given Product Planning's request for the release of a new 426 cu. in., 2-4 bbl., Hemi-head street package for 'B' and 'C' Series. The 'B' Series package has been designated as the A102 program and will be offered as a special equipment engine option on all 'B' Series Belvedere, Coronet, Plymouth, and Dodge models except station wagons. Because of the timing involved, this engine option is to be handled as a late product package."

This meant that production of cars with Hemi engines would begin later than the normal start of model-year production in August.

The memo continued: "The 'C' Series version (i.e., 1967 model year) of this street package has been designated as the A103 program and usage will be expanded to include Chrysler sedan models. In addition, several engine revisions such as the incorporation of hydraulic tappets and thermal-controlled cast pistons are intended, and air conditioning is desired for 'C' Series 'B' and 'C' Bodies."

The memo clearly stated that at that phase of product planning, it was envisioned Chrysler would offer the street

The left side of the 426 street Hemi had the greatest number of interferences. The brake booster had to be moved and the valve cover required a detent to clear the battery. In addition, the left exhaust manifold had to be designed to clear the power steering. Chrysler

Plymouth designers never missed a chance to have some fun when they had the opportunity. The Air Grabber graphic on the sides of the pop-up hood scoop is just one example. They took performance seriously but not too seriously. David Gooley

The only Hemi identification on the 1970 GTXs so-equipped was the word Hemi at the back of the hood bulge, facing the driver. David Gooley

339

This production 426 street Hemi on a display stand shows the system to provide exhaust manifold heat to the intake manifold using heat riser tubes, and heat control valve to provide faster warm-up and smoother operation. Chrysler

Hemi package as an option in full-size Dodge, Plymouth and even Chrysler cars. During the early months of 1965, this was dramatically scaled back. It was decided to initially offer the 426 Hemi in the new Dodge Charger and the Plymouth Satellite for 1966.

With the introduction of the street Hemi, the famous Maximum Performance Package race Hemi cars that had been offered in 1964 and 1965 would be canceled. This made sense because the new street Hemi could be raced stock or modified to compete in the class desired by the racer.

In September 1965, the Chrysler Corporation Engineering Office issued a publication titled, "Chrysler Corporation's 'Hemi-426' for 1966." It was meant to give a complete description of the street Hemi in response to countless requests from magazine editors, newspapers and interested individuals. In

part, the publication read, "Because of the increased demand and popularity, the hemi-head engine is now available as a regular production option for 1966 Plymouth Belvedere and Dodge Coronet. Belvederes powered by this high performance option are identified by the emblem 'HP2' on the fenders, Coronets by the '426 Hemi' medallion."

Initially, the HP2 emblem on 1966 Hemi-powered Plymouths raised the obvious question, What does it mean? It meant High Performance Plymouth. While the Dodge medallion was to the point and self-explanatory, the Plymouth badge was curiously vague. After several months' production, the HP2 medallion was replaced by the 426 Hemi emblem.

A supplement to this publication dated November 22, 1965, listed some changes and recommendations. The TorqueFlight-equipped Hemi cars now received a supplementary oil cooler mounted ahead of the main radiator to cool the transmission fluid. Optional front disc brakes were still in the works and would be available as a factory-installed option soon. The supplement went on to give recommended oil, and the changing interval for both engine oil and transmission fluid.

Building the 426 Street Hemi

The 426 street Hemi was assembled at Chrysler's Marine and Industrial division in Marysville, Michigan. The street Hemi went through its own pre-production testing program almost as tortuous as the race Hemi. These tests were run to verify its rated output and determine its durability.

Horsepower ratings of the day were always the topic of conversation and speculation. The enthusiast magazines debated where a given engine was grossly overrated or deliberately conservative. It turned out the factory rating of the 426 street Hemi was literally truth in advertising.

"The factory rating for the street Hemi of 425 horsepower was right on," Ted Flack recalls from his days in the dynamometer labs. "When we did a scuff test, we'd fire up a green engine—no hours on it—and run it at max horsepower for two hours. Those things made 425 horsepower like clockwork."

To enthusiasts familiar with the racing Hemi, the beauty of the street Hemi was knowing the engine underwent the identical manufacturing and assembly procedures as the circle-track and drag-racing engines. This had to be the case because the 426 Hemi Dodges and Plymouths now available in Chrysler showrooms truly were street/strip machines. Chrysler could not afford to suffer reliability problems with this engine which had achieved such notoriety in NASCAR, NHRA, AHRA and USAC competition. It had to uphold the Hemi's racing heritage. Chrysler maintained this level of excellence by constant quality control.

"I remember when that engine went to the Marine & Industrial area," Oscar Willard says. "We had continuous checking for them. From every batch of blocks they received over the years from the foundry they would usually send one or two of them into Highland Park, strain gauge them, then cut them up with a big bandsaw into minute pieces to determine residual stress level in that batch of blocks."

Selling the 426 Street Hemi

With all the excitement surrounding introduction of the 426 street Hemi, the automotive magazines couldn't wait to get their hands on a 426 Hemi Charger, Coronet, Belvedere or Satellite. *Car Life* was one of the premier high-performance car magazines during the muscle-car era and tested a Hemi-powered 1966 Plymouth Satellite with Torque-Flight automatic transmission. The performance figures were 0–60 mph in 7.1 sec. and the quarter-mile was covered in 14.5 sec. at 95 mph. However, a 1966 Plymouth Satellite powered by a 325 hp 383 ci V–8 bolted to a TorqueFlight was just as quick to 60 mph. It was only at the end of the quarter-mile that the Hemi showed its abilities. In elapsed time, the Hemi-powered Plymouth was the fastest car that *Car Life* tested in 1966. But clearly, the Hemi was hamstrung with Blue Streak street tires and a closed exhaust system.

Next page
The Plymouth Road Runner was one of the most clever and memorable cars from the muscle-car era. It was meant to be a low-buck performance car and came standard with a 383 Magnum V–8. However, if cost was no object, you could order the optional 426 Hemi. This one is from 1969. Musclecar Review

A production 426 Hemi bolted to a Chrysler heavy-duty four-speed manual transmission. Dipstick was thermally shielded to protect it from exhaust manifold heat. Chrysler

Another view of the same engine. This photo shows the air cleaner with a matte silver finish. Production air cleaners would be chrome-plated. Chrysler

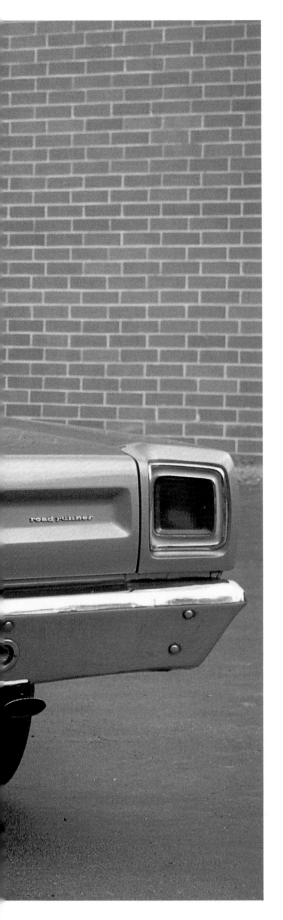

The Road Runner was, in fact, as close to the stock-car look as you could get at the time, typified by the exposed steel wheels with small hubcaps. Note the small Road Runner decal above the trunk lock. Musclecar Review

The Road Runner was based on the Belvedere, and the interior remained unchanged to keep the Road Runner affordable. The leather-wrapped steering wheel is not stock. Musclecar Review

This Road Runner's engine compartment is filled with the 426 Hemi and functional Air Grabber fresh-air hood. On Hemi-equipped Road Runners, there was a

unique Coyote Duster decal on the air-cleaner cover. The guys at Plymouth obviously had fun designing their performance cars. Musclecar Review

The 426 street Hemi received its namesake color: Hemi Orange. With its contrasting black engine pieces, it visually stated that it was all business. Chrysler

The 426 street Hemi truly was a racing engine in street clothing. The cross-bolt for the first main-bearing cap can be seen just above the oil pan. Chrysler

Bert Bouwkamp has an amusing story of a private test of a new Hemi-powered Coronet.

"When I was Chief Engineer for Dodge," Bouwkamp remembers fondly, "I got a request to host Tom McCahill of *Mechanix Illustrated* at the proving grounds with a 1966 Dodge Coronet Hemi convertible. This was to be a picture session. It wasn't to involve any high speeds, so there was no ambulance like we normally have. After driving it around and having pictures taken, Tom said he wanted to take it around the oval. He wanted the pictures to show just himself in the vehicle.

"So, his associate set up the camera and Bob Ludwig and I were standing on the side. The first time Tom came by we thought he was going pretty fast. The next time we knew he was wide open. He made three or four laps. Bob Ludwig was extremely upset, because this wasn't supposed to happen. But when the magazine came out, our public-relations people were really happy because there was a yellow band across the cover that read, 'Tom McCahill tests the world's fastest convertible at 144 miles per hour.' It was a wonder the top didn't blow off, it was ballooning so much."

Advertising for performance cars in the sixties was a genre that has not been duplicated since. Some of the most clever ad lines, ad copy and graphics made up the advertising of the era to draw the youthful buyer and the young at heart.

An ad promoting the 1966 Charger also featured the 426 Hemi. It pictured a Hemi-powered Charger at speed, with "Boss Hoss" and then a picture of the 426 Hemi below. The ad read in part, "Dodge Charger with a big, tough 426 Hemi up front makes other steeds look staid. Both for show and go. Charger looks beautifully quick just standing still. And the optional Hemi V-8 supplies a kick to match, with 425 muscular horses. Not a pony or a kitten in the bunch. The hot setup? You bet."

Over the next two years, *Car Life* tested two other Hemi-powered Mopars. In 1967, they tested a Boss Hoss Hemi Charger, again equipped with a TorqueFlight automatic transmission. The car reached 60 mph in 6.4 sec. and covered the quarter-mile in 14.2 sec. doing 96 mph through the timing lights. Top speed was 134 mph. The 1967 Hemi Charger had the lowest ET and the high-

A close-up photo of the 426 street Hemi induction system. The engine was rated at 425 hp at 5000 rpm—but 5000 rpm wasn't its redline! Chrysler

The 426 street Hemi as installed in a 1966 production car. The sound of those mechanical lifters in the morning was music to the Hemi-lover's ears. Chrysler

This photo of the engine compartment showed a different brake booster than the one used for the pre-production checkout at Chrysler engineering. Chrysler

This early production photo taken in the summer of 1965 showed the production chrome-plated air cleaner, but minus the 426 Hemi decal. Chrysler

est top speed of all the cars the magazine tested that year.

In 1968, *Car Life* tested a 426 Hemi Plymouth GTX. Performance was nearly identical to the Charger tested the year before. With TorqueFlight automatic transmission, the GTX took 6.3 sec. to reach 60 mph and covered the quarter-mile in 14.0 sec. doing 97 mph through the lights. Top speed was 144 mph.

In 1969, *Popular Hot Rodding* tested a pair of Chargers—one with a Torque-Flight and the other a four-speed manual transmission. The automatic car covered the quarter-mile in 14.01 sec. at 100 mph. By advancing the ignition and removing the air cleaner, the car reached the end of the quarter-mile in 13.75 sec. at 104 mph. The Hemi Charger equipped with the four-speed manual did much better. The ET was 13.60 sec. at 107.44 mph. And this was with a 3.23 Sure-Grip rear end and vehicle weight of more than 4,100 lb.!

In 1970 Chrysler rebodied the Plymouth Barracuda and introduced the new Dodge Challenger to the pony-car wars. Both of these handsome E-bodies were designed from the outset to accept the 426 Hemi. *Road Test* magazine tested a 1970 Challenger R/T with 426 Hemi, four-speed manual transmission and 4.10 Sure-Grip differential, for the June 1970 issue.

"It takes courage to specify the Hemi option in a Challenger," the editors wrote. "You must face a drive-train warranty foreshortened to six months, a whopping $1,227.50 increase in the $2,953 list for a basic Challenger V-8 to cover the Hemi and its mandatory related accessories, insurance and operating costs matched by no other U.S. nameplate except maybe a Hemi Plymouth and the certainty that no fuzz will let you pass by unnoticed.

"In return, you get power that can rattle dishes in the kitchen when you start it up in the driveway, extra attention in any service station, respect from owners of 428 Fords and SS427 Chevys, a measurable bonus in pride of ownership and immediate status as *the* car expert on your block."

Road Test recorded a quarter-mile ET of 14.0 sec. at 104 mph. In summary, the editors wrote, "If brute power over all other considerations is your forte, the Hemi is still boss on the street and if you'll note what most people put under

348

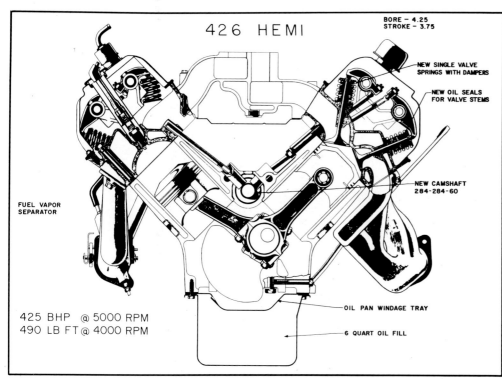

426 HEMI

BORE – 4.25
STROKE – 3.75

NEW SINGLE VALVE
SPRINGS WITH DAMPERS

NEW OIL SEALS
FOR VALVE STEMS

NEW CAMSHAFT
284-284-60

FUEL VAPOR
SEPARATOR

OIL PAN WINDAGE TRAY

6 QUART OIL FILL

425 BHP @ 5000 RPM
490 LB FT @ 4000 RPM

Peter Monteverdi was a Ferrari dealer based in Basel, Switzerland, who decided to construct his own series of sports cars and high-speed limousines. In 1969, he showed the prototype for his ultimate car, a mid-engined sports car built around a 426 Hemi, called the Hai 450 SS. Hai stood for "shark" in German; 450 stood for the horsepower Monteverdi was able to produce from the Hemi. With the mid-engine layout feeding the 490 lb-ft of torque to the rear tires through a five-speed ZF transaxle, the car was reported to accelerate from 0–60 mph in 4.9 sec. and top 175 mph. He planned to hand-build about one car per month, although in the end only three Hai 450 SS cars were constructed. Automobile Quarterly

Chrysler made numerous refinements in the 426 street Hemi for 1968. Chrysler

The 1966 Dodge Charger with optional 426 Hemi had to have muscle to back up its performance styling. You had to look fast to spot the 426 Hemi medallion on the front fenders. Chrysler

For those who wanted a lower profile than a Dodge Charger, you could order your 426 Hemi in a Dodge Coronet 500. This was a 1967 model. Chrysler

a supercharger in Top Fuel Eliminator, it's boss on the strip as well."

Perhaps the most distinctive Hemi-powered car Plymouth ever built was the Hemi 'Cuda, introduced in 1970. It wasn't a distinct model in the new 'Cuda line that year, but when you ordered the 426 Hemi in your 'Cuda it was identified as such on the standard shaker hood scoop with "hemicuda" on the sides of the scoop. The rear quarter panels received subdued graphics with the word Hemi as additional identification. It was the only Mopar during the 426 Hemi's production between 1966 and 1971 where Hemi was used in the name of the car. Despite being an option in the 'Cuda, the ads for the Hemi 'Cuda gave the implication of being a distinct model.

One ad showed a 1970 Hemi 'Cuda in a field of psychedelic-colored flowers. Then there was the famous Bob Grossman airbrush illustration of the Hemi 'Cuda that appeared as a two-page spread. The car was shown in caricature, a typical Grossman technique with the accompanying line: "The Rapid Transit Authority." The ad stated, "It's Hemi 'Cuda. Our angriest, slipperiest-looking body shell wrapped around ol' King Kong hisself." Not many supercar ads caught your attention like this one.

End of the Hemi Line

Few enthusiasts could foresee the end of the golden performance car era. Fewer still found out that 1971 would be the last year of the Chrysler 426 street Hemi. Those who read the industry journals learned of this and some of the enthusiast magazines hinted that the end might be near for all high-performance engines, but Chrysler wasn't about to admit it was stopping production of its most famous high-performance engine. Those who did see the handwriting on the wall and knew this would be their last chance to buy a street

When Dodge restyled the Charger for 1968, they also changed the Hemi medallion, dropping the 426. This was a 1969 Charger with optional 426 Hemi. Chrysler

Hemi prudently did so. And there were precious few 1971 street Hemi Dodges and Plymouths built.

Many Mopar enthusiasts in general and Hemi enthusiasts in particular wish they had had the wisdom—and the money—to walk into a Dodge or Plymouth showroom in the fall of 1970 to place an order for a 1971 Hemi-powered car. Better yet, to have ordered two—one to drive and the other to keep in storage with zero mileage, for true investment appreciation. But then, car collecting has always been this way. Certain cars are never thought of as collectible during their day, only years, perhaps decades, later.

Perhaps the most coveted Hemi Mopars in 1971 were the Hemi-powered Challenger and Hemi 'Cuda convertibles. Current owners love stating how few of their particular models were built. In fact, production numbers are some-

times an issue of heated debate and a matter of pride for the Hemi Mopar owner.

This raises the question of just how many 426 street Hemi Dodges and Plymouths were built between 1966 and 1971. Good estimates are between 10,000 and 12,000 cars.

It was perhaps best that Chrysler didn't attempt to put the 426 Hemi through an emasculating emissions certification program, but there were other pragmatic reasons for stopping production in 1971 as well.

"It was a matter of qualifying it for emissions," Tom Hoover says, "and the fact the insurance companies had come down hard on the people who were buying the cars at the time. It was prohibitive to own one, and the market dried up. If I had it to do over again, I would have used my influence to make it a single four-barrel engine in the street version instead of the eight-barrel version that was built."

Changes to the 426 Street Hemi

Throughout its six years of production, the 426 street Hemi's performance remained the same: 425 hp at 5000 rpm

with 490 lb-ft of torque at 4000 rpm. Had it remained in production beyond 1971, it would have suffered the same eventual fate as the other engines in Chrysler's line-up in particular and the auto industry in general. Tightening emissions controls and lower-octane unleaded gas forced the lowering of compression ratios, retarded ignition timing and conservative camshaft profiles. Government legislation of the automobile was forcing the de-emphasis of performance. It did not make fiscal or marketing sense to attempt to certify the 426 Hemi in the face of these realities, and 1971 was chosen as the last year of production.

Despite its steady power ratings over its six years, the 426 street Hemi did receive some modifications. The engine block remained unchanged until 1970, when a new block designed for supercharged and fuel-burning racing applications with heavier main webs and cylinder walls was introduced. According to Chrysler, all Hemi blocks with a casting date on the side of the block after January 19, 1970, had these improvements.

Plymouth introduced a new performance model for 1967—the GTX. The standard 440 ci V-8 could be deleted in place of the optional 426 Hemi. Identifying medallion was different from Dodge. Chrysler

Three different camshafts were used in the 426 street Hemi. For 1966 and 1967, the mechanical-lifter cam had 276 deg. of intake and exhaust duration with 0.46 in. lift. In 1968, Chrysler introduced enough changes to the 426 Hemi to call it Stage II. It included a camshaft with a longer duration of 284 deg. for both intake and exhaust, and a slightly higher lift of 0.47 in. The factory rating of the engine, however, remained unchanged.

Additional changes for the Stage II Hemi included single instead of double valve springs having 279.5 lb. spring pressure at 1.37 in., full rubber umbrella-type valve stem seals instead of the Teflon scraper-type, new Moly-filled piston rings, and a 6 qt. oil pan with windage tray.

In 1970, Chrysler introduced a hydraulic-lifter camshaft having the same specifications as the 1968 and 1969 mechanical cam to reduce maintenance. Interestingly, Chrysler did not do away with the adjustable rocker arms, but retained them. The hydraulic camshaft was carried over for 1971. Due to the new hydraulic lifters, new pushrods had to be designed. New springs were also used having 320 lb. pressure at 1.37 in. This engine is considered by some to be Stage III, and this Hemi is the most troublefree to maintain.

The Elephant Motor Reigns Supreme

Chrysler's decision to stop production with the 1971 model year had long-term positive effects. It retained for the Hemi an image of the ultimate street performance engine; all street Hemis were horsepower kings. Regardless of whether it was a 1966 Charger or a 1971 Hemi 'Cuda, each churned out 425 hp. Consequently, there were no 250 hp 426 street Hemis with anemic camshaft timing, wheezing through a single-exhaust system with catalytic converter.

The largest and most powerful beast to walk the face of the earth is the elephant, and for this reason the 426 street Hemi earned the nickname Elephant Motor. Ceasing production of the street Hemi in 1971 kept it that way. The

353

The tunnel rear window was used on all 1968–1970 Dodge Chargers except the Charger 500 and the Daytona. The second-generation Dodge Charger was one of the finest performance styling statements of the muscle-car era. Musclecar Review

The restored 426 Hemi of the 1970 B Body Charger R/T. Restoring a Hemi-powered Mopar is exacting work. Chrysler used numerous parts suppliers during the muscle-car era and so there are many variations in components from model to model and year to year. Debate still rages as to what component or finish may be accurate for a given model in a given year. Musclecar Review

This Hemi-powered Dodge Charger has Chrysler's beefy four-speed manual transmission with the terrific pistol-grip shifter. The design for the pistol-grip shifter was the brainchild of Chrysler's Bruce Raymond. For the Mopar enthusiast, it doesn't get any better than this. Musclecar Review

Hemi's bloodlines, so to speak, remained pure, untainted by any emissions-choked evolution.

Chrysler seriously looked into building a big-block for the seventies having Hemi heads with numerous modifications to reduce manufacturing costs and to comply with upcoming emissions standards. Known as the Ball-Stud Hemi to those working on the program, the A279 engine program was intriguing in its concept. The idea was to combine the hemispherical-combustion-chamber cylinder head with current B and RB cylinder blocks. It would feature a new, less-complicated valve actuation using ball-studs at each stamped-metal rocker arm, instead of the forged rocker arm and shaft.

The head-bolt pattern of the B and RB engines was to be retained. To literally get around this problem—the same one encountered when the 426 Hemi was being designed—the intake and exhaust valves were rotated around the hemisphere. This was a necessary compromise to achieve economical valve-train assembly.

The A279 Hemi actually reached the engineering prototype stage and several engines were built. The engines were tested in the dyno labs that were still running tests on the 426 Hemi. Output was disappointing at first, but it soon surpassed that of the 440 V–8, although it stopped short of the 426 street Hemi. This engine could have served a variety of large-displacement applications in Chrysler cars and trucks, without tarnishing the image of the 426 street Hemi, but the corporation decided not to approve production of the A279.

The void left by Chrysler when it ceased production of the 426 would eventually be picked up by the great names in racing engines and, two decades later, by Chrysler Corporation itself.

355

The owner of this 1970 Hemi Charger R/T chose wider aftermarket wheels to put more rubber on the road. For the stoplight grand prix, this is the way to go. Musclecar Review

Previous page
The 1970 Dodge Charger was the last year of this body design before changing for 1971. When you ordered the R/T, reverse-facing scoops were fitted over the scallops on the doors. No fresh-air hood was optional on the 1968–1970 Charger but one was available on the rebodied Charger for 1971. Musclecar Review

Plymouth released the Superbird in 1970. Based on the Road Runner, it used a similar nose and rear wing as the NASCAR stocker to permit Plymouth to race the car. Richard Petty raced his number 43 Superbird with great success. David Gooley

The standard engine in the Superbird was the Chrysler 440. The 426 Hemi was optional and the original owner of this car obviously made the right decision. No form of fresh-air hood scoop was available on the Superbird. Note the bold 426 Hemi sticker on the air-cleaner cover. David Gooley

The most awesome display of power
projection on the street during the sixties
was the 1969 Dodge Daytona. It turned
heads everywhere it was driven. Chrysler's
Larry Rathgeb was the chief engineer
behind the wind-tunnel testing that shaped
the Daytona. Musclecar Review

Previous page
This Daytona is fitted with the rare optional
aluminum wheels. The standard engine was
the 440 V–8. When the optional 426 Hemi
was ordered instead, a low-key medallion
was affixed to the doors between the
scallops. Musclecar Review

The interior of the Dodge Daytona was stock Charger. Nevertheless, it made a sporty, elegant statement. The TorqueFlight automatic transmission was superbly engineered to handle the mountains of torque put out by the 425 hp 426 Hemi. Musclecar Review

One of the most beautiful sights to the 426 Hemi enthusiast. On those 426 Hemi engines with the chrome air cleaner, this "426 Hemi Head 426" decal was affixed. Musclecar Review

A few Hemi 'Cudas were ordered with the optional factory rear-deck spoiler. This option was really more for show than function. Note the appropriate license plate. David Gooley

Identification under the hood on the Hemi 'Cuda took the form of lower-case letters on the sides of the Shaker hood scoop. It was low-key intimidation of the most subtle kind. Smart drivers pulling up next to one took the hint. David Gooley

364

In 1970, Plymouth redesigned the Barracuda, and a new era in Mopar muscle cars dawned. The E Body Barracudas and Dodge Challengers were an inspired combination of flowing lines and rawboned beauty. The Hemi 'Cudas took the look to the next stage with the Shaker hood scoop, hood pins, vinyl roof, rear-deck spoiler and hockey-stick Hemi graphics. David Gooley

The interior of the 'Cuda was unquestionably handsome. This car is equipped with the TorqueFlight automatic transmission. Driving a Hemi 'Cuda convertible was the ultimate in top-down cruising. It still is for a privileged few. Musclecar Review

The Shaker hood scoop was a much better system of fresh-air induction than the complex Air Grabber or Ramcharger designs on other Mopars. Here the Shaker has been removed, exposing the dual four-barrel carburetors with their staged linkage. Musclecar Review

The Ford Mustang launched the pony-car era in Detroit, but the most handsome embodiment of the period has to be the 1970 Plymouth Barracuda. The performance version was simply called 'Cuda. When the option 426 Hemi was ordered, it became the Hemi 'Cuda. Musclecar Review

Chrysler designed what was probably the best-looking hood scoop in the industry to go on its high-performance 'Cudas and Dodge Challengers. Chrysler coined the name Shaker for its hood scoop—and shake it did, particularly on top of the 426 Hemi. David Gooley

The Hemi Today

The Elephant Engine Lives On

The guy who has a Hemi race car sitting in his garage as well as the guy who has a Hemi car for restoration—this is where we obviously knew we had a market and that's why we did it.

—Larry Shepard

Through the sixties and seventies, both the first-generation Hemi and the 426 Hemi continued to be the most successful engines used in sanctioned drag racing. This continued success motivated aftermarket companies to offer parts for the 392 and 426 Hemi engines. Eventually, it became economically feasible for some firms to offer aluminum-block versions, and these engines took on new life.

Ed Donovan

During the 1950s, many racers felt the 392 Hemi was the best thing to ever happen to the sport. Despite being designed as a passenger-car engine, the largest first-generation Chrysler Hemi was horsepower-maker supreme. Many manufacturers produced parts for use with the 392 and its popularity continued into the sixties.

One of the true believers in the 392 Hemi's virtues was Ed Donovan. He had raced Ford flatheads in the forties. Later, he gained valuable engine-design experience working for Offenhauser. He continued racing and was drawn to drag racing in particular. He saw the need for stainless-steel valves that could endure the rigors of racing, and began machining them at home. Slowly, he branched out, making other parts, which con-

The Plymouth Road Runner Superbird was Plymouth's answer to Dodge's Charger Daytona, and again only a small number were fitted with the 426 street Hemi, above. Left, the Shaker hood scoop on a 1970 Hemi 'Cuda. Emissions controls and noise-limit regulations would doom such performance, but the Hemi lives on in the 1990s. David Gooley

sumed more of his time. In 1957, he left Offenhauser and opened Donovan Engineering to devote full time to his burgeoning business.

Racing was always the vehicle for producing and testing his parts to prove their durability and performance. In 1962, Donovan built a 270 ci blown Offenhauser dragster that reached 186 mph in the quarter-mile. Still, the small Offy was never designed for such applications, and Donovan looked to the big American V–8s for inspiration.

The Chrysler 392 Hemi had become a popular engine to use in drag racing, and Donovan produced parts for this engine to meet the demand. Despite the advent of the Chrysler 426 Hemi in 1964, the 392 Hemi continued to be a popular engine on the quarter-mile strip. Donovan felt the 392 Hemi could be improved upon but the cost of doing so was, at first, prohibitive.

By the end of the sixties, Donovan's performance parts business had grown rapidly, matching the explosion of drag racing's popularity. With his resources and manufacturing capability, Donovan could realistically consider filling a need for a truly durable engine based on the 392 Hemi head but designed strictly for drag racing. Donovan had been harboring the dream of designing an aluminum

A full-tilt Keith Black aluminum 426 Hemi is capable of churning out thousands of horsepower. Keith Black

engine block that embraced the advantages of the 392 while eliminating its weaknesses. It had to be able to withstand the fearsome stresses imposed by the use of nitromethane, the most powerful and volatile fuel used in drag racing. With so many stock and racing parts available for the 392 Hemi, a racer could literally build a strong racing engine around the new block Donovan had designed.

Donovan spent countless hours with his small design and manufacturing team before the block configuration was finalized, and work began in 1970. All major dimensions—deck height, camshaft centerline to crankshaft centerline, and bore-to-bore centers—were retained. Bore diameter, however, was increased

from 4.00 to 4.125 in., boosting displacement to 417 ci. Instead of being a solid block, it was an open-block design using centrifugally cast chrome-moly steel wet-sleeve liners. The result was a much lighter yet stronger block, and the sleeves were interchangeable and easily replaceable. This design made it possible to develop greater horsepower than was possible before.

The second major component of the engine was the main bearing girdle, also of aluminum, that provided massive support to the crankshaft. In the stock 392 Hemi, this was a weakpoint from a racing standpoint. This new bottom-end in conjunction with the new block permitted almost unrestricted application of supercharging with nitromethane fuel.

Together, the aluminum block, girdle and steel cylinder liners tipped the scales at just under 200 lb. Steel studs were used throughout the engine to

permit repeated teardown and reassembly without galling otherwise tapped holes.

Donovan's chief engineer, Bob Mullen, produced the drawings for the engine. Arnold Birner made the precision wood patterns for the block, girdle and cylinder liners. Dick Crawford established the tooling requirements for drag racing's first aluminum engine block.

After the casting and machining procedures unique to the Donovan 417 were worked out, the engine was offered to eager drag racers in 1971. The engine made its debut at the NHRA Super-Nationals in John Wiebe's rail, setting a low ET for the racers of 6.53 sec.

Proof of the 417's viability and durability is the fact the engine is still manufactured and sold today. Donovan went on to offer an aluminum 350/400 small-block in 1978. He followed this with an aluminum-block 427/454 in 1983.

When Ed Donovan died of cancer in May 1989, his wife Kathy became head of the company, continuing the long-standing Donovan Engineering reputation.

Keith Black

In Keith Black's office is a book that he has been working on for years. It's titled: "All I Know About Racing Engines." Inside, all the pages are blank. It's always good for a laugh, and it says a great deal about the man.

"I'm not a writer," Black says. "I'm a doer."

The name Keith Black is known to thousands of drag-racing enthusiasts as one of the sport's finest engine designers and builders. In a sport and profession that is fiercely competitive, he has remained uncompromising and forthrightly honest.

He was born in Lynwood, California, in 1926. Like many other teenagers in southern California, he became interested in hot rodding while in high school during the early forties. After graduating, he entered the Army Air Corps cadet program but World War II ended before he was called to action.

He married his high school sweetheart and set about the task of making a living in the postwar economy. Early on, he displayed an uncanny ability repairing and hot-rodding engines. His career actually started with boats, not cars. It all began when a friend asked him to fix the carburetor problems in his boat. A hobby became a career, and he started working out of his backyard.

"As I became successful at it," Black says, "more people would come to me and ask, 'Would you work on my engine?' I worked on a few Cadillac and Oldsmobile engines because they were the first ones out [with V–8s]. The first time I got into a race deal, where I had something that was of some size, I went into a Chrysler Hemi because I felt the engine was more of a race engine than the rest of the engines were. At that time, I did engines for boat racing that were 246 cubic inches, from the small Dodge [Hemi] engine. We built those up fuel-injected—some of them methanol. We also did a 265 cubic inch DeSoto."

As his business grew, he moved to Atlantic Avenue in South Gate, California. Black continued building boat racing engines into the early sixties, setting new national and international records every year. In 1965, Bob McCurry took over the Marine and Industrial division of Chrysler. McCurry learned of Keith Black's skill in building marine racing engines and flew out to California to meet with him.

"He came out and met me in my shop," Black recalls, "and he said, 'OK, I want to do for marine racing what Holman and Moody did for Ford, and I want you to do it.' We started in 1966 in the program to develop the late Hemi engine. Bob McDaniel was my immediate boss at Chrysler who worked for McCurry."

In the latter part of 1966, Black was called to help sort out the problems experienced by the twin-engine, Hemi-powered *Miss Chrysler Crew*.

"McDaniel said, 'Build up six engines, get started now. We'll start next year,'" remembers Black. "We built the engines and in 1967 we maintained the engines, went with the boat during the year and we ended up with second place in high points for the year."

In June 1967, Black moved to larger facilities on Scott Avenue in South Gate. It proved good timing because his involvement with the Hemi was about to grow dramatically.

"At the same time," Black continues, "I was told to make the late Hemi run as a fueler. Well, we put Barry McCown in the hospital from his drag boat at the time and it scared me. I said, 'You know, it's tough to develop these things in the boats because of trying to find a place to run them and all the things that are involved. I can do it much quicker in a car.' Bob McDaniel said,

The Chrysler Hemi continues to be the engine of choice in Top Fuel drag racing. Gene Snow shows what Mopar performance is all about. Thompson Advertising

'Then do it!'

"So we did the *Hawaiian II,* driven by Mike Sorokian. In fact, it said Chrysler Marine across the top of the rocker covers. The *Hawaiian I* ran a 392 Hemi. We did the development work on the *Hawaiian II* until it was far enough along where we did away with the second car. We put the [426 Hemi] engine in the primary car and we never looked back. By that time, the end of '67, Dale Reeker was my boss, but Bob McCurry started it all. McCurry came to me with the confidence to get the job done, and I thank him to this day for the opportunity."

The end of production of the 426 Hemi was a key event in the creation of the Keith Black aluminum 426 Hemi. The other key event was the arrival on the drag-racing scene of the Donovan 417.

"We had talked about an aluminum Hemi and I presented it to Chrysler but they looked at it and said, 'Well, we don't think there's any point in us building an aluminum Hemi. We're in the business of building cars.' And I had to agree. I couldn't argue with them, so we never did anything.

"Finally, Donovan built an aluminum early [392] Hemi. They took it to the racetrack and ran the thing. They announced it over the loudspeaker and called it the Donovan aluminum engine. All the guys around me who said they couldn't afford it started ordering it. I thought, 'These guys tell me they can't afford it and they're ordering it. That means that's baloney. They'll buy whatever they've got to have.' So I sat down and decided to make a late Hemi.

"So, I went to work on it. Bob Cahill at Chrysler called me and said, 'Did you know that Don Alderson is building a late Hemi also?' So I called Don, because we knew each other and talked about it. But he knew what he wanted to do and I knew what I wanted to do, so we both did it. The only thing was, it took me three years; it took him about a year. I did it [that way] because I couldn't afford it and nobody was paying for it but me. So I paid for it as I went.

"When I told them (Chrysler) I was going to make an aluminum Hemi, they said, 'Fine. Can we help you?' And I said, 'Yes, what can you do for me?' And they said, 'Anything that doesn't cost money.' So I said, 'Send me the current drawings for the Hemi, so I'll have that to work from for dimensions.'

"In the meantime, Alderson had his out in the marketplace and sold some.

Hemis have been used in Funny Cars ever since the 1965 A/FX cars Chrysler built—the original cars that coined the classification. A Hemi gives the Hawaiian Punch Dodge Daytona its punch. Bruce Biegler

We'd even put some together for some of our customers. Then we came out with our part. There was both of us in the market, then pretty soon he was gone."

Black initially encountered difficulties in finding a foundry that could produce a high-quality aluminum block. He visited two foundries, but found they couldn't do the job to his satisfaction. Then, through a pattern maker, he learned of another place that had the capabilities to do the job. He started offering his aluminum 426 Hemi block in 1974.

He followed this by offering cast-iron Hemi cylinder heads because of his desire to run on nitromethane, but Black says he could never make the iron heads work successfully on nitro. He switched to aluminum heads, but the foundry couldn't produce heads up to the quality he wanted, so he took over this operation himself.

Thanks to the 426 Hemi's incredible success on the drag strip over the decades, Keith Black expanded the list of parts available for his Hemi where today

372

he sells everything from the intake scoop to the oil pan.

"Our business has been mostly motivated by people wanting something," he says, "or we knew needed something and we'd make it. I started out making nothing and finally ended up making everything!"

Mopar Performance

Today, Mopar enthusiasts view the passing of the 426 Hemi as a milestone. As with most milestones in automotive history, the former glory of a particular car or engine remains just that. When Chrysler struggled to cope with the emissions and safety standards in the seventies and reorganization and rebuilding the corporation in the eighties, performance was not a major issue in the product offerings. Seeing the return of the iron-block Chrysler 426 Hemi was as plausible as turning water into gold.

Implausible perhaps, but not impossible. Certain events occurred in the late eighties that made the prospect of Chrysler offering the venerable 426 iron block to Mopar enthusiasts a serious possibility.

When Larry Shepard joined Chrysler in 1966, the reputation and popularity of the 426 Hemi were growing dramatically. In 1970 he moved to the race group and concentrated on drag racing. Chrysler received many requests for information regarding the 426 Hemi as well as their other engines, and per-

formance tips from both professional and amateur racers alike. Shepard worked alongside Dave Koffel, who handled the professional racers; both men reported to Tom Hoover.

"Back in those days," Shepard remembers, "Koffel worked with the contract racers, but they didn't have someone for what we'd call the 'door slammers'—someone to coordinate with our customers who had questions. Koffel would receive countless letters asking questions concerning performance, and there weren't enough hours in the day to handle them."

That job fell to Shepard. He began sifting through the filing cabinets full of letters with questions and began sorting them according to their specific query. These covered the gamut, from each of Chrysler's engines to the cars themselves. He also fielded phone calls with promises to get back to them with an answer. Koffel would often direct him to the engineer with specific knowledge regarding the performance area in question. Shepard felt he should never have to ask any question twice, and always wrote down the information. He began cataloging the answers to questions and putting them into binders. Still, this was far from ideal.

It occurred to Shepard that it would be more practical to write a bulletin in a given area and send that in response to a query, rather than responding to each letter or phone call individually. He began writing technical bulletins addressing key performance issues that were most frequently asked and originally these bulletins were given away. Later, the bulletins were sold through the Hustle Stuff parts catalog. Eventually, these bulletins were compiled into one book and sold through Chrysler's Direct Connection parts catalog. This book grew to such a size, it was decided to split it and publish two books, one for engines and the other for chassis.

In 1987, the Direct Connection name was changed to Mopar Performance. This name was readily identifiable by every enthusiast and tied in with existing parts sold by Chrysler. With the name change came the mandate to emphasize hard parts —the parts Mopar enthusiasts wished to buy—such as engine blocks, cylinder heads, intake manifolds, crankshafts, pistons, camshafts and so on.

"Looking back over our shoulder," Shepard says, "that decision has allowed us to become more visible in the performance marketplace and opened the door to very large dollars to allow capital-intensive programs."

At drag races around the country and such events as the Mopar Nationals, the Mopar Performance traveling display always draws crowds. Shepard never misses these events because it keeps him in tune with the enthusiasts who use Chrysler products. He began hearing complaints on the scarcity of 426 Hemi blocks and the outrageous prices that were being asked. Many of these blocks were more than twenty years old and had seen hard use. Additional demand was placed on the market by restorers of street Hemi cars, and those simply interested in putting a 426 Hemi in their Dodge or Plymouth or in a custom street rod.

The resurging interest in the 426 Hemi led Shepard to the conclusion that Chrysler should offer the 426 Hemi iron block to meet this demand.

"The guy who has a Hemi race car sitting in his garage as well as the guy who has a Hemi car for restoration—this is where we obviously knew we had a market and that's why we decided to do it."

The decision to reissue the 426 Hemi iron block was the biggest commitment Mopar Performance has ever made in terms of dollars and in overcoming some serious obstacles.

"The Hemi tooling was lost many years ago," Shepard admits, "so we would have to go back and make the tooling all over again. We've built up slowly up to this point, making intake manifolds, crankshafts, camshafts and so forth. Our goal at Mopar Performance was to be able to build a Hemi engine from top to bottom from our parts catalog. Will having Hemi parts change the way people think about the Hemi? We think so."

With its firm decision to reissue not only the 426 Hemi iron block but also cylinder heads and every part needed to build a complete engine, Chrysler has ensured its most famous V–8 will be available to Mopar enthusiasts for generations to come.

Appendices

1948–1971 Hemi Prototypes and Production Engines

A161
This was the 1947 Hemi-head research and development test engine with a Hemi head added to a straight-six Chrysler engine.

A182
The 1948 Chrysler 330 ci Hemi V–8 prototype.

A239
The 1948–1950 331 ci Hemi V–8 prototype that became the Chrysler FirePower engine. Shorter and lighter than the A182.

A864
The 426 race Hemi V–8, developed initially in 1963–1964 by adding a Hemi head to a raised-block 426 ci engine.

A925
Prototype 1964 426 race Hemi with four valves per cylinder and double overhead camshafts.

A990
Drag-race lightweight 426 Hemi developed initially in 1964 using aluminum-alloy cylinder heads and other alloy parts as well as a cast-magnesium intake manifold.

A117
Circle-track 404 ci race Hemi developed initially in 1966 based on the A864 426 race Hemi but using a shorter, 3.558 in. stroke.

A148
Prototype 1965–1966 426 race Hemi based on the shorter, 3.558 in. stroke of the A117 but with a larger 4.363 in. bore and larger valves. Aluminum-alloy and iron cylinder heads were experimented with, as was a gear-driven camshaft and a flat crankshaft.

A102
The 426 street Hemi, initially developed in 1965.

A103
The 426 Stage II street Hemi, initially developed in 1967–1968.

A279
The Ball-Stud Hemi 440 ci big-block prototype initially developed in 1968 as a low-cost challenger to Chevrolet's big-blocks. Ball studs were used instead of the forged rocker arms, and the Hemi heads were added to a 440 ci Chrysler block. Program was canceled in 1970.

Chrysler FirePower Specifications

	1951 FirePower	1957 FirePower	1958 FirePower EFI
Displacement (ci)	331	392	392
Bore (in.)	3.81	4.00	4.00
Stroke (in.)	3.63	3.90	3.90
Compression ratio	7.5:1	10.0:1	10.0:1
Horsepower	180 @ 4000	390 @ 5200	390 @ 5200
Torque	312 @ 2000	435 @ 3600	435 @ 3600

Dodge Red Ram Specifications

	1953 Red Ram
Displacement (ci)	241
Bore (in.)	3.44
Stroke (in.)	3.25
Compression ratio	7.1:1
Horsepower	140 @ 4400
Torque	220 @ 2000

DeSoto FireDome Specifications

	1952 FireDome	1957 FireDome
Displacement (ci)	276	345
Bore (in.)	3.63	3.80
Stroke (in.)	3.34	3.80
Compression ratio	NA	9.25:1
Horsepower	160 @ 4400	345 @ 5200
Torque	NA	355 @ 3600

426 Hemi Comparative Specifications

	1964–1965 Track	1966 Track	1964 Drag	1965 Drag	1966 Street
Displacement (ci)	426	426–404	426	426	426
Bore (in.)	4.25	4.25	4.25	4.25	4.25
Stroke (in.)	3.75	3.75–3.558	3.75	3.75	3.75
Compression ratio	12.5:1	12.5–12.0:1	12.5:1	12.5:1	10.25:1
Cylinder block	Cast iron stress relieved	Cast iron stress relieved	Cast iron stress relieved	Cast iron stress relieved	Cast iron stress relieved
Bearing caps	Mall. iron tie bolted	Mall. iron tie bolted	Mall. iron tie bolted	Mall. iron tie bolted	Cast iron tie bolted
Crankshaft	Forged steel shot-peened and nitride-hardened 0.015 in. journals	Forged steel shot-peened and nitride-hardened 0.005 in. journals	Forged steel shot-peened and nitride-hardened 0.015 in. journals	Forged steel shot-peened and nitride-hardened 0.015 in. journals	Forged steel shot-peened and nitride-hardened 0.015 in. journals
Main bearings	Trimetal	Trimetal	Trimetal	Trimetal	Trimetal
Main journal diameter (in.)	2.75	2.75	2.75	2.75	2.75
Crankpin diameter (in.)	2.375	2.375	2.375	2.375	2.375
Piston	Impact extruded aluminum	Impact extruded aluminum	Impact extruded aluminum	Impact extruded aluminum	Impact extruded aluminum
Piston weight (gm)	852	813	852	848	843
Top of skirt to bore clearance (in.)		0.008			0.003
Piston pin offset (in.)	0.060 toward minor thrust side	0	0.060 toward minor thrust side	0.060 toward minor thrust side	0.060 toward major thrust side
Piston pin					
OD (in.)	1.0936	1.0936	1.0936	1.0936	1.0311
ID (in.)	0.751	0.750. S6 taper	0.751	0.751	0.685
Type	Pressed	Floating	Pressed	Pressed	Floating
Connecting rod	Forged steel	Forged steel	Forged steel	Forged steel	Forged steel
Centers	6.861	7.061 426 7.174 404	6.861	6.861	6.861
Intake valve	Silchrome XB	Silchrome XB	Silchrome XB	Silchrome XB	Silchrome XB
Head diameter (in.)	2.25	2.25	2.25	2.23	2.25
Stem diameter (in.)	0.309 solid	0.309 solid	0.309 solid	0.309 solid	0.309 solid
Stem finish	Chrome	Chrome	Chrome	Chrome	Chrome
Exhaust valve	21–4N	21–4N	21–4N	21–4N	21–4N
Head diameter (in.)	1.94	1.94	1.94	1.94	1.94
Stem diameter (in.)	0.308 solid	0.308 solid	0.308 solid	0.308 solid	0.308 solid
Stem finish	Chrome	Chrome	Chrome	Chrome	Chrome
Valve springs installed height					
Outer (in.)	1.86	1.86	1.86	1.86	1.86
Inner (in.)	1.64	1.64	1.64	1.64	1.64
Valve closed load					
Outer (lb.)	85	85	85	85	105
Inner (lb.)	40.5	40.5	40.5	40.5	50
Valve open load					
Outer (lb.)	280	288	272	280	184
Inner (lb.)	94	96	92	94	91
Wire size					
Outer (in.)	0.216	0.216	0.216	0.216	0.187
Inner (in.)	0.128	0.128	0.128	0.128	0.128
Water pump body	Cast iron	Cast iron	Cast iron	Cast iron	Cast iron
Impeller diameter (in.)	3.32	3.32	3.67	3.67	3.67
Water pump housing	Cast iron	Cast iron	Cast iron	Aluminum	Cast iron
Oil pump body	Cast iron	Cast iron	Cast iron	Aluminum	Cast iron

	1964–1965 Track	1966 Track	1964 Drag	1965 Drag	1966 Street
Oil pump cover	Cast iron with cooler tubes	Cast iron with cooler tubes	Cast iron	Aluminum	Cast iron
Oil suction pipe	Dual-fixed and swinging	Dual-fixed and swinging	Single	Single	Single
Intake manifold type	Aluminum conventional single 4 bbl	Aluminum plenum-ram single 4 bbl	Aluminum plenum-ram dual 4 bbl	Magnesium plenum-ram dual 4 bbl	Aluminum two-level tandem 4 bbl
Manifold heat	None	None	None	None	Exhaust gas
Exhaust headers	Steel casting and tubes	Plate and tubes	Steel casting and tubes	Plate and tubes	Cast-iron manifolds
Carburetors	Single Holley	Single Holley	Dual Carter	Dual Holley	Dual Carter
Choke			Manual	Manual	Automatic hot air
Rod bolts (in.)	7⁄16–20	1⁄2–20	7⁄16–20	7⁄16–20	7⁄16–20
Bolt load	0.008/0.0085 stretch	0.0095/0.010 stretch	75 lb-ft	75 lb-ft	75 lb-ft
Cylinder head	Cast iron machined hemisphere	Cast iron machined hemisphere	Cast iron machined hemisphere	Aluminum machined hemisphere	Cast iron machined hemisphere
Chamber radius (in.)	2.42	2.42	2.42	2.42	2.42
Chamber depth (in.)	1.34	1.34	1.34	1.34	1.34
Chamber volume (ci)	172.7	172.7	172.7	170.4	172.7
Camshaft	Hardenable cast iron	Hardenable cast iron	Hardenable cast iron	Hardenable cast iron	Hardenable cast iron
Cam sprocket attachment	Single 7⁄16–14	Three 3⁄8–16	Single 7⁄16–14	Single 7⁄16–14	Three 3⁄8–16
Timing chain	Double roller	Double roller	Silent	Double roller	Double roller
Intake duration	312	328	300	312	276
Intake max. open	112 ATDC	106.5 ATDC	114 ATDC	112 ATDC	106 ATDC
Exhaust duration	312	328	300	312	276
Exhaust max. open	112 BTDC	109.5 BTDC	110 BTDC	112 BTDC	114 BTDC
Overlap	88	112	76	88	52
Intake valve lift (in.)	0.54	0.565	0.52	0.54	0.48
Exhaust valve lift (in.)	0.54	0.565	0.52	0.54	0.46
Rocker ratio					
Intake (in.)	1.57	1.57	1.57	1.57	1.57
Exhaust (in.)	1.52	1.52	1.52	1.52	1.52

D Series 426 Race Hemi Cylinder Heads

D1

Alternate cylinder heads for the 426 race Hemi initially developed in 1969 using the same intake and exhaust valves but with larger exhaust valve ports.

D2

Alternate cylinder heads for circle-track racing initially developed in 1969 with a 0.02 in. overbore giving 429 ci.

D3

Alternate cylinder heads for the 426 race Hemi initially developed in 1969 using larger intake and exhaust valves.

D3.5

Alternate cylinder heads for the 426 race Hemi initially developed in 1969 using the larger intake valves and ports of the D3 and larger and straighter exhaust ports of the D4.

D4

Alternate cylinder heads for the 426 race Hemi initially developed in 1969–1970. It used the same intake valves and ports as the D1 but with larger area, higher exit and straighter exhaust ports.

D5

Alternate cylinder heads for the 426 race Hemi initially developed in 1970 with all of the improvements of the D4 but cast in aluminum alloy and using two spark plugs for each cylinder.

D20 Magna

Alternate cylinder heads for the 426 race Hemi initially developed in 1970 with substantially larger ports and a wider iron head to house the ports.

D21 Magna

Alternate cylinder heads for the 426 race Hemi initially developed in 1970 as an aluminum-alloy version of the D20 Magna.

426 Street Hemi Specifications

Engine

Type	90°V
Number of cylinders	8
Bore	4.250 in.
Stroke	3.750 in.
Compression ratio	10.25:1
Piston displacement	426 ci
Engine output:	
horsepower	425 hp @ 5000 rpm
torque	490 lb-ft @ 4000 rpm

Combustion chamber specifications

Combustion chamber volume	168 cc min.; 174 cc max.

Distance from top of piston to block deck	0.502 to 0.547 in.
Maximum variation between cylinders	30 psi

Cylinder numbering

Left bank	1–3–5–7
Right bank	2–4–6–8

Cylinder block

Material	Tin-alloyed cast iron
Cylinder bore	4.250 to 4.252 in.
Cylinder bore finish	0.020 to 0.035 in.
Tappet bore diameter	0.9050 to 0.9058 in.

Intake manifold

Material	Cast aluminum
Type	Double level

Crankshaft and main bearings

Type	Forged counter-balanced, shot-peened and chemically treated (hardened journals)
Bearings	Tri-metal—copper–lead alloy with steel backing (MS-2355)
Diameter main bearing journal	2.7495–2.7505 in.
Diameter crankpin	2.374–2.375 in.
Clearance	0.0015 to 0.0025 in. (selective fit)
End play	0.002 to 0.0085 in.
Finish at rear seal surface	Diagonal knurling
Interchangeable bearings	Lower nos. 1, 2, 4, 5
	Upper nos. 2, 4, 5
Main bearing bolt torque	100 lb-ft
Main bearing tie bolt torque	45 lb-ft

Connecting rods and bearings

Rods:

Type	Drop forged I-beam
Length	6.861 in.
Weight (less bearing shells)	1084 gm

Bearings:

Type:	Tri-metal—copper-lead alloy with steel backing (MS-2355)
Diameter and length	2.376x0.927 in.
Clearance	0.0015 to 0.0025 in.
Side clearance (two rods)	0.009 to 0.017 in.

Camshaft

Drive	Double roller chain
Bearings	Steel-backed Babbitt
Number	5
Thrust taken by	Cylinder block
Clearance	0.001 to 0.003 in.

Camshaft bearings

Journal diameter (mean)

No. 1	1.9985 in.
No. 2	1.9825 in.
No. 3	1.9675 in.
No. 4	1.9515 in.
No. 5	1.7485 in.

Bearing clearance	0.001 to 0.003 in.

Timing chain (Special roller type)

Adjustment	None
Number of links	66
Pitch	⅜
Width	0.86 in.

Valves—intake

Material	Silicon-chrome XB
Head diameter	2.25 in.
Stem diameter	0.309 in.
Stem to guide clearance	0.002 to 0.004 in.
Angle of seat	45°
Lift	0.460 in.
Duration	276°
Lash (cold)*	0.028 in.

*Due to the high overlap, long duration and high lift of the camshaft, special care must be taken to be sure each tappet is on the base circle of its cam lobe when clearance is set.

Valves—exhaust

Material	21–4N chrome-manganese with welded stellite face
Head diameter	1.94 in.
Stem diameter	0.308 in.
Stem to guide clearance	0.003 to 0.005 in.
Angle of seat	45°
Lift	0.460 in.
Duration	276°
Lash (cold)	0.032 in.

Valve springs

Number	16 (inner); 16 (outer)
Free length	2.20 in. (inner); 2.47 in. (outer)
Installed height	1.83 in. min.; 1.89 in. max.
Load when compressed: Valve closed: inner	47–53 lb. @ 1.635 in.
outer	102–108 lb. @ 1.86 in.
Valve open: inner	86–96 lb. @ 1.175 in.
outer	179–189 lb. @ 1.40 in.
Valve spring diameter (outer)	1.090 in.
Surge damper	Spiral type

Tappets

Type	Mechanical
Clearance (in block)	0.0010 to 0.0023 in.
Body diameter	0.9035 to 0.9040 in.

Pistons

Type	Domed forged aluminum

Material	Extruded aluminum alloy, tin-coated
Clearance at top of skirt	0.0025 to 0.0035 in.
Weight	843 gm

Piston rings

Number of rings per piston	3
Compression	2
Oil	1
Ring side clearance	
Top compression	0.0015 to 0.003 in.
Second compression	0.0015 to 0.003 in.
Oil ring (steel rails)	0.0002 to 0.005 in.

Cylinder head

Material	Cast iron
Combustion chamber	Hemispherical
Valve seat run-out (maximum)	0.002 in.
Intake valve seat material	Integral
Intake valve seat angle	45°
Intake seat width	0.060 to 0.080 in.
Exhaust valve seat material	Integral
Exhaust valve seat angle	45°
Exhaust seat width	0.05 to 0.07 in.
Cylinder head gasket material	Stainless steel
Cylinder head gasket thickness when compressed	0.025 in.
Cylinder head bolt torque	70–75 lb-ft*

*Uses new, special hardened cylinder head bolt washers.

Engine Lubrication

Pump type	Rotary full pressure
Capacity	5 qt. (add 1 qt. with filter change)*

378

Pump drive	Camshaft
Oil pressure	1000 rpm to 8 psi (hot) 45–65 psi (cold) @ 40–50 mph
Oil filter type	Full-flow

*Check oil level indicator (dipstick) and change if necessary to correspond to correct level. Maintaining proper oil level is necessary during acceleration trials.

Fuel pump

Type	Mechanically operated, diaphragm type
Pressure	6–8 psi

Carburetor

Type	Two, 4-bbl. downdraft
Model	AFB-4139S front AFB-4140S rear
Throttle bore	
Primary	1 7/16 in.
Secondary	1 11/16 in.
Main venturi	
Primary	1 3/16 in.
Secondary	1 9/16 in.
Idle speed (engine hot)	750 rpm
Idle mixture (both screws open)	1–2 turns

Ignition system

Distributor type:	Double breaker, automatic advance
Basic timing	12° BTC
Advance—centrifugal (crankshaft degrees @ engine rpm)	0° @ 1000 rpm 9° @ 1400 rpm 17° @ 2800 rpm
Advance automatic—vacuum (distributor degrees @ inches of mercury)	0° @ 6 to 9 in. 4.5 to 7.5° @ 12 in. 8.25° to 11° @ 15 in.
Breaker point gap	0.014 to 0.019 in. (use dwell meter for final setting)

Dwell angle	
One set points	27 to 32°
Both sets points	37 to 42°
Breaker arm spring tension	17 to 21.5 oz.
Rotation	Counterclockwise
Spark plugs	
Type	N-9Y
Size	14MM 3/4 in. reach
Gap	0.035 in.
Firing order	1–8–4–3–6–5–7–2
Coil	PN 2444242 PN 2444241
Primary resistance @ 70–80°F	1.65–1.79 ohms 1.41–1.55 ohms
Secondary resistance @ 70–80°F	9,400–11,700 ohms 9,200–10,600 ohms
Ballast resistor Resistance @ 70–80°F	0.5–0.6 ohms

Current draw (coil and ballast resistor in circuit)

Engine stopped	3.0 amps
Engine idling	1.9 amps
Clutch	
Free-play adjustment	1/2 in. min.; 3/4 in. max.
Rear axle	
Axle shaft end clearance	0.13 in. min.; 0.023 in. max.
Ratio	3.23 automatic 3.55 manual

Torqueflite transmission

Line pressure	90 psi @ 1000–1100 rpm
Oil (engine)	Only oils labeled "For Service MS" should be used. Note: SAE 30 is recommended for acceleration trials

Transmission fluid	
Manual	SAE 80–90 gear oil
TorqueFlight	Use automatic transmission fluid Type A suffix A

Capacities—transmission	
Manual—four-speed	7 1/2 pt.
TorqueFlight	18 pt.

Index